The Netball Handbook

Jane Woodlands

**HUMAN
KINETICS**

Library of Congress Cataloging-in-Publication Data

Woodlands, Jane.
 The netball handbook / Jane Woodlands.
  p. cm.
 Includes index.
 ISBN-13: 978-0-7360-6265-7 (soft cover)
 ISBN-10: 0-7360-6265-3 (soft cover)
1. Netball--Handbooks, manuals, etc. I. Title.
 GV889.6.W66 2006
 796.32--dc22

                               2006006027

ISBN-10: 0-7360-6265-3
ISBN-13: 978-0-7360-6265-7

Copyright © 2006 by Jane Woodlands

Acquisitions Editor: Jana Hunter; **Developmental Editor:** Amanda M. Eastin; **Assistant Editor:** Christine Horger; **Copyeditor:** Patricia L. MacDonald; **Proofreader:** Erin Cler; **Indexers:** Robert and Cynthia Swanson; **Permission Manager:** Carly Breeding; **Graphic Designer:** Nancy Rasmus; **Graphic Artist:** Tara Welsch; **Photo Manager:** Dan Wendt; **Cover Designer:** Keith Blomberg; **Photographer (cover):** © Sport The Library; **Photographer (interior):** Photos by Tim Walker and Barry Walker unless otherwise noted. Photos on pages 5, 8, 103, 202, and 212 courtesy of The Advertiser. Photos on pages 136 and 221 © Empics; **Art Managers:** Kareema McLendon-Foster and Kelly Hendren; **Illustrator:** Argosy; **Printer:** Sheridan Books

We thank ETSA Park in Adelaide, South Australia, for assistance in providing the location for the photo shoot for this book.

Human Kinetics books are available at special discounts for bulk purchase. Special editions or book excerpts can also be created to specification. For details, contact the Special Sales Manager at Human Kinetics.

Printed in the United States of America   10   9   8   7   6   5   4   3   2   1

Human Kinetics
Web site: www.HumanKinetics.com

United States: Human Kinetics
P.O. Box 5076
Champaign, IL 61825-5076
800-747-4457
e-mail: humank@hkusa.com

Canada: Human Kinetics
475 Devonshire Road Unit 100
Windsor, ON N8Y 2L5
800-465-7301 (in Canada only)
e-mail: orders@hkcanada.com

Europe: Human Kinetics
107 Bradford Road
Stanningley
Leeds LS28 6AT, United Kingdom
+44 (0) 113 255 5665
e-mail: hk@hkeurope.com

Australia: Human Kinetics
57A Price Avenue
Lower Mitcham, South Australia 5062
08 8277 1555
e-mail: liaw@hkaustralia.com

New Zealand: Human Kinetics
Division of Sports Distributors NZ Ltd.
P.O. Box 300 226 Albany
North Shore City
Auckland
0064 9 448 1207
e-mail: info@humankinetics.co.nz

To Alexander, Sebastian and Adam; Margaret, David, Simon, Sarah, Aurelio and Lisa. You support me and my ventures unconditionally and always make me want to do better.

Dedicated also to the players: my former team-mates and all the spirited young women and men I have had the privilege to work with, learn from and celebrate with.

Special thanks to my mother, Margaret, who took me to the courts when I was seven and shaped my overall vision of the game.

CONTENTS

KEY TO DIAGRAMS

☐	Player
GS	Goal shooter
GA	Goal attack
WA	Wing attack
C	Centre
WD	Wing defence
GD	Goal defence
GK	Goal keeper
D	Dummy
X	Opponent
△	Marker (cone)
●	Ball
∿∿⟶	Ball movement
⟶	Player movement (strong move)
------►-----	Player movement (clearing move)
∧∧∧∧∧	Player movement (quickstep)

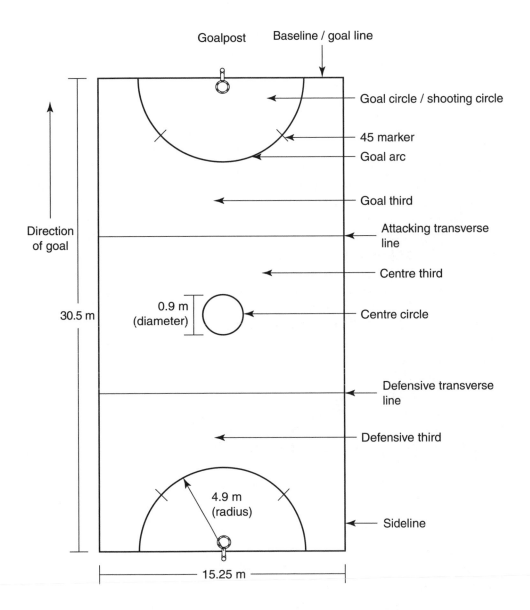

Note: The 45 marker indicated on the diagram is not an actual court marking, but rather is a reference point frequently referred to in drills.

PREFACE

"When each team member strives for individual excellence, when the achievement of the team's objectives are a passionate priority for each member, when members are proud to be in that team and when the distinction between individual and group is blurred, those are qualities that define a great team."

~ Anne Sargeant, Former Australian Team Goal Attack and Captain,
Two-Time World Champion

The Netball Handbook presents an inspiring range of netball concepts and solutions pitched in dual focus for players and coaches. The book is a total reference guide to the game's mechanics and finer points in the form of skills, drills, strategy and the wider aspects of one of the world's most interconnected team games. *The Netball Handbook* aims to assist and encourage its readers in their quest to maximise total skill potential. While touching on the fundamentals, the text's primary focus is on attaining advanced skills in all areas of the game. The best of traditional skills are updated and blended with contemporary ones in a fresh coverage of the skills of the game.

Players will perfect their craft by discovering the secrets of succeeding in their playing positions. They will also be able to assess and fine-tune their skills in ball handling, off-the-ball play, goal shooting, attacking and defending. By taking on the skill-specific drills at the end of these chapters, players will be well on their way to understanding best-percentage plays and gaining edges over opposition. For netballers hoping to play their best game consistently, the text provides motivation and direction for maximising their individual potential.

Coaches are presented with a complete skills package that identifies individual skills and how they should be executed. In addition to a wide range of individual playing skills, the text presents detailed, innovative discussions on transitions, set plays and strategy to get a team playing as a successful unit. For coaches aiming to maximise their team's performance, the book provides sequential themed drills in ready-to-go format, as well as a games log featuring a collection of high-transfer games for training. Coaches will be able to create a complete playbook for the team and will benefit from training tips for making sessions slick in design, content and execution.

Both players and coaches will be challenged to address the once-peripheral, increasingly mainstream aspects of the game in netball-specific conditioning and mental skills. Players and coaches will also be enlightened by the examination of teamwork and will receive practical guidelines for how to improve their personal skills to get the team functioning as an enthusiastic, integrated unit.

Readers will benefit from concise photographs and strategy diagrams as well as illustrated drill packages complementing the skills at the end of relevant chapters. Topical quotes from the world's most decorated players and coaches (past and present) punctuate major concepts for readers to gain direct insight from the experts. A sample statistics team sheet, periodisation guidelines, and pre-season and competition phase training-session samples are all provided for use. Performance points supplement major concepts as an additional feature that completes this comprehensive collection of modern netball concepts and solutions. All this and more make this book a must-read for netball connoisseurs dedicated to the continual improvement of their performance in the game.

ACKNOWLEDGMENTS

A number of talented and generous people contributed their technical expertise most graciously to this project. I would like to offer my sincere thanks and appreciation to Catherine Foreman for her patience and time with all sorts of technical assistance, Todd Miller for his hours of tracking down netball experts across the globe, Barry Walker and Tim Walker who took the photographs and Margaret Angove OAM, Sarah Vidmar, Claire Drummond and Ian Goldsworthy for their expert checking. I would also like to thank Netball SA, the ETSA Park staff, the Western Jets Netball Club, the Medibank Adelaide Thunderbirds Netball Team, Louise Souter and Sarah Vidmar again for their enthusiastic assistance with the photo shoot.

I was blown away by the willingness and professionalism of the world-class netball icons who contributed their insightful words of wisdom in their skill area and would like to acknowledge Ruth Aitken, Margaret Angove OAM, Natalie Avellino, Margaret Caldow, Michelle den Dekker OAM, Liz Ellis, Kathryn Harby-Williams, Donna Loffhagen, Sharelle McMahon, Anna Rowberry, Lesley Rumball, Rebecca Sanders, Anne Sargeant, Kendra Slawinski OBE, Peta Scholz, Irene van Dyk, Natalie von Bertouch and Vicki Wilson OAM.

My extreme gratitude also goes to the fantastic models who were very patient and professional in their work for the technical photos, thank-you Kristen Heinrich, Nadia Mapunda, Natalie Medhurst, Adam Pearce and Natalie von Bertouch.

Finally, I would like to thank the team at Human Kinetics for their enthusiasm, guidance and encouragement from beginning to end. Thanks in particular to Jana Hunter, Mandy Eastin and Chris Halbert.

CHAPTER 1

Positional Roles

The beauty of netball is in the intrinsic way seven players interact and function as one on the court. Every playing position is specific in netball, and different teams have slightly different job specifications for each position. Coaches and players should be clear as to what each position's individual objectives are. Each positional patch (bib) dictates the fundamental objectives for the player, identifies her direct opponent and defines her playing area boundaries. To maintain team flexibility and be able to counteract opposition positional permutations, players need to be adaptable to cover another position in their area, but the mechanics of their assigned position should first be sound. Genetic make-up (e.g., extreme height or speed) predisposes many players to certain positions, as does natural attacking or defensive inclinations. As each position has markedly different demands and movement patterns, to be outstanding in a position, a player should specialise in one and be strong in another.

Players need to balance time spent developing general game skills with time honing the specifics of their position. This chapter puts on-court positions under the microscope and examines the skills needed to be successful in playing them.

Goal Shooter

"The most important skills for a shooter to have are vision, variety of shot, strong core stability, movement in a confined space; short, sharp, definite movements."

~ Irene van Dyk, Silver Ferns' Goal Shooter, Former South African
Goal Shooter and Captain, World Champion, Commonwealth Games Gold Medallist

As one of only two players who can score goals for the team, a goal shooter's brief is simple—get into a good scoring position to receive the ball, and shoot as many goals as possible! The priority is straightforward, but the mechanics of making it happen are a little more complex. A goal shooter must possess an attacking instinct and eagerness to take on the role of chief goal scorer for the team.

The most fundamental quality for an effective goal shooter is shooting accuracy. Accuracy is achieved foremost by a sound, smooth, consistent technique and a predisposition for scoring. Proficient mental skills as well as a range of shot variations such as side-stepping and penalty techniques are essential for thriving in all pressure situations. Successful goal shooters must display a variety of potent preliminary moves and leads to enable them to shake off a close-marking defender, to work the tight spaces assigned to them and to present as a target. They must have a good blend of out-leads (leads that take them strongly out of the goal circle to meet the ball) and finishing moves (leads that are towards the post, culminating in a shot for goal). Fitness-wise, the goal shooter's work is predominantly anaerobic, with speed over the first five metres, power and overhead strength the priorities.

As the only player with a complete view of the entire team attack, the goal shooter is responsible for calling appropriate leads and systems (as detailed in chapter 5) as well as providing critical vocal cues to the attacking unit in front. The goal shooter must work closely with the goal attack to play fluently as a goaling pair, functioning as a team within the team.

In addition to shooting and attacking skills, the goal shooter has a major role as the first line of defence after a turnover in the attacking third. Quick recovery and transition to defence, strong hands-over-the-ball pressure, and the ability to double defend and communicate are assets in a shooter's defensive repertoire.

Goal Attack

"You need great timing, the ability to use change of direction and pace, a good fitness base to do the work outside the circle as well as the composure to put through the shot to get to the top and stay at the top as a premier goal attack."

~ Sharelle McMahon, Australian Goal Attack and Captain, World Champion,
Two-Time Gold Medallist in the Commonwealth Games

The goal attack has two main priorities: sharing the scoring responsibilities with the goal shooter and combining with the feeders to deliver the ball to the goal circle. Playing up-court from the goal shooter, the goal attack covers much more court space and has to regularly change up from running the open flanks to working the tight confines of a crowded goal circle. A position favoured by natural athletes, goal attacks are ideally instinctive, dynamic playmakers who work in tandem with the goal shooter, regularly finishing the play with a goal.

Being the other of only two team members who can shoot, shooting accuracy is a fundamental prerequisite for a goal attack. Shot variation, advanced ball-handling skills, strong mental skills and a range of effective preliminary moves and leads as for a goal shooter carry similar weight in a goal attack's brief. The position is more aerobically demanding than that of goal shooter, so a goal attack's conditioning program should vary accordingly (see chapter 10 for sample programs) so she can do all the movement work required outside the circle and still shoot without fatigue. Mobility, agility, strength, speed, balance and a healthy split of aerobic and anaerobic fitness ratios are ideal.

As well as responding to the shooting partner's commands in systems, the goal attack must communicate to combine efficiently with the wing attack at the attacking transverse line to orchestrate centre-pass moves. Defensively, the goal attack must mark the opposition goal defence tightly in one-on-one defence all the way to the opposition attacking transverse line, or act as the teeth of a flooding or zone defence (see chapter 6 for defensive options). Attention to detail and tenacity will net the goal attack valuable defensive touches.

Wing Attack

"When playing wing attack, it is your job to take control of the centre pass through communicating with your centre and goal attack, and to give quality balls into your shooters through your positioning, speed and vision."

~ Anna Rowberry, Silver Ferns' Wing Attack and Former Captain,
World Champion, Commonwealth Games Gold Medallist

A wing attack's brief is to be the key feeder to the shooting circle and the first-priority lead at the centre pass. The wing attack is the link between the centre third and goal arc and should possess a focus on the goal circle and a tenacity to drive the ball onto the circle's edge to connect with the shooters. Wing attacks aspire to shift momentum from running flat out on the end of a bullet pass to pulling up, rebalancing and threading a delicate placement pass to a shooter. A skilled wing attack in full flight is really something to watch.

Getting the ball is the first priority for the wing attack. Often double defended at a centre pass or throw-in, the wing attack must power through tight spaces when an opening occurs and use a range of short, sharp preliminary moves as well as fast-breaking longer leads in the open spaces to break clear of the opposition defence. As often the primary attacking ball handler, the wing attack needs an extensive armoury of passes and advanced throwing and handling skills. Wing attacks who can pass from either side of the body are an enormous advantage for hitting the shooters off a centre pass and feeding into the goal circle.

Wing attacks need adept mental skills to hold the attack together under pressure and support the shooters. Decision making is pivotal in all positions, but with the attacking unit down-court ahead of them in limited spaces, wing attacks are often faced with complex passing options. Successful wing attacks exhibit calm, flexible thinking. They are clear-headed in a crisis and shift to alternative plans effortlessly without panicking. A proficient wing attack can scan the options and calmly choose the best available target consistently and quickly. In the fitness department, wing attacks (like goal attacks) need a healthy split of aerobic and anaerobic fitness ratios to cope with the demands of longer clearing leads and repeated short, intensive efforts. Agility, speed and balance also feature in the positional conditioning program.

The wing attack must forge constant links with both goalers (goalies) and the centre (see Linking the Attack Together in chapter 5) to patrol the goalmouth and retain court spacing until the shot is taken. At the centre pass, the wing attack must coordinate with the goal attack to share the space at the line or run a set play to enable the centre pass to move forwards to an open target. However offensively talented a player is, her repertoire is not complete without a defensive game. The opposition wing defence is often a prime mover in delivering to the attacking unit, and if the wing defence can be shut down, it can create stress for the opposition attack, which is drawn up-court too far. Consistent halfback defensive efforts by the wing attack in tandem with the goal attack will not go unrewarded.

Centre

> *"At centre, you know you've had a good game when you have combined well with the attacking players, made very few unforced errors and have limited your opponent's influence on the game by working hard in defence to stop their drives and keep them off the edge of the circle."*
>
> ~ Natalie von Bertouch, Australian Centre

The centre is the engine of the team and the connecting agent between defence and attack. Centre is the only position in which a player can operate in all thirds of the court. Top centres enjoy the freedom of running unrestricted and operate well in open spaces. A major role for the centre is to get the team off to a good start by placing the centre pass accurately time after time, as this player starts with the ball after every alternate goal. Ideally, centres are steady, balanced players who possess natural attacking and defensive skills and good spatial awareness.

To get possession, a centre often has to make the transition from a mobile start to a sharp sprint towards the ball. These leads are blended with long drives down-court to receive high passes, combined with the art of stopping suddenly to hold position and create space for a team-mate. Dynamic balance is an asset, as many plays will place the centre in the midst of a full-court attack requiring catching and a run-on pass without stopping. In conjunction with constant effective movement action, the position demands advanced ball-handling skills, both

Aerobic fitness, dynamic balance and a combination of attacking and defensive skills are hallmarks of the centre position.

while stationary (placement of the centre pass) and on the move. In terms of mental skills, centres should have a sound grasp of match-day mental techniques. Although there is little time for centres to stop and weigh things up as they are in constant motion, there is no room for panicky passes out of the centre circle or into the goal circle in a tight situation!

Fitness skills that enhance a centre player's performance include aerobic fitness, speed, agility and balance. The centre is involved in nearly every pass as a primary, complementary or back-up lead, so the physical workload is extreme. High levels of aerobic fitness are required to patrol the court effectively. Centres need to train their aerobic fitness more than the rest of the team if they are to rise above fatigue and execute their skills precisely late in the game.

In an evenly matched contest, the centre can spend as much time in defence as in attack. The development of tight-marking and space-marking defensive skills is critical for a complete centre player. Centres act as the teeth of defensive third zones and the middle of flooding defensive configurations (see chapter 6 for details), and they are responsible for keeping the opposition centre out of the prime feeding channels. The centre must also be able to operate in conjunction with the wing defence to double defend at the opposition centre pass.

Wing Defence

*"As part of the defensive unit, a wing defence must promote the ball to inter-
cept for themselves or others, prevent fast feeds into shooters, stop drives
onto the circle edge, disrupt the link between the feeders to shooters, prevent
'in and out' feeds around the circle edge, apply the most appropriate style of
defence and be a link and strong driver in attack. A wing defence is a tireless
worker often with little direct reward, but loves the challenge!"*

~ Lesley Rumball (nee Nicol), Silver Ferns' Wing Defence,
Former Captain, World Champion

Athletes who play wing defence have a very distinct job description. They must
shut down the opposition wing attacks and negate their impact on the game.
Their opponents are often the key in attack, and if a wing defence can close out
the opposition's primary avenue of supply, the team has an excellent chance of
winning. A wing defence should display natural defensive tendencies and strive to
strike a balance between guarding an opponent and intercepting a stray ball.

Wing defence skill requirements include nimble footwork, shadowing ability, elevation and excellent techniques in hands-over-the-ball defence. A wing
defence must also be adept at different styles of defence, including switching
between one-on-one and floating defensive techniques (see chapter 6 for techniques and drills). To get the ball in defence, wing defence players should have
a commanding presence when pressuring an opponent's pass. They should also
be able to tag opponents and stay with them on a range of preliminary moves.
When the opportunity presents itself to have a go at the ball, a skilled wing
defence recognises it instantly and leaves her player to deflect or intercept. A
wing defence should be able to direct an opponent to the flanks and away from
the central passing channels, increasing the difficulty of passing angles. Mentally,
wing defences need resilience and the disposition of a true team player, as they
often do the hard groundwork in applying pressure so that their team-mates
end up with possession as a result; patience, persistence and a thick skin all
help the cause.

Good wing defences have discipline to defend within the framework of the
rules. If a wing defence gives away excess penalties and is constantly out of play,
this puts the circle defenders under enormous pressure to defend the goal circle
with no front line. Because wing defences largely follow the movement of wing
attacks, their fitness requirements are much the same. Balance near the circle's
edge is critical to avoid giving up free passes in the goal circle for offside or penalties for contact. Communication skills are vital at wing defence, as it is the first
line of defence at the centre pass. Wing defences require excellent teamwork with
the centre and goal defence to be able to pressure the opposition attackers and
shut them down at the centre pass to prevent easy passes forward. A critical role
for wing defence is to provide vocal cues for the circle defenders. An extra set of
eyes in the opposition goal circle is an asset for the defensive unit.

A wing defence also needs to be a prime mover in a full-court attack. For defensive-third throw-ins, the wing defence is usually responsible for bringing the ball smoothly out of defence into attack, requiring slick ball handling and direct down-court vision. When attacking out of defence, top wing defences should be proficient at mixing up long driving leads and short cutting leads. At their own centre pass, they act as one of four options in the form of providing back-up leads, covering their attackers in an emergency.

Goal Defence

"The most important skills for a competitive goal defender to have are good fitness levels, which allow you tenacity, quick reflexes, quick feet and determination."

~ Michelle den Dekker OAM, Former Australian Goal Defence
and Captain, Two-Time World Champion

The goal defence's job is to negate the opposition goal attack's influence on the game by denying her the ball and starving her of scoring opportunities. Goal defences must try to figure out an opponent's strengths and weaknesses early in the game to get the upper hand. Once the basic weaknesses have been uncovered, a goal defence must prey on them and calculate when to strike and have a go at the ball. Quality goal defences command an imposing presence, have a natural hunting instinct and enjoy patrolling halfback on the prowl for an interception.

Goal defences must be able to guard a player tightly, apply hands-over-the-ball pressure and know when to leave their player and focus on intercepting or deflecting the ball. They must continually attempt to direct their opponent wide and out of the goal circle, and once they are in, try to keep the opponent from the post. To do this successfully, a goal defence must have a few different options in defensive stances (see chapter 6) as well as the ability to operate in tandem with the goal keeper by switching and double defending. Goal defenders must have a range of defensive techniques (one-on-one and floating styles) and an effective lean or jump on an opponent's shot for goal. They are often natural athletes, as a lot of what they do is reactive, and are often matched up against the more dominant players on the opposing team. Skills that make an ideal goal defence include mobility, footwork, speed, recovery, reactive agility, elevation and the ability to intercept. Rebounding ability is essential, as defenders can usually claim the best position for rebounds when their opponent sets for a pass-off. A good spring to the ball and a two-hand grab-and-twist technique will serve a goal defence well and limit the number of second chances for the shooting team.

Patience, persistence, a thick skin and discipline are specific traits of classic netball goal defences. They need good mental strategies to cope when an opposition goal attack starts to dominate so they can ride out the tough period and refocus to chip away again. Aerobic and anaerobic systems share the demand

Courtesy of The Advertiser.

A skilled goal defence is instrumental in driving the ball out of defence and into attack.

for goal defence. These players have a lot of territory to cover and need to mix long runs at the ball in the mid-court and short, sharp footwork patterns in the goal circle. Overhead strength, power and speed are other essential fitness components a goal defence must train. Elite goal defences understand their special relationship with their defensive partner, the goal keeper. If they work together, they can cover each other and will reap rewards of combined pressure. They need to establish a good working relationship to form a formidable circle defence and be in tune with each other, sensing when to change up the defensive tactics from one on one to zone or other alternatives.

Once the ball has turned back to the team's possession, a goal defence needs to be instrumental in ensuring the ball is transported safely to the team's attacking third. Although she should be mindful of leaving an opponent unguarded near the goalmouth, the goal defence is needed to drive the ball out of defence and into attack in harmony with the wing defence and centre.

Goal Keeper

"To have a major impact on the game, a goal keeper must annoy the goalers, frustrate them into making mistakes and missing shots. This allows you to take risks and get spectacular intercepts."

~ Liz Ellis, Australian Goal Keeper and Captain, Two-Time Commonwealth Games Gold Medallist, Two-Time World Champion

The goal keeper's brief is to deny the opposition goal shooter attempts at goal. Often matched up against the opposition's major goal scorer, the goal keeper must be able to work the tight spaces and patrol the goal circle with authority, keeping the ball and the opponent away from the post. Quite simply, the goal keeper is the last line of defence between the opposition and the goal.

Specialist skills that need constant honing to play goal keeper well are footwork, reactive agility, defence over the shot, rebounding, shadowing and floating defence (see chapter 6 for details). Quality goal keepers will familiarise themselves with attacking preliminary moves and goal shooter–specific leads and movements (see chapter 5 for details), plus develop an armoury of defensive stances and techniques to combat them. Successful goal keepers continually change their stance and direct their opponents to the flanks and away from the central feeding areas and preferred scoring positions. Mentally, goal keepers are tough, resilient, persistent and unforgiving. They need to have good goal-setting ability to stay on track if the front line of defence is getting beaten. Successful goal keepers are also adept at knowing when to change up the tactics or systems to mentally dominate their opponent. A top goal keeper will bide her time, applying constant pressure and picking the right balls to go for, rather than go for every ball and cough up too many penalties, resulting in easy goals for the opposition.

The goal keeper's fitness program should mirror the goal shooter's. It is largely anaerobic work, requiring repeated short-burst, multi-directional movement. Overhead strength, agility, speed off the mark and balance are core elements to train. As mentioned in the previous section, the goal keeper and goal defence need a particularly good understanding and communication link. It is much more effective to operate in pairs or groups in a fast-flowing game where the attackers have considerable advantage. The goal keeper provides the eyes at the back of the defensive unit and should provide vocal cues to assist the goal defence and wing defence in front of her. A goal keeper's role in attack is primarily to start the full-court attack by getting a good pass away from a throw-in or opposition turnover, so static passing skills need to be proficient.

Bench Players

A team is only as good as its bench. Being on the bench or on the substitute players' list is an important and sometimes difficult role. One type of game that is evolving is one of running substitutes on and off through the mid-court so that an opposition centre or wing defence will continually have to battle fresh legs. Traditional teams use their benches more sparingly. Whatever the circumstance that sees a player on the bench, she must deal with a situation she cannot change and therefore needs to make a choice of whether it will be a positive or a negative experience. Players on the bench need as much support, coaching and inclusion as those on the court. With good communication skills from the coach and a specified role to fill on the day, the best team players will take the opportunity to develop some off-court skills so they will be wiser, stronger and respected when they enter or re-enter the line-up. Some examples of these skills are tracking potential opponents and noting strengths and weaknesses; observing team-mates' moves, strengths and weaknesses so they can blend with them better; and supporting team-mates vocally at breaks and during play.

Bench players should assume they will enter the game at every break, tune into the play, and be ready to go if called upon. Entering the game with enthusiasm, prior knowledge and fresh legs can produce a big impact. Bench players can also be of great assistance to the coach and manager by helping with timing, drinks or other off-court tasks pertaining to the smooth running of the team.

CHAPTER 2

Individual Ball Skills

In a 60-minute game where players cannot travel with the ball and must dispose of it in less than three seconds, the value of the fundamental skills of passing and catching cannot be underestimated. Constant honing of ball skills is a critical component of a player's continuing overall development. Even the greatest players in the sport need to devote a considerable percentage of their training time to improving and fine-tuning their individual ball handling. For maximal development, players need to work on both individual and team ball-handling skills. These include ball control, catching with safe hands, developing an expansive passing repertoire, passing placement, selecting the best target, gaining possession of loose balls and decision-making speed.

Ball Control

A player's ball control can be defined by how well she handles the ball from the second she touches it to its arrival at its next destination. Good ball-control skills start with the ability to use peripheral vision to sight incoming balls earlier than opponents do. Once she has tracked the ball accurately, the receiver should snap in the ball with strong hands and snatch the ball rapidly to the body's midline. Players with well-developed ball control can pass accurately on and off balance, pass from both sides of the body and display a range of sound passing techniques.

Good ball-control skills are evident in players who fluently shift from receiving to releasing and maintain dynamic balance while simultaneously selecting the correct pass for the correct target. These players tend to save a high percentage of inaccurate passes from team-mates and use quick hands to move the ball very quickly in the right situations. By closely observing the world's top feeding players, we note that they are able to thread passes through a congested area with pinpoint accuracy, use good deception with fake passes, and look smooth and poised, performing skills seemingly effortlessly. It would be an interesting exercise to run a skills battery test to see how many points players in a team can honestly tick off as mastered!

Ball control is a package of skills often neglected in the training regimen. It is regularly taken for granted that when players move beyond junior level they have adequate ball-control skills. Some players never reach their full potential because of underdeveloped skills in this area. A frequently underutilised fundamental is passing from the non-preferred side. A complete player in the passing department is able to throw successfully from both sides of the body. Centre-court players in particular can limit their team's success in attack by delivering the ball from one side only. Passes need to be practised with the non-preferred hand (or a hybrid two-hand technique on the non-preferred side) in isolation as well as in team drills. Therefore, it is also important when setting drills to reverse them halfway through (i.e., start drills from the other side or adjust them so that players are releasing, reading and moving from the opposite side). This way, athletes are able to train themselves to be polished double-sided players and an asset in any attacking play. Well-developed ball control in attack can tear opposition defence lines apart. Teams that have developed this skill are exciting to watch and set their goalers up with plenty of high-percentage opportunities in the goal circle.

Catching

It is the responsibility of both the passer and the receiver to complete each pass. Despite players' familiarity with catching and passing skills, it is always worth revising their correct execution in a game so reliant on ball handling. In such a fast-paced intrinsic team game as netball, where each player is allowed to handle the ball for less than three seconds at a time, catching is a simple skill that takes on enormous importance. Players who have sloppy catching techniques may find themselves attracting too much whistle from the umpires and costing the team possession because of replayed balls. There are several recognised catching techniques; the predominant ones are two-hand catch, one-hand catch, a one-hand variation known as tap and collect (or bat and catch), and a split-foot reception catch (in the goal circle).

Two-Hand Catch

Catching with both hands is always the desirable option as it maximises strength and control. To be in the best position for the catch, the receiver should sight the ball from when it is released, track it and move early into the best place to receive. Applying two hands if possible, the receiver should spread the fingers wide and place them firmly behind the ball, thumbs together (see figure 2.1). If the ball is above the waist, fingers point up. If the ball is below the waist, fingers point down. For balls in the middle, fingers point outwards. Players should watch the ball until it is securely in possession to see the catch being made. In today's game where the majority of balls are fiercely contested, the simple two-hand catch has fashioned itself into a snappy, smart take. It essentially involves finishing the catch with finesse by snatching the ball and whipping it away from the opponent to protect possession and leave the umpire

Figure 2.1 Catching safely with two hands.

with no doubt as to who had it first. When catching on the run to receive a wide ball, players should try to land on the outside foot with respect to the thrower. This will give some extra reach in raking in wide balls as well as enable the receiver to turn faster in the direction of play (inside turn is the fastest) and have a better chance of hitting the quick lead down-court.

One-Hand Catch

The one-hand catch is sometimes essential for reaching balls placed very wide or high of the receiver or for retrieving balls from over a boundary line. The balls are raked in with one hand and brought to the other quickly. One-handers can also be used to add a few centimetres to a player's vertical elevation. If it is not possible to reach the ball with two hands, the receiver should go with one and extend the body, arms and fingers (see figure 2.2) to rake the ball in to the body's midline, then get two hands on it quickly.

Tap and Collect

Tapping to collect is more difficult to execute than standard one- and two-handed catching. It is used when a player is contesting from behind to outjump an opponent in front of her and tap the ball to a space behind to gather it safely. It is a technique seen in rebounding, particularly carried out by players trying to outreach a taller opponent. If a player is in an intense aerial contest for the ball or is the back player in a rebound situation, she should elevate off two feet to maximise extension, avoiding contact with the opponent, and tap the ball to an area away from defenders (see figure 2.3). Players need to be careful to catch the ball or direct it to another player after one controlled tap to avoid breaking the playing-the-ball rule.

Figure 2.2 Catching a high ball with one hand.

Figure 2.3 The tap and collect.

Split-Foot Reception Catch

Split-foot receptions (split-foot landings) involve coordinating a two-hand catch with hands fully outstretched with some precise footwork and balance. A style of catching almost exclusively employed by goalers receiving in the goal circle, this is a catch made with the feet placed very wide apart in a forward lunge position, with the aim of gaining ground towards the post for a closer shot.

The two versions of the split landing are aerial and grounded. To land aerially with split feet, the goaler takes a high ball with both feet off the ground, splits the feet apart before landing, then grounds both feet simultaneously. In accordance with the footwork rule, the player may choose either foot as the first grounded one, and this by design is the one closer to the post. The grounded split is set up as the goaler positions her body to her advantage next to the defending opponent. When she has good coverage of the space to cut off from the defender, the goaler lunges towards the thrower, anchoring the back foot (see figure 2.4). With arms and fingers outstretched and the body held strong, she is ready to receive the feed-in from the edge of the circle.

Rules to keep in mind for the split landing reception are stepping, contact (accidentally with the foot) and short pass, if the feeder and goaler are in proximity. Players adopting the split-foot landing technique need to be aware of the footwork rule, as both feet must hit the ground at *exactly* the same time for them to be able to make a choice of grounded foot, sometimes a difficult move to pull off if a player is stretched to receive the ball. Athletes should always be aware of where the other players are when executing this landing. It should also be noted that this manoeuvre should be practised from a basic grounded model before aerial split landings are attempted. Executed at full stretch and game speed, split-foot landings can be hazardous for knees and ankles unless the player has a good technique and can land safely with knees and ankles in line.

Figure 2.4   Catching with a grounded split-foot reception.

Performance Points for Catching

- Sight the ball early, and prepare to receive by tracking it and setting up in perfect position.
- Extend arms and spread fingers wide to meet the ball, then snap the ball away from opponents when it comes into reach, using two hands if possible.
- Make the transition from catching to throwing or shooting smoothly and quickly.
- Work hard on catching difficult or misdirected passes at training and in matches.
- Goalers should use a split-foot reception in the goal circle at every opportunity to minimise shooting distance.

Passing

Players should keep some principles in mind when aiming to improve and fine-tune their passing skills. Acronyms serve as easily remembered cues that can help players check the elements of a skill or concept and target areas for development. Acronyms help to sequentially cement the cues and positively transfer to better skills on court. Effective passers tend to SPUR:

- Scan: Take a quick snapshot of the situation down-court upon reception, scan the options, select and zero in on the target.
- Place: Place the ball to the optimum space, considering speed, boundaries and pursuit of the defender.
- Unleash: Unleash the best-choice pass, delivering it with crisp "zing".
- Reoffer: Upon release, drive to a free space to reoffer as a receiver.

With SPUR in mind, extra skills need to be in accompaniment for consistent, effective, polished passing. Upon reception, players should turn quickly to face the goal (in the air if practicable) and scan their options. Standing up straight will assert the thrower's advantage by allowing maximum vision and range. Throwers should look down-court in the first second of possession and seek the target nearest the goal. If a clear down-court option exists, the pass should go. Options may be available for only a split second, so targets must be hit when they are open, not before and not after.

"Mastery of the fundamentals of throwing and catching comes down to peripheral vision, quick hands and the ability to read the play one step ahead."

~ Natalie Avellino, Australian Wing Attack and Goal Attack, World Champion

Passers must place the ball where a defender cannot get it. The optimal passing space is a vital concept to understand and apply if players are aiming to hit their passing targets with precision while maintaining the flow and speed of an attack. The optimal passing space is simply the best possible location the ball could be placed to allow the receiver to gather it safely, to avoid a defensive contest and to set the receiver up as quickly as possible for the next pass.

Coaches should draw the group's attention to optimal placement in dynamic ball drills (refer to the drills section at the end of this chapter) to help players train their eyes to cue in to the optimal space. Optimal placement can be much more difficult to master when executing fake passes, so it is best to fake the ball early in possession to allow sufficient time to cue in to the optimal space. While applying the principle of optimal space, throwers must not telegraph their passes, thereby making them easy for the opposing defenders to read. Players need to practise the skill comprehensively in drills and practice matches in order to master the timing. With passing, players should train to be adaptable to changing situations, such as throwing against a floating defence (see chapter 7), to complete their pass effectiveness.

Traditional passes (used since the game's inception) co-exist with others evolving through the increasing speed and tactics of today's game. The pass used for each particular situation should best fit the circumstances. Types of passes can be categorised as one-hand or two-hand execution. The one-hand techniques include the shoulder, hip (bullet), lob, bounce and flip (underarm) passes, while the two-hand versions are the reverse shoulder (side), overhead, chest and sling passes. These passes are detailed in this section. (See table 2.1 for a summary of the most commonly used passes.)

Table 2.1 Characteristics of Various Netball Passes

Type of pass	Distance	Applications	Frequency	Users	Features
Shoulder pass	Long to mid	Any quick pass in general play; centre passes; throw-ins	Very high	All players	Can cover maximum allowable distances easily; simple to execute; arrives at the target hard and fast; allows for quick disposal and enables extra decision-making time

(continued)

Table 2.1 *(continued)*

Type of pass	Distance	Applications	Frequency	Users	Features
Hip pass	Mid to long	Throwing over defenders with vertical-arm defence; exposing wide passing corridors	Moderate to low	All players	Provides a viable long-distance alternative to the shoulder pass if over-the-ball defence is high
Lob pass	All	All over the court where the target is in a clear space behind an opposition defender	High	All players	Can cover all situations where the target is behind an opponent and protecting the space
Bounce pass	Short	Low feed to shooters in the goal circle; any time there is good hands-over defence in high or wide passing lanes	High for feeds in to the goal circle; lower for general play	WA and C feeders; all attackers in general play	A valuable weapon for feeders to reach a stationary goaler in a lunge closely guarded by a defender; also great to use with a step around a close defender to set up a double play
Overhead pass	All	Passes in general play where target is in line with the thrower; when defender over the ball has hands set wide, exposing the centre passing corridor; in penalty passes with a fake to disguise the target	Moderate	All players for throw-ins, penalty passes and close one-on-one down-court play; WAs upon reception of centre pass	Very versatile Can hit long-distance targets in direct lines; low risk of deflection by the close defender due to high release point; good control and direction

Type of pass	Distance	Applications	Frequency	Users	Features
Chest pass	Short	When no defenders are between the passer and receiver; used for attacking through zone defence or for a penalty pass when close defender is out of play; good for some feeds to wide leads in the goal circle	Low	C; WA when feeding from the arc; defenders and mid-court players playing through a zone	Simplicity; accuracy; speed

Shoulder Pass

The shoulder pass is indispensable for many players, and a high passing average on the statistics sheet can be built around it. It is a strong, fast and direct pass from the throwing shoulder of the passer to the space ahead of the receiver in the direction of movement. Used with a step past the defender on release, this pass sets up a good double-play option.

To execute the shoulder pass, a player should establish his balance while facing his goalpost. The ball should be positioned quickly on his preferred throwing side, slightly behind the shoulder, with the throwing hand firmly behind the ball and fingers spread (the supporting hand front and low on the ball). The player should always stand up tall when passing (except for goal circle feeds), maximising his height, vision and throwing angles. The next steps in the process are scanning the court situation (*S* of SPUR) and selecting the most appropriate target. For optimal

Figure 2.5 The shoulder pass.

balance and power, the thrower needs to have the opposite foot forward from the throwing arm when passing (see figure 2.5); he should adjust his feet accordingly within the rules before release.

While making these adjustments, the player should cue in placement (*P* of SPUR) of the ball in the optimum space for the target (taking into account the target's speed, proximity to the boundaries and defensive pursuit). With the feet in place and the optimal space targeted, the thrower should open the shoulders, drop the supporting hand and whip the ball away, with simultaneous explosive forward extension of the elbow and wrist (unleash—*U* of SPUR) while transferring weight forward. The thrower should be sure to clear the defender's arms if they are up over the ball. Stepping past the defender to throw or raising the ball slightly will assist if defensive pressure is a problem. To finish the pass, the thrower should follow through with a swish of the wrist and fingers to add poise and control.

Reverse Shoulder Pass

The reverse shoulder pass, or side pass, is a great pass to develop, as its mastery makes a player truly two-sided. It is especially important that wing attacks master this technique so they are able to hit a goaler on a strong drive forward after receiving a centre pass. With little margin for error in this connection, the pass must be released to the space very quickly. If a wing attack is two-sided, with sound technique and timing, the speed at which the ball can be released increases because the ball doesn't need to switch sides of the body. The steps involved in the execution of the reverse shoulder pass are identical to those of the regular shoulder pass except for a few amendments. The player releases the ball from the non-preferred throwing side. The preferred hand moves behind the ball at the top, and the non-preferred hand behind the ball underneath (the two thumbs should be in line behind the ball). The thrower steps towards the target with the opposite foot to ball side, ensuring that two hands remain on the ball to whip it away with simultaneous forward extension of both elbows and wrists (see figure 2.6). The thrower then should follow through with a swish of both wrists and both sets of fingers.

Figure 2.6 The reverse shoulder pass.

Hip Pass

The hip pass, or bullet pass, is a fast and forceful low, flat pass executed from the hip (see figure 2.7). It is a useful weapon when a defender up over the ball has her hands high rather than wide, exposing a greater range of wide passing corridors. The leads down-court should be adjusted by increasing width to give the passer greater vision and to make use of the exposed corridors. The hip pass is more difficult to perfect, as it is executed away from the body's midline; therefore using the preferred hand is ideal. If the lead appears on the non-preferred side, the passer can scoop the ball through underarm style for a very wide angle but should change to reverse shoulder if no lateral leads are forthcoming.

To execute the hip pass, a player should set up identically as for a shoulder pass on the preferred side at hip height, with the elbow tucked in to the side and the ball held out to the side of the body.

Figure 2.7 The hip pass.

The throwing hand should be behind the ball, with fingers spread, and the supporting hand in front of the ball. To release, the thrower opens the forearm towards the target, drops the supporting hand and whips the ball away with explosive extension of the elbow, wrist and fingers, transferring weight forward.

Lob Pass

The lob pass, or high pass, is used for the specific purpose of throwing over a defender to hit a team-mate. It is a slow-release, more obviously placed pass with a loopy trajectory (see figure 2.8). Short lobs are primarily used by feeders into the goal circle or in set plays and throw-ins with a close target. Medium to long lobs are frequently used to bring the ball down-court out of defence on the run or to pass to a shooter on a long breaking move to the post. A well-executed lob to a good holding lead (see Preliminary Moves, chapter 3) is almost impossible to stop without breaking the contact rule.

Figure 2.8   The lob pass.

To execute the lob pass, a player should set up identically as for the shoulder and hip passes. The ball is positioned quickly on the preferred throwing side, with the throwing hand under the ball and fingers spread. The supporting hand should be in front and high on the ball. The thrower opens the shoulders towards the target and extends the arm slightly forward of vertical, transferring weight forward and releasing the pass with a swish of the wrist and deliberate finger control to guide the ball to its target in the back space. A receiver who puts up his back arm as a target provides valuable visual cueing for the thrower.

The lob is a very successful pass if used from the goal circle's edge to finish a well-timed drop move by a goaler. It is often the easiest pass to initiate a down-court attack from a defensive-end throw-in. It is also used to exploit mismatches in height.

Bounce Pass

The one-hand bounce pass appears in the game in many forms. It is a versatile throw that is very effective in passing around a defender with a long reach. It is also virtually unstoppable when executed correctly as a feed into a goaler positioned in the wide-split lunge. The bounce pass is usually used as a feed to goalers from the edge of the goal circle, a very short drop to the back foot (see figure 2.9), or as a ball put out early to a lead a long way in front of a moving target so that the ball will hold up for the receiver to run onto it. Another use is as an outlet pass from goalers in the goal circle across the circle to a feeder to reposition. The key to success in the bounce pass is placement. One thing to keep in mind when electing to bounce pass is that it is a slower route to the target, so it needs to be chosen appropriately and should not replace the quick pass to a short-range target. The bounce pass has a low release point and should travel below waist height at all times. Some of the best feeds to goalers in the circle stay at sock height.

Figure 2.9   The bounce pass as a feed to a goaler.

To execute the mid-range bounce pass, a player should set up identically as for the shoulder and hip passes. The ball is positioned quickly on the preferred side at hip height, knees bent to a slight crouch. Fingers should be spread on the throwing hand behind the ball, with the supporting hand in front of it. The thrower steps towards the target, being sure to clear the opposition defender's arms, opens the shoulders and flicks the ball to the floor with explosive elbow and wrist extension, transferring weight forward. The ball should hit the ground two-thirds of the way to the thrower. The pass should be followed through with a swish of the wrist and fingers.

When using a bounce to feed from the edge of the circle to a goaler who is positioned in a set split-foot lunge, the pace needs to be taken off the ball so that it sits low and just drops to the receiver's foot (with respect to the passer). The receiver will invariably have a defender right on her.

Reverse Bounce Pass

The reverse bounce pass is implemented when a player wants to use a bounce pass from the non-preferred side, primarily for feeding from the goal arc when an opponent applies defensive pressure on the preferred release side. This pass is chosen in favour of a regulation bounce pass with the non-preferred hand because passing low and one-handed from this side magnifies control and power limitations. The steps involved in the execution of the reverse bounce pass are identical to that of the regular bounce pass (mid-range and feeding bounce passes) except that the grip changes to preferred hand behind and top, other hand behind and bottom of the ball, with both thumbs together. The step to the target (except for passes on the goal circle edge) is made with the opposite foot to throwing side. To finish the pass, players should follow through with both wrists and all fingers.

Flip Pass

A flip pass is a more recent addition to the game and can be best described as an underarm feed from the edge of the goal circle to a goaler positioned in the split-foot lunge at close range. It involves a quick give to the fingertips of the goaler's outstretched arms and hands. The flip is a soft pass that just floats the short distance out of the defender's reach. It is usually delivered by the wing attack or centre, with a wide stance around the arc from the opposite side of the body to which the defender is standing. The flip is a common method of delivery in attack.

To execute the flip pass, the thrower places the ball at knee height to the side away from the defender on the edge of the goal circle, knees bent. When the target opens, the thrower flicks the ball in an underarm motion using the wrist and fingers (see figure 2.10), floating the ball to the receiver's fingertips.

Figure 2.10 The flip pass.

Overhead Pass

The overhead pass starts high and moves quickly in a flat flight path. It is an excellent weapon to combat long-reaching defenders' arms, as well as a standard pass for players who do not have height on their side. The overhead pass allows for a lot of control, as it is executed from the body's midline with two hands, so it is great for a quick pass in a higher passing corridor. It is a recommended choice when the target is straight down-court from the thrower in the clear.

To execute the overhead pass, the thrower brings the ball quickly to the body's midline above the head, gripping it with both hands behind the ball, fingers pointing up and thumbs together. After selecting the target, the thrower should step towards the target, propel the ball in a straight path to the optimal space and transfer weight forward (see figure 2.11). To finish the pass, the thrower follows through with wrists and fingers.

Figure 2.11 The overhead pass.

Chest Pass

The chest pass is one of the traditional passes that have been used since netball's infancy. It is the simplest short-range pass and is usually deployed from the edge of the goal circle by a feeder. It has limitations in the contemporary game in general play because of its low central release point and the short distance it covers. In today's fast-paced game, it is rare to see the situation where there is no defender over the ball as well as no defender in front of the receiver.

To execute the chest pass, players follow the same procedure as for an overhead pass, changing the release point of the ball to the chest region and aiming for the receiver's chest. It should be reinforced that unless a target is in close range and unopposed, with no defence between the thrower and receiver, the chest pass is probably not a suitable option.

Sling Pass

The sling pass has evolved more recently with the game. It is a short-distance underarm "scoop" pass used primarily by feeders at the edge of the goal arc delivering into a goaler. The sling is released with two hands, like a reverse bounce pass minus the bounce (so it gets there faster). The release point is very low, with the thrower crouched down to clear a low corridor, or "tunnel", between herself and the goaler (see figure 2.12). The ball travels either knee-to-knee height or knee-to-ankle height if a circle defender is in a position to deflect. The procedures and features of the sling are the same as for the reverse bounce pass with the exception of the flight path of the ball, which remains straight.

Figure 2.12   The sling pass.

Fake Pass (Baulk or Dummy Pass)

The fake pass is a fantastic offensive tool that can leave defenders clueless as to where the ball is going (or even where it went!). Highly skilled players can execute two types of fake with ease and regularity, having developed the strategy into an integral skill in their offensive armoury. In fact, it becomes second nature to those dedicated enough to perfect it. The fake takes a lot of practice to get right, and it can be very entertaining for all when a team tackles the development of the skill.

In the first kind of fake, the ball (or pump) fake, the passer pumps the ball towards a dummy target sharply as if she were going to release it, unfoots the defenders, redirects and makes the actual pass to the real target. Needless to say, it requires a two-hand technique. The second, more perceptually difficult fake is the eye fake (or no-look pass), when the passer looks one way and executes in another direction (see figure 2.13) without subsequently sighting the receiver. This is heads-up netball at its best. Receivers in the entire vicinity of play must be cued in on the passer and keep their eyes peeled if they don't want to cop an embarrassing ball to the back of the head! Fakes can precede any pass, and their use should be encouraged. Fakes are used primarily in attack, but it is great to see them sneaking into creative full-court plays by adventurous defenders. Players who fake add to the skill level and excitement of the game, and the best of the super-skilled players can execute both types of fakes within the allowable time limit. A player needs to develop a sense of appropriate application for the fake. If overdone it has the drawback of leaving frustrated team-mates on the fast lead unused and stranded out of position.

Figure 2.13 The eye fake.

Performance Points for Passing

- Remain on balance throughout the pass, and scan down-court for targets first.
- Select the best target, determine the most appropriate pass for the situation, and cue in the optimal space to place it.
- Develop and fine-tune a repertoire of passes, and aim to become a two-sided player.
- Practise passing techniques and placement in every individual and team ball drill, and welcome the chance to practise passing under pressure.
- Work on your weaker techniques to add to your overall effectiveness and reliability.

Toss-Ups

When players simultaneously gain possession, knock the ball out of court, go offside or contact each other, a toss-up should be called. It may also occur if the umpire is unsighted or unsure as to who last touched the ball before it went out of court. Skills needed in taking the toss-up are essentially fast reactions with hands and body. Players require excellent concentration, steely control and lightning-fast reactions to beat the opponent—who faces them only .9 metre away—to the ball.

To be effective in the toss-up situation, players should track the ball from the moment the toss-up is called. They must move into position quickly, watching the ball at all times. Players should adopt a balanced stance, with one foot forward or both feet shoulder-width apart (one foot forward mirrors natural catching position more closely, but it really is preference). Both hands should be by the players' sides, their arms slightly bent. Fingers should be spread slightly in anticipation, ready to grab the ball. The rules dictate that the body must be still, but to initiate movement on the whistle just that little bit faster, it helps to be moving a body part, even if it is slight, so that momentum is not being generated from a motionless state. Twitching the toes or the little finger is about all a player would be able to get away with. On the blast of the whistle, players explosively propel their arms forward and up to snatch the ball, transferring weight forward. They should aim to twist the ball away from the opponent to secure possession. If a player is beaten to the ball, she should either jump back to the .9-metre mark to defend or move off quickly to locate her positional opponent if that person is not her toss-up opponent.

Decision Making on the Move

Each person can handle the ball for less than three seconds at a time. If the same 14 players stay on the court for an entire 60-minute match and we take out time when the ball is dead and add decisions made off the ball, it is possible that each player would average around 70 decisions per match just in relation to passing and moving! There would be even more for the team's chief ball handlers and more again when the coach throws in a lot of tactical plays. In this game, decisions are thrown at the players thick and fast. The netball court is no place for the hesitant. It is obvious that decision making is a critical skill to develop and one that must be nurtured constantly. In a pressure situation, players who remain composed and make clear, definite decisions set themselves apart from their peers. With passing, the chief decision-making process involves

- whom to throw to,
- when to throw,
- which pass to use,

- where the defenders are,
- whether a fake is needed and
- where the optimal space is.

This is a lot for a human brain to compute and get right within three seconds—not including the time to physically gather the ball, turn and release it. Some fundamental guidelines can enable players to make good, quick decisions on a consistent basis. Once a player has secured possession, she should balance as fast as possible while scanning for the next target. If it is impossible to regain total balance, she should off-load the pass to the nearest safe option, with the objective purely to save possession. Once the player in possession is balanced and the scanning process has begun, she should seek options in the same or adjacent corridors, avoiding cross-court passes over opponents, which are the easiest to read and intercept. After narrowing the field of choice, the thrower should look down-court first while calculating the opposition's movements, then choose the safest target. High-scoring attacking teams play direct netball, always seeking the option nearest the goal first. When bringing the ball down-court, players can be a little more selective with their targets as there is more space with more options. When play is concentrated around the goal circle, with eight players on or inside the edge of the goal circle, throwers should hit the first target that momentarily pops open. Throwers must avoid being overprogrammed or robotic with their decision making or they become too predictable. Instead, they should strive to apply the fundamental processes while injecting creativity and using instinct.

So many steps must be performed simultaneously. A player can be successful with speedy, complex decision making only through constant exposure and quality application to well-designed drills and practice situations. Drills need to replicate and intensify the decision-making process so that players' brains and bodies respond accordingly in pressure situations. Including many decision-making opportunities in drills is simple with a bit of thought and effort. Coaches and players will certainly reap the rewards of their labour.

Ball-Handling Drills

Ball-handling drills make up the bulk of most netball training drills. Ball handling is such an intrinsic part of the game that constant development and fine-tuning are an essential part of the journey to become a complete player. Drills for handling the ball range from very simple to multi-tracking complex. There is always opportunity to consider doubling up the skill content to maximise players' time invested in these drills. For example, a drill to develop fake passing could include preliminary moves, timing of leads, reverse pass techniques and fitness work.

Even with the most basic of ball-handling drills, a few points should be kept in mind for drill design. Foremost, the specific purpose of the drill must be established. Once that has been identified, other elements can be added to the drill to build it up and make it more interesting, thereby adding motivation and extracting the highest levels of application in its execution. Elements such as alternative footwork, reverse side passing, reversing the drill's orientation, fitness and conditioning, as well as decision making, can add to the drill. The more the player needs to think to get the drill sequence right and keep moving, the greater application is needed and the more players will get out of it (short of overcomplicating the drill so it becomes static as nobody can figure it out!). In brief, once the objective of the ball drill has been identified, consider adding additional interesting aspects, including defensive pressure. Players enjoy drills that look sharp, involve advanced skills, and flow. They tune in to good drills so much sometimes that they do not know just how hard they are working! Even the simplest of variations to a ball drill can keep it fresh and lively.

Individual Ball Drills

Ball-handling drills for individual practice aim to develop dexterity and static ball control. These elements are essential for achieving the foundation skills needed for more complex multi-process ball sequences and demanding team drills that simultaneously tax gamelike requirements of decision making, timing and ball skills. All these drills require one ball per player.

VERTICAL BALL TOSS

OBJECTIVE

To develop aerial ball control and overhead kinaesthetic awareness by developing whole-arm coordination and control when the ball is out of the direct line of sight. This is an excellent drill for defenders, who are often unsighted when striving to maintain a bi-focus of player and ball; it also develops general dexterity in all players.

REQUIREMENTS

One player, one ball

METHOD

1. Place the ball in front of the body at waist height, knees and elbows slightly bent.
2. Toss the ball back so it passes about 40 centimetres above the head. Swing arms behind body quickly, and try to catch ball behind back without looking.
3. After 30 seconds, reverse the drill. Start in finishing position, and flip ball forwards over head to catch in front.

When repeated frequently, rapid improvement should occur.

BACK DROP, BOUNCE THROUGH

OBJECTIVE

To develop ball control, dexterity and kinaesthetic awareness by improving general upper- and lower-body coordination as well as eye–hand skills

REQUIREMENTS

One player, one ball

METHOD

1. Start with ball at back of neck, leaning slightly forward at the waist.
2. Drop ball down spine and swing arms behind back to catch ball before it hits the ground.
3. From this position, bounce ball back through legs and catch it in front of body.

WALL WORK

OBJECTIVE

To develop dexterity, control, passing strength and accuracy with two- and one-hand techniques. This drill overloads reflex ball skills of gathering and disposal by reducing reaction time; it applies to any situation where quick hands are needed, particularly feeding in attack and deflecting in defence.

REQUIREMENTS

One player, one ball, a suitable rebounding wall

METHOD

Two-hand technique:

1. Stand facing a wall about one metre away.
2. With fingers pointing up, hold the ball straight above the head and slightly forward; flick with wrists to release forwards to rebound the ball off the wall. Quick catch and release are essential. Aim for 30 with speed and control.
3. Take another step back. Slow the speed to run the sequence of "high, middle, low, middle, high" passes off the wall, including targets at shoulder and below waist levels. The worker must rapidly make hand adjustments from fingers up, to wide, to down.

One-hand technique:

1. Stand facing a wall about one metre away. Grip the ball in preferred hand, above and forward of head, fingers spread wide—check that daylight can be seen between palm and ball.

2. Flick ball forwards to rebound off wall, slowly at first then in rapid succession. Work for 30 seconds.

3. Change to non-preferred hand and repeat.

To extend and develop control in the extremities of reach, start with the ball just above waist height and flick to wall, moving hand towards vertical about 10 degrees every catch. When ball reaches vertical, smoothly continue through the range with the other hand until almost at waist height.

Pairs Ball Drills

Ball work with a partner is an essential part of every training session. Individual ball skills must be coupled with the involvement of another player to replicate a gamelike situation, incorporating judgment, timing and assimilation of team-mate driven cues. Pairs drills maximise activity for the worker and need to be done in conjunction with team drills. For these drills, one ball per two players is needed, except for "Double Ball", which requires one ball per player. The first partner will be represented by *A* and the second by *B*.

QUICK FEET AND LUNGE

OBJECTIVE

To develop coordination and speed in footwork, receiving with outstretched arms and fingers, and coordination of hand–foot timing for obeying the footwork rules

REQUIREMENTS

Two players, one ball

METHOD

1. A stands with the ball and faces B five metres away.
2. B commences fast foot tapping and lunges sharply left to take the pass from A.
3. B returns with a shoulder or reverse shoulder pass and repeats the process with a forward lunge, then repeats again with a lunge to the right.
4. B returns the last pass, takes off towards A, cuts around her, and returns to the original starting position as A throws a lob to challenge B to gather upon return.
5. A and B swap roles. Players repeat the drill three times each.

LINE BALANCES

OBJECTIVE

To develop static and dynamic balance when in possession of the ball and to improve the technique of using the ball as a support in an offside area. The drill enhances players' effectiveness to retain possession and dispose of the ball quickly and safely while obeying the rules governing leaning on the ball in an offside area.

REQUIREMENTS

Two players, one ball, straight or goal arc court line marking

METHOD

1. A stands with the ball and faces B five metres away along a transverse line. A stands on the line, and B stands beside it.
2. A places an easy high ball to the offside area (the opposite side of the line that B is on). B retrieves the ball by raking it in, then returns it to A.
3. A progressively makes the passes more difficult to receive, varying them in width and height.
4. After 10 passes, B swaps sides of the line and works the other side. Players rotate roles.
5. Add movement at the next rotation, with B starting three steps off the line and moving towards it, having to stop, balance and retrieve.

Centre-court players should do this drill around the goal arc for control around the circle. When players rake the ball in but are unable to bring it to their midline, using the ball to balance their hands for support in the offside area is allowable under the rules, providing no body part touches the ground in that area.

VERBAL RESPONSE TEST

OBJECTIVE

To develop a player's responses to verbal cues on court, fine-tuning responses to team-mates' verbal commands when reacting to surprise balls

REQUIREMENTS

Two players, one ball

METHOD

1. A stands five metres behind B, who is facing the same way as A.
2. A passes an easy ball in one of four directions (left, right, up or down), simultaneously calling the direction.
3. B responds by turning quickly in the direction of the call and catching the ball before it hits the ground. Players rotate roles after 10 attempts.
4. At the next rotation, B moves her feet up and down rapidly on the spot to add movement and tries to catch the ball at an earlier point than in the last attempt. Players rotate roles after 10 attempts.

With practice, players should aim to start the drill with quick feet and jump to turn with arms outstretched to receive.

PERIPHERAL VISION

OBJECTIVE

To develop peripheral vision and be able to track ball and player movement earlier, reacting to it faster

REQUIREMENTS

Two players, one ball, straight line court marking

METHOD

1. A stands along a line with the ball five metres from B, who is also on the line facing sideways at 90 degrees, looking straight ahead.

2. A chest passes an easy ball to B slightly ahead of the line. B attempts to track the ball upon release and catch it as soon as possible.

3. After 10 attempts, A passes to B's other side. Players rotate roles. At the next rotation, B starts with quick feet, tapping them up and down to add movement, and tries to extend the arms earlier, progressing to jumping towards the thrower to pounce on the ball as quickly as possible.

REFLEX BALLS

OBJECTIVE

To develop faster reflex reactions and dexterity from a very short distance and coordination of fast hand- and footwork. With practice, the worker should improve skills in toss-ups and intercepting an opponent's pass from the one-on-one hands-over defence position.

REQUIREMENTS

Two players, one ball

METHOD

1. A stands with the ball and faces B, who is two steps away, holding the ball at waist height with an underarm grip. B is focussed on the ball, knees slightly bent, weight forward and hands on sides of legs.

2. A flicks the ball forwards softly but quickly in a random direction for B to snap hands forward and take possession, snatching the ball away in a smart take.

3. B returns ball quickly to A and resets for the next repetition. Players rotate roles after 15 attempts.

4. Next rotation, B adds quick feet for a mobile start. The pair moves slowly down-court to complete the drill, maintaining the same distance between them and ensuring the footwork rule is not broken while in possession of the ball.

SLINGS

OBJECTIVE

To develop the sling pass technique and coordinate it with a split-foot reception, fine-tuning goalers' footwork in the split landing. Goalers using the split landing at every opportunity can condense their shooting range to almost exclusively short to middle distance, making them a very serious threat to opposition defence.

REQUIREMENTS

Two players, one ball

METHOD

1. A starts with the ball and faces B five metres away.
2. A passes to B using the underarm sling technique as B times an aerial split to catch the ball with feet wide, grounding them simultaneously.
3. B returns with a sling from the split position to A, who splits aerially and receives with feet in a simultaneously grounded lunge.

A and B continuously exchange sling passes in this fashion, switching front feet in alternate lunges to work both sides on the lunge and the pass. Time the sequence for one minute.

CROSS-BODY WORK

OBJECTIVE

To develop finger strength and hand control while training the brain to respond to cues on both sides of the body. The drill also develops the ability to receive or deflect a ball with either hand on either side, an advantage for defenders attempting to deflect balls when an opponent is between themselves and the ball, as it avoids contravening the contact rule.

REQUIREMENTS

Two players, one ball

METHOD

1. A starts with the ball and faces B three metres away.
2. A places an easy ball at head height to B's left side. B, who is standing with knees bent and weight forward, focusses on the ball, extends the right arm up and across, dipping the left shoulder away slightly, and returns the ball with a controlled tap to A's chest.
3. A places the ball to B's right side, and B returns with the left hand, crossing the body in the same fashion.
4. A continues to send in alternate balls, left and right, for 30 seconds. Players rotate roles.

5. Add movement at the next rotation, with B starting with quick feet and stepping with the foot opposite to the hand when receiving.

6. Placing balls randomly to the right or left will challenge the worker's brain–limb coordination.

VARIATION

A places the ball (still easy and at same height) such that B has to take two steps to reach it. A places random left or right high balls, then adds in the bounce pass so it sits up to B. B returns a bounce with a cross-body bounce, then rolls back (turning outside) to starting position. Players can try this when the fundamentals of rolling as a preliminary move have been achieved.

DOUBLE BALL

OBJECTIVE

To develop fast hands, ball control, eye–hand coordination and concentration by providing the best possible ratio and overload for maximal development of eye–hand skills

REQUIREMENTS

Two players, two balls

METHOD

Chest–Bounce

1. A and B face each other with a ball each, rear feet five metres away. Both are stepping towards each other, their weight forward.

2. A releases a firm chest pass as B releases a regulation two-hand bounce pass such that it sits up for A to receive without reaching. They simultaneously swap balls as fast as they can with control until the coach calls, "Swap!" and they switch roles (A bounces, B chest passes).

Have a recorder count errors for 45 seconds, then the players try to beat the previous score.

Shoulders

1. A and B set up as for the chest–bounce combination but instead pass firm shoulder passes from the right shoulder to the partner's left shoulder. The balls should travel roughly parallel to each other.

2. Upon reception, players must swing ball rapidly from left shoulders to right and release the next pass as quickly as possible.

3. After 30 repetitions, players reverse so that passes are made from left to right, working the reverse shoulder pass technique if favoured over the non-preferred hand. (Left-handers will work reverse shoulder pass first.)

High–Low

1. A and B set up as for the chest–bounce combination. A raises ball high and uses the overhead pass technique to pass down to B's abdomen. B simultaneously tunnels a "chest" pass from waist height to A's abdomen.

2. A has to work the arms hard to recover from a high release to a take in the midsection. A has to be quick to avoid wearing one right in the breadbasket!

3. Players rotate roles after 30 seconds.

To keep basic ball drills fresh, motivating and fun, try the following:

- Time players and record their scores so they can try to beat them next time.
- Include thinking and cross-body work to challenge and develop concentration.
- Reverse the drill, or work with the opposite hand.
- Use drills as recovery exercises for conditioning drills and pre-season work.

Choreograph the session so the players move from drill to drill continuously for 5 to 10 minutes for great time efficiency and maximal skill development. Adding music to the sequence is even more motivating.

Small-Group Ball Drills

In a well-designed training session, individual and pairs ball work progresses to small-group ball drills. The ratio of maximal individual participation is still high, as the number of variables and cues and the rate of decision making increase. The inclusion of directional elements and reorientation adds to the development of ball and movement coordination. For these drills, players 1 to 4 are represented by *A*, *B*, *C* and *D*, respectively. One or two balls are needed for each drill.

DOUBLE TOUCH–JUMP

OBJECTIVE

To develop fast footwork and weight transfer skills in combination with ball position awareness while developing power in vertical elevation

REQUIREMENTS

Three players, two balls

METHOD

1. A, B and C form a triangle about two steps apart. A holds a ball with two hands overhead; B holds the other ball with two hands in front, just below waist level.

2. C (with A on the left) steps forward with the left foot and touches A's ball, slip-steps back quickly to change feet and steps with the right foot to touch B's ball.

3. C then quickly slides the front foot back and elevates powerfully off both feet to receive a short lob from A, who releases the ball at the same time as C touches B's ball.

4. With a snappy, smart take, C rakes the ball in with one hand and returns it to A. Sequence repeats immediately in reverse as C starts the routine at B's ball.

Players rotate roles after 30 seconds. After every player has had a turn to be the worker, A and B can place the ball wherever they like for C to touch, while C must react to changing situations, thereby increasing concentration.

TRAMLINE TURNING

OBJECTIVE

To develop and incorporate turning efficiently into the ball-gathering and -disposal sequence, replicating the situation for players running an attack down-court. This drill also works on optimal space technique for passing precision at a static level.

REQUIREMENTS

Three players, one ball

METHOD

1. A starts with the ball and faces B 10 metres away, with C in the middle facing A. C breaks left to receive a shoulder pass from A, who focusses on placing the ball in the optimum space.

2. C catches, turns on outside foot, balances and delivers a shoulder pass to B and returns to starting position in the middle of the throwers.

3. B then takes A's role of starting the sequence. After four repetitions, C breaks to the right first, and A uses a reverse shoulder pass to rehearse optimal space technique, and likewise for B.

After four more repetitions, players rotate roles.

VARIATION

Add defenders over the ball for A and B at .9 metre to work on finding gaps for passing in the central corridor. Passers may need to choose a more appropriate technique to place their passes successfully.

T PASSING

OBJECTIVE

To enhance eye–hand coordination, rapid disposal, peripheral vision and concentration

REQUIREMENTS

Four players, two balls

METHOD

1. A, B and C stand along a line, each person three metres apart, all facing D who is opposite B. A, D and B form one passing triangle, and B, C and D another one that operates simultaneously and independently of the other. As the primary worker, B's job is to focus on D, the source of all direct passes, and alternately pass laterally to A and C. All passes are chest passes.
2. A passes to D as D passes to B.
3. B passes laterally to C as D passes another one to B. D keeps passing to B, and B keeps passing left then right without shifting focus from D. A and C keep returning passes to D.

The timing is split so that B receives a constant stream of passes, never two at the same time. A's and C's pace is a bit less frantic. D (like B) has to handle the ball double time in receiving from A and C alternately and passing straight down the line to B. This drill looks great when it is mastered, and it keeps every mind fully absorbed.

VARIATION

For those with superior coordination and multi-tasking ability, try adding cross-brain footwork to the task. As B dishes the pass left, she simultaneously taps her right foot on the ground. When dishing right, she taps with the left.

Team Ball Drills

These drills are based on eight players unless specified otherwise. All drills can be modified to cater for larger numbers by adding players, rotating them in, creating an extra station or reducing the dimensions and working two smaller groups. One or two balls are needed for each drill.

PRECISION PASSING

OBJECTIVE

To enhance optimal space technique with a fast-moving target; to catch hard, wide balls and develop timing of leads. The drill also promotes slick gathering, balancing and turning as well as release combination work.

REQUIREMENTS

Nine players, one ball

METHOD

1. Nine players form three queues (Q1, Q2 and Q3) as detailed in figure 2.14.
2. The player at the start of Q1 sprints forward to receive a shoulder pass from the player at the start of Q2, receiving it as close to the projected point of intersection of lines two and three as possible. The thrower from Q2 runs to the back of her line after releasing the ball.

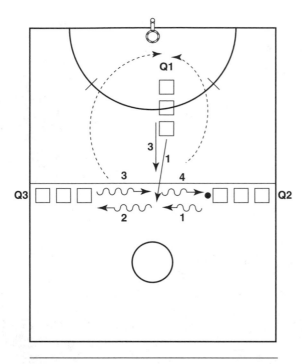

3. The receiver balances, turns quickly and shoulder passes back to Q3 (receivers always pass to the queue they did not receive from), then returns with a clearing move outside the congested area to the end of her original queue.

4. The drill repeats as the first player in Q3 throws to Q1's new runner. The thrower then runs to the back of her line.

All leads are from Q1 to the projected point of intersection of the other two queues, and all plays are sequenced in order of run, catch, turn, pass and clear. Players remain in their own queues until the coach calls a rotation.

Figure 2.14 Precision passing.

VARIATION

Add a static defender to the projected point of intersection. The defender does not attempt to intercept at this stage but adds pressure to the return pass when the receivers are in the middle.

THE TRIANGLE

OBJECTIVE

To develop the skill of reoffering, moving in the opposite direction (as an alternative to following the ball); to enhance technical aspects of finishing off passes, transferring weight forward in the direction of the pass before rebalancing and sprinting in the opposite direction. The drill can also be used as a pre-screening activity to train players' bodies to move away from the ball, as well as the planning of moves off the ball. The drill also provides chances to improve concentration, reaction time, group thinking and collaboration.

REQUIREMENTS

Nine players, one ball

METHOD

This drill needs at least nine players; three for each queue is ideal.

1. Form three queues (Q1, Q2 and Q3) in a triangle formation, 10 metres apart.

2. The player at the start of Q1 shoulder passes to a player at the start of either remaining queue and sprints to the back of the opposite queue.

3. Players continue the sequence of throwing one way, driving another. Players need to exercise their judgment and decision making to keep the queues relatively even and ensure there is at least one player in each queue.

4. After a few minutes, add an occasional fake pass before the balls are released. Be sure players are working a variety of passes and both sides of their bodies, including reverse shoulder passes, hip passes and overhead passes.

VARIATION: THE SQUARE

For larger groups (minimum of 12), add another queue and run the drill from a square formation, with 10 metres between each queue. If the player with the ball chooses the queue to her right or left, she runs to the laterally opposite queue as for the original version. If she chooses the queue diagonally opposite, she runs to the shortest queue to keep numbers equal. If the queues are the same length, a quick choice must be made between the two.

CHAPTER 3

Off-the-Ball Moves

With one ball for 14 players, each player spends the great majority of time during a game without the ball. During this time, players are reading the play, timing leads, leading for the ball, planning play sequences or defending against opponents. Sound body movement dynamics are an integral part of the overall performance of a netballer no matter what position she plays. Developing skills that do not involve possession of the ball carries considerable importance. It is critical that a player develop good body control so she can shift from dynamic, free-flowing movement in running for the ball to a more static mode to take possession of the ball and stop, elevate or pivot.

Players need to understand that court balance and movement without the ball can be just as important in setting up scoring opportunities as moves involving the ball. Apart from speed, which can be improved only marginally with proper training, all movement dynamic skills can be significantly improved from a basic level. This chapter defines and outlines these skills and provides base drills for targeting development in each of the broad off-the-ball attacking movement areas (specific defending techniques are featured in chapter 6). The areas examined are elements of movement without the ball, as well as preliminary moves and lead variations.

Body Movement

To be complete all-round players, athletes need to understand and apply the concepts of maximising their effectiveness when not in possession. Players should always have their eyes up and be switched on, looking for involvement at all times, moving with purpose and without hesitation. The chief components of body movement in netball are balance, footwork, speed, agility, elevation and timing.

Figure 3.1 The ready stance with good static balance—low centre of gravity and wide base.

Balance and Control

Balance can be considered in two forms, static and dynamic. Players with good static balance will keep their feet in a contest and not be pushed over easily. These players have a low centre of gravity in their body position before take-off, or their ready stance. A player in the ready stance features a flexed and upright trunk, weight slightly forward on the balls of the feet, arms symmetrical at the sides and elbows bent (see figure 3.1). The player has a wide base from which to spring into action, with feet shoulder-width apart and the opposite foot to preferred hand slightly forward in a splayed stance.

Effective static balance requires good muscular strength, particularly in the quadriceps. Training muscular groups in opposite pairs (e.g., quadriceps and hamstrings) as well as stabiliser muscles is important to develop balanced strength in each major muscle area. Static balance can be developed through drills that involve movement recovery and that transfer momentum from the passive ready stance to take-off, acceleration, deceleration and back to ready stance with varying speeds and footwork combinations.

Dynamic balance is essentially balance on the move (e.g., passing on the move or in the air). The ability to maintain good control of body and ball while mobile is an acquired skill that needs to be constantly developed and honed. Dynamic balance can be cultivated through ball drills (detailed at the end of this chapter) and most team warm-up drills.

Body control develops in unison with balance. Without appropriate balance skills, control is impossible to maintain. Body control begins with moving safely and knowing when to accelerate into a space and when to wait, as well as possessing sound running, jumping and passing techniques. It also involves knowing which balls players should attempt to contest or intercept without risking injury or breaking the rules. Body control is essential for player safety. Players without adequate control of their bodies on the court are a danger to themselves and others as well as a disaster on the team statistics sheet.

Attempting to keep streamlined, with limbs close to the body's midline, is a good starting point for fluent, controlled movement on the court. When a ball is involved, the primary body control objective is to land safely after gaining or attempting to gain possession. Landing on two feet is the safest option, taking care to align body joints as much as possible before grounding to prevent injury. When a two-foot landing is not possible, bringing the ball to the midline of the body as quickly as possible helps regain balance and control and allows the player to move quickly onto both feet.

Sometimes the safest landing option is not to stop at all. If a player is running at full speed and is extended to reach a ball, it is sometimes impossible to pull up safely in two steps. If the path ahead is clear (most likely because the player has outrun her opponent), passing on the run (the step-on pass—see figure 3.2) is the best option. Players up-court who have read the play well will read that the passer is going to run two steps with the ball and should provide a quick forward lead on the same side of the court to provide an obvious target for the mobile passer.

Figure 3.2 Passing on the run. Good dynamic balance is needed for a step-on pass.

Footwork

Netball footwork is very intricate, and players need a highly developed aware-ness of their feet in relation to their bodies. Footwork rules need to be obeyed at all times when playing the ball; to contravene the footwork rule ever so slightly incurs a loss of possession for the team. Footwork needs to be worked in with movement that is adjusted for speed, stopping and turning (pivoting). Footwork must be crisp in games to avoid being penalised for stepping or dragging the grounded foot. Players should always practise sharp footwork in drills and warm-ups, making stopping safely a priority.

- **Speed.** The element of the game that has possibly evolved the most is the speed at which it is played. Netball is one of the fastest team sports, and play-ers benefit from having speed. People can develop great skills, work ethics and attitudes, but speed is one ability that has a ceiling. Players should all aim to maximise their speed, regardless of their genetic predisposition. A player who is lucky enough to be blessed with great raw leg speed, particularly speed over the first five metres, has a head start on her peers and should develop her game to exploit it.

  Training for speed in netball needs to be very game specific to maximise development (refer to chapter 10 for details). If players' movements were electroni-cally tracked, it would become apparent that the majority of recorded sprinting distances in a game would be approximately within the 3- to 10-metre zone, before a change of direction occurred. Therefore, sprint training should be engineered to reflect this (taking into account overload and building an initial base). Exercises to improve sprinting performance could include resistance work (e.g., sprinting against a force such as a team-mate holding a towel around the waist as a harness to develop strength), pool work (low impact as well as resistance) and altering take-off style. Players should remember that although speed is a wonderful asset, it needs to be balanced with control and nurtured in combination with ball skills and decision making.

- **Stopping.** When a player is moving without the ball, it is generally easier to slow down, stop safely or change direction than when she has the ball. When changing direction, players should incorporate a few standard procedures into their motion. Shortening the stride length into the turn and transferring weight smoothly through the stop will protect the knees as well as enhance take-off speed in the new direction. Players should dig in with their feet by momentarily anchoring and pushing off from their outside foot and take short, quick steps out of the turn, using their arms for balance and stability. Hips, knees and ankles should be kept in line at all times, avoiding twisting. While completing the stop-ping action, players must keep their eyes on the ball and the play at all times.

  Stopping with the ball is more difficult because the focus is on the ball and often the player is at full stretch, moving with speed, and has to pull up cleanly in two steps. It is especially difficult for players transferring from other sports such as basketball; often footwork has to be taken right back to the basics and relearned. Stepping tends to be called a lot in beginners' grades, then eases off through intermediate levels, reappearing again at higher levels as the pace and intensity of matches pick up and many more sophisticated leads are used. With the pace so fast as well as increased rolling, spinning and turning in the goal circle and faster ball work, the degree of difficulty of the footwork rises to a completely new level.

• **Pivoting.** Whenever a player receives the ball while facing in any direction other than that of the next target, she needs to turn quickly and legally to sight down-court options or set up to shoot. As players can pivot an unlimited number of times in the same possession, they should use the pivot correctly to fully open their bodies to the target for optimal technique, balance and power and not pass or shoot with a closed or twisted stance. Players should try to land on their preferred throwing side's foot or on two feet so that the opposite foot to hand is movable and forward, completing a balanced passing technique.

At the top levels of the game, where elite players have mastered the fundamental passing and footwork techniques, hybrid combinations of landing foot, passing action and throwing side come into play to gain release-time advantages. These hybrid, or fusion, techniques are executed only after years and years of polishing the foundation models and achieving a high level of passing accuracy and strength in combination with superb footwork and body control.

Agility

The netball court is only 30.5 metres long and 15.25 metres wide, and space is shared by 14 players. In a closed goal circle, with 4 players in and 4 around the goal circle's edge, each player in the circle gets about 9.4 square metres of foot space (area of a semi-circle with radius 4.9 metres divided by 4 for the mathematically curious . . .). Netball is definitely a game of working the tight spaces, and players with great agility who can combine nimble footwork, speed, changes of direction, smooth momentum transfer and elevation enjoy distinct advantages over less agile opponents.

Agility in netball includes the interchangeable transference of forwards to backwards; acceleration to deceleration to stopping; pivoting to stopping to acceleration; and long strides to short strides. Side-stepping, or slip-stepping (side-together-side foot pattern in the same direction), is used when the distance to cover is too short to effectively break into a running technique. An extension of this is diagonal side-stepping forwards and backwards. Sprinting to stopping to jumping; consecutive jumping; and jumping to landing to accelerating sequences are all frequent combinations in a mobile player's repertoire. Speed in crossing body sides with feet or hands is a distinct hallmark of the agile, coordinated player.

All agility movement combinations need to be considered in agility drill design. Over a unit of training, it is ideal to train the body to perform all the specific netball combination movements by including them in agility drills (such as the ones at the end of this chapter) or adding them to regular ball drills. A carefully designed drill could easily incorporate all of them.

Elevation

Elevation involves the distance a player can get from the ground when jumping. Four elements of jumping that determine elevation are technique, run-up, take-off and muscular development. Jumping can be vertical or diagonal. High leapers use power primarily from their legs, and two legs are much more powerful than one. To maximise height in vertical (standing) jumps, a combination of two feet and one hand should be used, as one hand can reach higher than two can; however, two hands are more likely to bring the ball down securely. Adding a run-up to the sequence (running jump) will increase momentum and, therefore, power. Each situation must be judged according to the circumstances (e.g., the height of the ball and who will be contesting it). Most of the time, other than rebounding and holding leads, the high ball will be wide of the receiver's midline. The receiver should aim to accelerate into the jump, extend her arm diagonally and forward if practicable to get first touch of the ball, and make the last stride a long one. Again, using a two-foot take-off and two hands to catch, if possible, will increase chances of snapping the ball into possession.

Training methods to improve vertical jump are still traditional. Plyometrics (an explosive form of power training) and weight-training programs aim to increase strength and power in the legs and improve technique. Like speed, each individual's elevation can be improved relatively marginally compared with other skills such as ball handling and decision making. However, when all things are relatively equal among athletes and teams, it is the one-percenters that count. Maximising individual elevation is another facet of being a complete player.

Timing and Deception

Timing and deception can be linked to both moving and passing. This section focusses on the body movement dynamics of these elements. Deception in relation to passing is detailed in the section on fake passes in chapter 2.

In netball, making a move to the ball too early quickly leads players to a boundary line as well as allows defenders to easily pick off balls. Moving too late causes the team to pass backwards or incur held-ball infringements that lose possession for the team. To engage the passer, shake a defender off, time a lead and receive the ball safely within three seconds is an impressive juggling act. To get the timing of leads right and maintain forward momentum of a team attack, a player needs to combine several skills including reading the play, knowing who is on the lead, knowing team-mates' strengths and capabilities (e.g., how quickly they turn, if they pass from both sides of the body, speed and common movement paths), knowing when to make a preliminary move and knowing when to lead for the ball. Knowing when to slow down the timing of a lead by turning (rolling) or changing direction, as well as confidence to turn off the ball, can be gained through many different simulated down-court play drills. Timing can be greatly improved by regular practice of well-designed drills. Timing is an aspect of nearly every ball drill, so opportunities to fine-tune it are plentiful. To isolate timing and feature it as the focus for improvement, group movement drills without a ball are useful.

Deception works intrinsically with timing to create consistently well-executed leads. Players should mix up their speed on court with sprint, clear, stop, sprint actions rather than a standard cadence jog. Players who run the same speed with little variation are much more predictable and less effective at presenting as clear targets (unless the target towers over the opponent, in which case a very predictable holding lead the whole game might be the smartest move!).

To be deceptive in movement and keep one step ahead of a defender, the attacking player can do several things. If being guarded in a standard one-on-one front defence stance, she should be conscious of moving to the side her opponent is *not* looking to begin a lead (see figure 3.3). This will unsight the defender straightaway. For example, an attacker making a lead makes a sharp dodge left when the opposition defender has adopted a defensive position looking over the right shoulder. Mixing up running speeds, changing direction frequently and including sudden stops in straight leads to make opponents overrun are all standard in a match plan of the effective attacking player. Mastering many different types of leads to develop an armoury of options will enable a player to deceive any defensive style. Incorporating rolling and dodging into the leading repertoire challenges a personal opponent's defensive range, and players should always aim to keep one step ahead in planning and action.

Figure 3.3 Using deception by making the first movement to the side the defender is not looking.

Preliminary Moves

Preliminary moves are individual movements a player completes immediately before presenting as a target on a lead for the thrower. The effectiveness of the preliminary move will determine if a player has lost a defender momentarily and is open as a clear passing target. Mastering a variety of prelims maintains mental focus, motivation, confidence and unpredictability. Some prelims are location specific and apply to players specialising in that position, such as the roll and drop for a goaler.

Preliminary moves can be grouped into two sections: basic (moves facing the ball) and advanced (moves turning off the ball or away from the play). Basic prelims are necessary for every player to develop, and advanced moves should be tackled to add depth to a player's range once she has mastered the basics. Players can develop a personal range of prelims that work for them according to their individual physical attributes and their position. Players with a complete range of prelims are exciting to watch and will often have opponents' heads spinning around trying to find them!

When working on their prelims, players should get close to the defenders to get open. It is easier to set an effective move from a definitive starting point. If the defenders move offline, attackers need to move back up to them to make a clear getaway. If the attackers do not set their prelims from close range, their leads will be hazy and mistimed. Attackers must create space to be able to use it.

To execute a prelim, attackers must read the play and time their moves well. After the prelim, the attackers flow into their explosive movement to lead and receive. All preliminary moves examined in this section will assume standard one-on-one defence. Each move is also detailed in table 3.1.

> "A player who uses a variety of moves off the ball will keep opponents guessing and will ensure that she is always that half a step ahead in whatever moves she makes."
>
> ~ Rebecca Sanders, Australian Centre, Two-Time Gold Medallist of the Commonwealth Games, World Champion

Straight Lead

The straight lead is a direct run to the ball, usually on the same side of the court as the thrower. It requires very rapid acceleration, as deception is not used in body movement. The key to executing a successful straight lead is timing. A straight lead executed at the right time and at the correct angle is usually successful because it allows the attacker to make an explosive move that is quicker than the defender's reaction move.

To execute the straight lead, the attacker should select the ball side if practicable (the same side of the court as the passer so the defender is less likely to catch up)

Table 3.1 Characteristics of Various Preliminary Moves

Type of move	Difficulty	Applications	Frequency	Users	Features
Straight lead	Easy	Used when slightly clear of a defender to begin with or when a defender's head is turned to the opposite side of the intended lead	Very high	All players	Very simple and quick to execute; keeps the ball moving and maintains the flow of play in a down-court attack
Cut-off lead	Moderate	Used when attacker wants to lead into a front space that is currently being occupied by the opponent	Moderate to high	All players	Prevents defenders from contesting ball on the next pass; assists thrower by reducing perceptual demands of optimal pass placement; gives the cutter good initial vision for the next passing target
Dodge	Easy	Used when the defender is playing very close to the attacker to get free relatively easily	High	All players	Easy move to execute with maximum impact; leaves defenders guessing right from the start as it begins on their blind side; can be deadly under the goalpost

(continued)

Table 3.1 *(continued)*

Type of move	Difficulty	Applications	Frequency	Users	Features
Half roll	Moderate	Used when a defender covers the dodge well or is agile and good on the lateral moves; also used as an alternative to moves facing the ball	Low	All players but mainly the attack line	Gives an attacker an extra weapon to use in presenting as an open target; disorientates defenders
Hold	Moderate	Used when a player has a clear space behind or to her side and wants to protect it so she can receive a lobbed pass there	High passing into the goal circle and from a throw-in; lower in dynamic mid-court play	All players except the goal keeper	Effective as a finishing move into the shooting circle; can exploit a height mismatch; provides an easy inbound option for a back-line throw-in
Screen	High	Used when two players work together to protect premium space to receive a ball in: one screens or blocks and the other makes the catch	Low; opportunity only presents in congested crossed-ball situations	Mostly goalers but also wing attack, goal defence and wing defence	Effective as a finishing move into the shooting circle; can provide a secure back target over congestion, create uncontested centre-pass targets or lose a close-checking defender
Roll-around	High	Used when an attacker wants to lead into a front space that is occupied by an opponent; great before an out-lead for a goal shooter off a centre-pass reception	Low to moderate	Predominantly goal shooter but also goal attack, goal defence and wing defence	Great for goal defence or wing defence off a back-line throw-in; great signature move for shooters of all speeds on an out-lead from the circle

and accelerate off the mark. The attacker then springs forward on an angle (about 45 degrees) towards the thrower to cut the defender's angle and time, reaching for the ball with arms and fingers extended. She should be sure to land safely, pivot and sight the next target or the goal.

Cut-Off Lead (Front Cut)

The cut-off lead is another basic move that should be in every player's prelim list. It is executed when an attacker positions slightly to the preferred leading side, swings the inside leg forward to cut off an opposition defender's space and moves towards the passer. This lead lets an attacker gain total front spot on a defender and increases the chances of a safe delivery pass, as the ball is uncontested on the catch.

To execute the cut-off, a player must read the play and time her move. Next, she should select the side to cut and position herself very close to the defender, with the outside foot almost level with the nearest foot of the defender. The attacker then bends the knees and transfers weight forward to suddenly swing the inside leg through the gap across in front of the defender's feet, sealing off the front space (see figure 3.4). The attacker must ensure that the defender is not committed to moving forward first, or the cut-off could cause contact. If the defender is guarding the opponent behind closely, the defender's weight will be over her feet and not forward. After the leg swing, the attacker should transfer weight forward again and accelerate off the mark, springing towards the thrower. As for all leads, the attacker should reach for the ball with two hands and arms extended to catch the

Figure 3.4 The cut-off lead.

ball, land safely and pivot to sight the next target or goalpost. After the attacker seals off the space and advances into it, she may add a variation by breaking left or right to optimise court balance or steer away from other defenders.

Dodge

Dodging before receiving a ball is a common sight on the netball court. Many players choose the dodge frequently, as it is both easy to execute and one of the most effective ways to lose a defender. The dodge begins before the passer is ready to release to allow time for the complete action. The attacker springs explosively to one side for two steps to complete one dodge (see figure 3.5). If the defender is still on board, the attacker digs in and dodges back the other way. As soon as the attacker senses she is free, she sprints out for the ball. The attacker should always take advantage by starting the dodge on the defender's blind side, the side she is not looking. The number of dodges should be determined by when a defender has lost track of the attacker. It is always amusing to see some attackers double dodge right back into the path of a defender even though they completely lost the defender on the first dodge!

Figure 3.5 The dodge.

After identifying the defender's blind side, the attacker accelerates off the mark to the blind side by taking two quick side-steps, keeping the feet uncrossed and using the arms for balance and power. If the defender has lost sight temporarily on the first dodging movement, the player should continue in a straight lead to that side. If the defender is still on board, the attacker keeps dodging until she loses the defender. Excessive dodging or dodging with too much lateral force can put strain on knee joints and lead to injury. It is important to mix up high-impact preliminary moves such as the dodge with rolling and holding moves to protect and conserve knees, particularly on unforgiving asphalt surfaces.

Half Roll and Roll-Off

The half roll is a very effective way to confuse a defender and protect knees at the same time. Any time a player turns back and away from a defender in front, she immediately gives herself the advantage of depth and width. By turning, the attacker disappears from the defender's field of peripheral vision. The half roll can be a great move for a centre pass or for any set play where there is dead ball time before the pass (e.g., penalties, throw-ins), giving the passer full view of the move from the start of the three-second ball-handling limit.

To execute the half roll, the attacker starts directly behind the opposition defender, feet shoulder-width apart, and pivots 180 degrees sharply to the defender's blind side, turning the head in line with the body and using the arms for balance (see figure 3.6). The instant the movable foot hits the ground, she spins back to the starting position. The movable foot creates a visual cue for the defender, who usually then turns her head and transfers weight to this side. As the head turns, the attacker spins back 180 degrees to her original position. The attacker then accelerates off the mark in that direction.

A variation, or rather a continuation, of the half roll is the roll-off. The mechanics are exactly the same as for the half roll except instead of spinning back 180 degrees to the original position, the roll is continued in the same direction to complete 360 degrees in two half turns. The attacker moves smoothly out of the roll in the same lateral direction and sprints out on a 45-degree angle for the ball. The downside of this spectacular manoeuvre is that it is slow compared with other moves that take the attacker's eyes off the ball. If the roll-off is not done rapidly and fluently, the defender has time to catch up by the time the roller has recovered.

Figure 3.6   The half roll.

Hold

The hold is used in conjunction with a lob pass. It is a stationary player-on-player move designed to protect space where the receiver can catch the ball, either behind or to the side of a defender. When setting up a hold, an attacker aims to seal off

Figure 3.7 The hold using a T-position technique, side-on to the defender.

a space to receive the ball by moving into it at the last moment. A player needs to leave enough room behind the protected space for a pass that comes in long or wide and calculate if other players in the vicinity are close enough to deflect the pass. The hold is likely to be the predominant move of a very tall goaler.

Two of the most effective techniques for a hold are the T position and the front to back. To set up the T position, the holder swings her body side-on to the defender such that her arm lines up with the defender's spine (see figure 3.7). A T-position hold telegraphs the target area but puts an extra body width between defender and ball, making the ball harder to deflect. With the front-to-back technique, the holder faces the thrower square-on and indicates with a raised arm which side she wants the ball to be placed. A front-to-back technique hides the target area from the defender, whose orientation is on the ball, but places the attacker closer to her opponent.

To execute the hold, the player must set it late. If a player indicates too early what she intends to do, a defender can easily foil the plan with a simple shuffle step around the body. Just as the pass is about to be released, the attacker provides a visual cue for the thrower by raising the appropriate target hand into the receiving space. The attacker then steps behind the defender to seal off the desired space using either a T-position or front-to-back technique. (The technique chosen comes down to personal preference of the holder.) The attacker should maintain body position with knees flexed as the ball sails in, holding strongly so that the defender is not able to nudge her out of position. When the ball passes over the defender, the attacker springs into the protected space and snaps the ball in with a smart take, landing with a split reception if possible in the goal circle.

Screen

Screening is an attacking preliminary move requiring advanced skills that has crept into goal circles worldwide to become a standard manoeuvre for high-performance teams. It is like a hold set up for a team-mate, and it is a two-player operation: one screens, one receives. The screen is a self-sacrificing move, as the player setting the screen forfeits her chance to lead for the ball. The goal circle is the best environment for screening, as the area is congested and the ball is crossed frequently, allowing set-up time. Screens can also be used at centre passes (e.g., GA screening the opposition WD for WA to pop out, as illustrated in figure 3.8), from throw-ins to create a clear space for a lob to go to a team-mate (e.g., GD screening for WD on a back-line throw-in) and to throw over a zone (e.g., WA screening opposition GD in a centre-court press for GA to receive at the back). Sometimes screens are used to guide an opponent into traffic to hold her up as the attacker cuts past (e.g., GA cutting into the goal circle, taking her opponent past the WA and opposition WD).

To execute a screen, players look for an opportunity in a congested space where the ball will be crossed from one side of the court

Figure 3.8 The screen (set by GA) used to protect a space to free up a team-mate (WA) as a target at the centre pass.

to the other. The screener communicates with the team-mate whom the screen will be set for. Often eye contact, a quick verbal signal or even grabbing the team-mate's arm when close by to position her is all that is needed. The receiver then splits her focus between the ball, the next receiver (if it is not her) and getting in the space being protected for her to finish the move. The screener sets a low and visible body block (with knees and hips slightly flexed, feet slightly more than shoulder-width apart) and defends the designated opponent from getting to the ball as it goes to the team-mate in the protected space adjacent.

Roll-Around

The roll-around, or screen and roll, is a slick move that has the same function as a standard cut-off. When executed correctly, a roll-around leaves defenders stranded behind and allows the receiver to run unopposed to the ball. It takes more time than the front cut because of the turning aspect but is less likely to incur a contact penalty, as the movement of rolling around the player directs limbs away from the defender, avoiding contact. It has another advantage over the front cut in that a defender cannot predict it, making the initial step across easier for the attacker.

To execute the roll-around, the attacker selects the side to roll to (ball side if possible) and starts moving early, as a full turn takes some time. She positions herself behind and very close to the opposition defender on the side to which she is rolling. The attacker takes a large step quickly and assertively with the front foot to seal off the defender's feet at the prescribed side as the ball is received by the thrower. The attacker then transfers momentum forward by pivoting on the front foot (outside with respect to the defender) and across the front of the defender, keeping knees bent and centre of gravity low, using the defender's nearest shoulder to act as a vertical axis to rotate around. As the ball is resighted, the attacker pivots back onto the other foot, staying as close as possible so she cannot break forward until a full 360-degree turn is completed and she is directly in front of the defender. The attacker then rebalances and sprints forward to receive the ball uncontested.

Lead Variations

Once players have preliminary moves under control, they can consider some simple variations when the run to the ball is under way. Variations are deployed if a defender is closing in on the attacker, to place the receiver in a more advantageous location or for variety.

- **V-Lead.** The V-lead is a straight lead with a hairpin bend in it. It is also like a dodge in the middle of the lead rather than at the start. After the first few steps of a lead, the attacker simply puts the brakes on suddenly, transfers momentum smoothly and springs off in another direction between 45 and 90 degrees to the original path. Usually the V-lead starts in a path leading away from the ball and ends up going to it.

- **Lead and Dodge.** Similar to the V-lead, the lead and dodge is a straight lead with a change of direction. While the V-lead is a smooth transition of momentum from one direction to another, the lead and dodge involves stopping the lead and dodging or double dodging to lose the defender, then recommencing the lead.

- **Up-and-Back Move.** The up-and-back move, or drop-back, draws the defender towards the thrower at full pace on the guise that the ball is going to be passed in front to a straight lead. The leader then digs in and doubles back, running away from the thrower down-court for a lob or overhead pass. The leader needs to turn her body in the direction she is travelling for speed and balance but should continue to sight the ball over her shoulder. The up-and-back move is pre-planned, so the attacker must ensure that the space she is going to double back into is clear for her to do so before breaking. A variation is to turn off the ball when doubling back to maintain momentum and make the move more difficult to pick for the defender.

- **Stop Dead and Lunge.** A defender can be brutally caught out by the action of this move because it is much faster than any reaction a defender can execute. If the opposition defender has gained ground on the attacker using a straight lead, the attacker pulls up abruptly (with consideration for joint safety and not so that the umpire deems it inevitable contact) from running at full speed to stopping suddenly without warning. If executed well, the defender invariably overruns, and the attacker simply digs in, lunges back towards the ball or leads in another direction to receive an easy pass. Care should always be taken in any sudden movement to cushion the ankles, knees and other body joints as much as possible. The stop-dead lead can be a good remedy for the attacker who has made her move too early.

Performance Points for Movement Off the Ball

- Strive to be in peak physical condition with a solid aerobic base to be a constant contributor off the ball.
- Practise footwork, timing and body control in every team or individual drill.
- Develop a wide range of preliminary moves, and constantly add to and fine-tune them.
- Aim for an acute sense of court spacing and balance—look to support, reoffer or screen for a team-mate.
- Exploit your natural strengths and tailor major movement patterns to enhance them.

Off-the-Ball Drills

Body control is intrinsic in almost every netball drill. Focussing on a particular developmental area or combining fitness work with body control can satisfy a number of objectives at once. It is not a waste of time doing drills without the ball on occasion. Working without the ball isolates particular body movements, enabling players to make corrections without the demands of coordinating the action with ball movement (e.g., in preliminary moves and timing). If the specific purpose of the body control drill is communicated to the players, it provides a focus and promotes awareness, and high-quality work is more likely to emerge. Setting a time limit or a skill-based goal for body control drills also sharpens the focus for the group or individual.

Individual Off-the-Ball Drills

Body mechanics drills designed for individual practice can be done either independently of team training or simultaneously with the group at training. They can be performed in any space roughly equivalent to one-third of a court. A set of markers is useful to mark distances when not using court markings. A good warm-up including adequate light movement and stretching should precede all sprint work. If possible, heavy-duty sprint work (such as in the pre-season phase) should be done on grass, firm sand or an athletics track surface to absorb the shock of this high-impact work. Players with pre-existing injuries or health problems should be screened by a health professional before participating in any high-impact or strenuous conditioning work.

SPRINT DRILLS

OBJECTIVE

To develop speed, leg power, elevation, footwork, dynamic balance, timing and body control. The drill set also overloads transitions from several different movements while focussing on running technique and balance.

REQUIREMENTS

One to 10 players, full netball court or equivalent space

METHOD

Every time a worker gets to an end of the court, she should pause for 10 seconds, turn and start the next step in the sequence.

1. Starting behind the baseline of the court, for the first third, run slowly forward with "high knees", raising knees to above waist level every step, maintaining balance and power to the transverse line. Cadence should be high, but there should be low horizontal speed. Keep the head steady and eyes straight ahead. Use arms for drive and balance. Jog through third two, and in third three change to "back flicks", running forwards and exaggerating the follow-through stage of each step by flicking heels up at the back, contracting the hamstrings.

2. Complete a graded run (jog, sprint, jog sequence) over the three thirds.

3. For the first third, complete high bounding strides using arms for lift and balance, focussing on elevation and knee drive to gain maximum height each step. Jog the second third and "quickstep" through the last third by taking very small steps as rapidly as possible to the end. Emphasis should be on the transition from jog to quickstep, keeping eyes up, stepping lightly on toes.

4. Repeat the graded run through three thirds.

5. For the first third, complete long bounding strides using arms for power and balance, focussing on maximum stride length. Jog through the centre third, then complete V-cuts in the last third by taking three diagonal steps left, then cutting three diagonals right, to the end of the court. Emphasis should be on pushing off the outside foot, using arms for balance and drive and keeping eyes up.

6. Sprint the first third, jog the last two, turn and repeat.

7. Sprint the first two thirds, jog the last one, turn and repeat.

8. Sprint the whole court length, turn and repeat.

9. Finish with another graded run.

Rest and repeat steps 1 to 9 twice.

These basic run-throughs can be mixed, split and recombined to keep them fresh. The number of repetitions should be adjusted to the level of the performers.

RAMPS

Running uphill is not always a crowd favourite with the team. It does, however, translate to an excellent challenge for players and provides a chance to develop mental toughness as well as speed.

OBJECTIVE

To overload the difficulty of sprinting by adding a gradient to translate to an increase in flat linear speed

REQUIREMENTS

Any number of players, a ramp. Ramps can be found at beaches (sand hills have the same effect), parks, buildings and other community places.

METHOD

Depending on the gradient and length of the uphill slope, sets of 5 (increasing to 10 or more over subsequent sessions) can be run, with a walk-back recovery in between. Straight runs or strength work (e.g., push-ups, sit-ups or triceps dips) can be added in as recovery or to extend the workout. If no ramps can be found, stairs serve as an excellent substitute. Players must take care to keep weight forward, clear the step height and be sure to always walk back down.

AGILITY COURSES

OBJECTIVE

To practise different common netball movement patterns and link them together to improve agility, court speed and fluency; to enhance the ability to get free for a ball, defend an opponent or area, provide back up or reoffer leads

REQUIREMENTS

Eight to 12 players, 19 markers

METHOD

Set the markers out according to the formation in figure 3.9. Athletes start at the 45-degree mark of the goal arc (see note on page ix), facing the baseline at the far end of the court.

1. Sprint through the zigzag course, pushing off on the outside foot around each marker, to the corresponding goal arc at the other end. Pass the outside of the final marker, and side-step to the top of the arc. Jump vertically with arms up to an imaginary overhead ball and land safely.

2. Quickly move back into a side-step to the marker at the other 45 mark. Pass the outside of this cone, and shift to a backwards sprint to the marker directly behind, level with the centre circle.

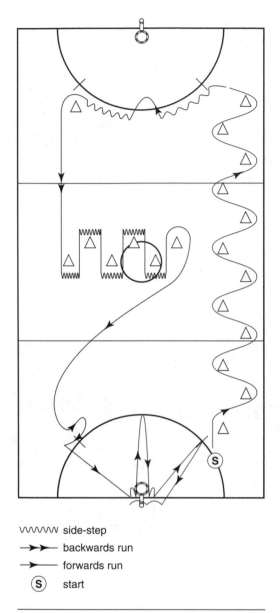

3. Pass the whole marker and begin "castle runs", side-step right twice, forward twice, right twice, back twice and so on through the course, ending at the final marker in the set.

4. Turn, pivot on the outside (right) foot and sprint cross-court to the final 45 mark of the goal arc.

5. Dig in and pivot on the left foot 180 degrees to meet an imaginary ball being passed from behind.

6. Pivot back on same foot and start the goal circle course, drive from the 45 to the post, touch the net, drive to the goal arc, return and touch the net, drive to the remaining 45, return and touch the net twice to finish the drill.

The coach should time the players and see if they can beat their times on the next attempt. If the next attempt is not to follow, be sure to set the markers at exactly the same places if comparing times to get an accurate result.

VARIATION

Reverse the drill. Make up your own agility courses to keep motivation high. Be sure to include different kinds of transitions as outlined.

vvvvvv side-step
→►— backwards run
→— forwards run
(S) start

Figure 3.9 Agility courses.

Pairs and Small-Group Off-the-Ball Drills

Body control drills can be completed in pairs and groups of three. Some drills replicate a specific game action and include a ball to provide a target or focus. Once players have mastered body movement drills to a sound degree, they should challenge themselves to coordinate their movement with that of their team-mates. To further develop their skills, players need to consider the positioning and movement of the ball in play with several players in a crowded vicinity. The following drill set details a graduated blend of the previously mentioned elements. Players 1, 2 and 3 are represented by *A*, *B* and *C*, respectively.

REPEATER JUMPS

OBJECTIVE

To increase elevation and improve recovery transitioning to sprint

REQUIREMENTS

Six to 12 players, 12 markers

METHOD

Set the markers out according to the formation detailed in figure 3.10, approximately one metre apart. Start at the first marker facing the row.

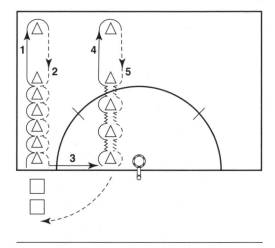

Figure 3.10 Repeater jumps, plus variations.

1. Complete six two-leg jumps over the markers, landing on two feet simultaneously.

2. As soon as the ground is touched after the sixth marker, make the transition to a sprint to the end marker. Approach the marker on the preferred side, push off on the outside foot, swing the inside leg across and pivot on it to turn 180 degrees back to face the markers.

3. Sprint back and complete two-leg jumps back to the start, tagging the next worker. (Rest while two team-mates complete the drill, for a 1:2 work to rest ratio.)

4. Repeat the sequence but after the jumps, pass on the other side of the end marker to develop turning on both sides.

5. Repeat the sequence again, but jump the markers facing sideways instead of forward. The sprint phase is the same.

6. Repeat previous sequence, facing the other way on the jumps phase.

VARIATION 1

Add another sequence of markers three metres to the side of and parallel to the first row, spaced three metres apart. After completing the return leg of the original row of jumps, side-step to the other set and jump the three-metre distance markers, completing quick-steps in between jumps.

VARIATION 2

Complete the routines hopping over the markers on one leg. Emphasis must be on balance and safe landings.

CENTRE-PASS MOVES

This drill replicates the agile movement patterns used at a centre pass.

OBJECTIVE

To fine-tune techniques and timing of dodges, half rolls, roll-arounds, cut-offs and up-and-back leads under pressure of one-on-one defence in a centre-pass setting. This is also a great drill for fitness and conditioning.

REQUIREMENTS

Three players, one ball, half a netball court

METHOD

A is the acting centre who starts in the centre circle with the ball. B is the worker who executes the attacking prelims from behind the facing transverse line (as for a centre pass). C acts as the defender on B.

1. A tosses the ball in the air behind the centre circle and jumps into it, landing on two feet to signify the start of the drill.
2. B uses any part of the transverse line to dodge past C and get over the line to receive the pass within three seconds.
3. Upon receiving, B lands on the outside foot, pivots and fakes a pass down-court using a shoulder, reverse shoulder or overhead pass as A drives to the transverse line on the opposite side to B, as a centre would to balance up the court space when driving towards the goal circle.
4. C attempts to intercept or deflect the pass from A. If successful, the ball returns to A for a repeat. If the pass gets through cleanly, C quicksteps to the hands-over position down-court, moving as quickly as possible to apply defence over the ball held by B.
5. After B fakes, A doubles back when she crosses the transverse line and returns to the centre circle to reset the drill.

The progressions of preliminary movements for B are dodge, half roll, cut-off, up-and-back lead, roll-around (adjust timing to start before A lands in the circle). Players repeat in the same roles one more circuit through, then rotate roles.

VARIATION

On the fifth centre pass (after the roll-around), A keeps driving through the transverse line to the 45 mark on the goal arc to receive a lob from B, who releases it this time. B then cuts to the opposite 45 mark to A, negotiating the blocker, C, who attempts to delay the drive forwards.

WALL WORK ROTATIONS

Players will need a brick wall for this drill.

OBJECTIVE

To improve a player's ability to work the tight spaces, react quickly to the rebounded ball and move around another player to get the ball without making contact

REQUIREMENTS

Up to five pairs of players, one ball per pair, a brick wall large enough for safe movement

METHOD

A stands three metres away from the wall with the ball, in front of B; both face the wall.

1. A lobs the ball onto the wall at overhead height.
2. After releasing the ball, A side-steps left once, diagonally back-steps right twice and moves forwards to receive again and to repeat. Meanwhile B has caught the ball, placed it back on the wall in the same position and carried out the same movement so that the two players are rotating closely around each other between each catch.

After 30 seconds, players change direction. Repeat for three minutes.

VARIATION

To work on forwards and backwards transitions and straight acceleration, the following adaptation can be made. Players stand side by side facing the wall, A with the ball standing slightly ahead of B. A passes the ball to a spot on the wall between both of them at just overhead height. A moves back as B accelerates forwards to the rebounded ball, places the ball back in the spot for A and moves backwards until the next pass presents. A and B continue to move back and forth in rhythm so that they are changing direction at the same time. Players work for 30 seconds, rest for 30 and repeat.

WORKING THE SQUARE

OBJECTIVE

To maintain and improve agility when tired

REQUIREMENTS

Up to 12 players in pairs, one ball per pair

METHOD

Mark out a three-metre square on the ground with markers. A stands outside the square two metres away with the ball. B starts as the worker in the square.

1. On "go", B completes an explosive combination of random netball-specific movements using the entire area of the square. Movements should include multi-directional sprinting, jumping, side-stepping, balancing, dodging, rolling, cutting, dropping back and touching the ground. B works for 30 seconds.

2. B tags A, who becomes the worker for 30 seconds.

3. Players repeat the task over a 20-second burst each.

4. Players repeat the task again for just a 10-second burst, maintaining equal work to rest ratios as they swap.

5. After the 10-second work period, they continue the sequences starting with 10 seconds and building up in 10-second increments to 20 and 30.

VARIATION

Repeat the drill with A throwing a ball in for B to chase down and return during the work phase. B must return to the movement work immediately after passing the ball back. Include the ball for all the work phases.

Team Off-the-Ball Drills

These drills are designed for a team of eight or more players in a group training setting. They combine a range of different netball skills but focus on body control and movement.

FOUR-POINT STAR COURSE

OBJECTIVE

To improve speed, agility and acceleration by racing against team-mates through a four-station "Star" course as quickly as possible

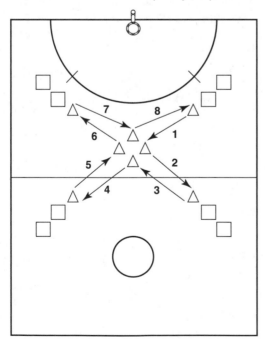

REQUIREMENTS

Eight players, eight markers

METHOD

Set eight markers in a double square formation as detailed in figure 3.11. The larger square should be approximately eight metres in length, the smaller square one metre. (Distances should be adapted according to level of the performers.) Two players position themselves at each point of the large square. Teams of two should be as even as possible in sprinting and agility capabilities to make for a challenging contest.

1. On "go", the four players at the start of the queues of the large square sprint to the corresponding marker of the small square, all moving in a clockwise direction.

Figure 3.11 Four-point star course.

2. They must bend to touch the marker with their hands then accelerate out to the next point in the large square, touch the marker and return to the next marker in the small square.

3. Players continue in this in-and-out pattern until they reach their original positions and tag their team-mates, who complete the same routine.

Each player completes the course three times. The team who finishes first wins. Reverse the drill so that players are moving anti-clockwise.

READ OFF

OBJECTIVE

To improve a player's ability to read the play down-court, in particular the lead in front to maintain court balance. Good understanding of reading off will maintain the flow and balance of the attack and reduce crowding.

REQUIREMENTS

Eight to 10 players, one ball held by the coach

METHOD

Players line up behind each other facing the coach at the baseline, about two metres apart.

1. On "go", the first player in line breaks sharply left or right three steps. The player behind reads off and makes the earliest possible judgment to move three steps the opposite way.

2. The pattern repeats down the line so that players in positions 1, 3, 5 and 7 end up on the same side, with players in positions 2, 4, 6 and 8 all on the other side. Movement should be as instantaneous as possible.

3. After four attempts, players should switch positions in the line-up.

4. When proficiency has improved, players change from a static start to a mobile start with quick-feet tapping.

5. When the group has mastered this, players add a dodge before take-off.

This exercise provides a few laughs initially, as a few players normally need a few attempts to get it right. The team goal is to have everyone on the correct side three times in a row.

VARIATION

Increase the distance to full court, with players spaced end to end, and start with player 1 throwing in from the baseline facing the line. On "go", players break as before, and the thrower chooses one of the first two leads and plays the ball down the line, with subsequent pairs of players making a new lead off every catch. Players finish with a shot for goal, then throw the ball in from the finishing end to reverse the drill. Players rotate up one position every sequence.

FULL-COURT RELAY MOVES

OBJECTIVE

To improve and add variety to a player's moves down-court when she does not have the ball by practising V-leads, recovery steps, lateral and diagonal side-stepping and short to long stride transitions

REQUIREMENTS

Eight players, eight markers, full netball court

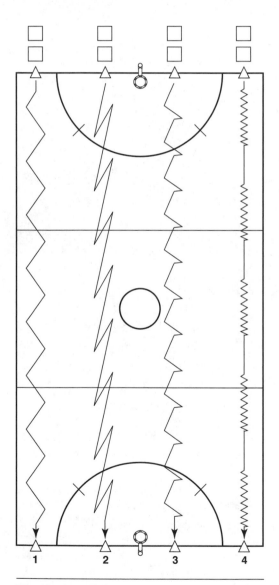

Figure 3.12 Full-court relay moves.

METHOD

Set four markers along one baseline, evenly spread at each end and in line with a corresponding marker at the opposite end. Two players line up behind each marker on the baseline (see figure 3.12). On "go", the four players at the start of each queue move down-court simultaneously using a prescribed movement.

1. Line 1: continuous four-step V-leads, moving four steps right first then four left

2. Line 2: sprint forwards four steps, dig in, back-step (recovery step), hands up in defensive position over the ball, pause one second, repeat sequence down-court

3. Line 3: V-leads moving three steps diagonally forwards to the right first, push off and change to three diagonally forwards left, dig in and complete two diagonal back-steps along the same path, repeat sequence down-court

4. Line 4: small rapid steps forwards for three seconds, sprint forwards three steps, repeat sequence down-court

When players reach the end of the court, they repeat the action back to the starting end and tag their partners (1:1 work to rest ratio). Players work for two minutes, then rotate one position to the left. The pair in queue 4 jogs back to the marker left vacant at queue 1. Repeat until each pair has completed each course.

FOUR CORNERS ROTATION

OBJECTIVE

To improve a player's ability to cut around another player using a triple-agility transfer action to meet the ball, pass accurately and recover for the next ball

REQUIREMENTS

Twelve or 16 players, four balls, four markers

METHOD

Set markers in a square formation, each about eight metres apart. Three players line up in a triangle formation at each marker, facing inside the square, one at the marker and two behind on either side. Two players at the markers diagonally opposite each other start with a ball (see figure 3.13).

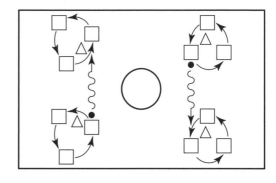

Figure 3.13 Four corners rotation.

1. On "go", the players with the balls pass to the adjacent clockwise queue as the receivers move to meet the ball forward of their marker.

2. After releasing the ball, the passers shuffle diagonally back two steps in an anti-clockwise direction, side-step right two steps and drive forwards (forming a triangle rotation pattern with the other two in the queue) to receive the incoming pass from their right.

3. The receivers pass onto the next adjacent clockwise queue and complete the same anti-clockwise triangle rotation (as mentioned in step two) with their group of three.

Players work for three minutes then restart the drill in the reverse direction (ball moves anti-clockwise and players move clockwise).

VARIATION

Add two balls to double the speed and decrease reaction time. All four players at the start of each queue have a ball. These players throw simultaneously to the second player at the next clockwise queue to initiate the drill.

CHAPTER 4

Goal Shooting

Accuracy, composure, toughness, precise technical work and rehearsed game pressure situations are the key ingredients to consistent, high-percentage shooting. If any of these elements are missing, the shooter is likely to go missing when the pressure is really on. In a game where only two of the team members can shoot, it is critical that they both be comfortable and eager to score at every opportunity. Every time the ball moves down-court, the aim is to get it to a shooter in a good scoring position. With the choice to play in goals comes the responsibility to do extra work to master the required skills: passing, catching, attacking, defending and executing set plays as well as carrying the load of making the shots count for the team. Shooters should focus on goal scoring and remember that their number one objective is to score as many shots for the team as they can. This chapter contains guidelines and drills for best-percentage goal shooting. It details shot selection, shooting techniques, the role of the shooting partner, mental rehearsal and rebounding. The drills section couples shooting with goaler-specific movement drills to maximise total goal circle performance.

Shot Selection

Shot selection underpins goal-shooting success. A shooter must weigh up—literally in a second—whether to take the shot, whether the other shooter is in a better scoring position and open, or whether to pass out to a feeder on the goal circle's edge and reposition. Four key points determine whether a goaler should shoot: balance, distance from the post, the goaling partner's actions and most important, how it feels.

- **Balance.** How quickly balance is maintained after reception is a critical factor in deciding whether to shoot. If a shooter takes a high ball close to her body's midline, it is easy for her to set up for a shot because the ball is almost in shooting position overhead and balance is reasonably intact. A tall shooter who plays a holding game receives a very high percentage of feeds overhead and close to the body's midline. These goalers are afforded not only the luxury of close-range shooting positions but also maximum set-up time for the shot as the transition from reception to a balanced shooting position is a simple, quick one.

Goalers who play more of a ground-cover game, darting around the circle and cutting *to* the ball, receive a lot more bounce passes, slings and short feeds for which they must stretch fully to take safely, often in a lunge or split-foot reception. It takes these goalers much longer to arrive in the balanced shooting position to take aim because they need to take the ball, which is often in the extremities of their reach or on the ground, move from a lateral wide position to a central tall position and raise the ball overhead to shoot. Any goaler who finds herself in an off-balance position to save the ball and knows that taking the shot would compromise her accuracy should attempt to pass off.

- **Distance.** After balance, distance is the next critical factor. Experienced shooters know their range and how far out they can shoot confidently. As a general guide, balls received halfway in or closer to the post should always be shot (barring special situations such as when both defenders commit to the shot, leaving the other goaler free under the post, or when the ball is received completely off balance). If the defensive pressure is not overbearing and other factors are in place, such as balance, a rebounder, no closer target and confidence, a shooter should take the shot from as far out as her technique's accuracy is reasonable.

"Speed, agility, and shooting daily (jump shot, step back, step to side, and fake shot) are key training fundamentals for commanding performances in goals. Players should always train at 100% focus on all aspects, not only shooting."

~ Irene van Dyk, Silver Ferns' Goal Shooter, Former South African
Goal Shooter and Captain, World Champion, Commonwealth Games Gold Medallist

- **Goaling partner.** Making the shots for the team is a dual responsibility shared between the goal shooter and the goal attack. Both have a job to do irrespective of who is taking the shot at the time. While the shooter takes aim, the partner looks to either screen the shot (close shots) or provide an off-load option (closer target for mid- to long-range shots) or sets up for a rebound. If the partner is screening or rebounding, the shooter shoots. If the partner sets up for a safe off-load and is in a better position, the decision is with the shooter. If the shooter is at a mid-range distance and is confident the shot will score, she should take the shot. If the risk of passing off and allowing the partner to make an easy shot is a higher-percentage option than the shooter's own more challenging shot, the shooter should off-load.

- **Feel.** When the balance, distance, partner and defensive factors are all in place, the decision to shoot is most likely the correct one. With an understanding of these variables, shooters get to the point where they automatically sense when to shoot and when to pass off. They need this instinct because there is not time to consciously go through each factor one by one for every shot. A goaler who has a sound technique and mental skills but suffers inaccuracy is most likely making poor choices on shot selection and needs to be taken back through the decision-making processes to relearn them so that instinct based on understanding can take over.

Shooting Techniques

Different circumstances call for different shots. A successful shooter must work towards mastery of a range of techniques to ensure that she is comfortable shooting against all types of defence and in all game situations. These techniques include the high-release standard shot, stepping back, stepping to the side, stepping in, the jump shot, the running shot and the fake shot. Wherever possible, goalers should opt for the high-percentage standard shot.

Standard Shot

An acronym that emphasises the critical elements of shooting is BEES. This easily remembered acronym provides a reminder and focus of netball shooting mechanics.

- B: balance
- E: eyes
- E: elbows
- S: swish

When making modifications to a technique, fine-tuning variation shots or ironing out inaccuracy from the previous match, players can always go back to BEES with the help of their coach to pinpoint technical errors and identify segments of the shot to be improved.

- **Balance.** To balance for a standard stationary shot, the shooter needs to square up to the goalpost by aligning the midpoints of the feet, hips and shoulders vertically to the post (see figure 4.1a). Fingers should be spread wide to grip the ball in the shooting hand so daylight can be seen between the palm and ball, with the other hand supporting on the side. A moment of stillness is ideal before release.

- **Eyes.** When balanced, the shooter should zone in on a very distinguishable and consistent focus point. The back eyelet of the net thread in line with the shooter on the back rim of the ring gives a specific and visible point on which to fix concentration. Focussing on this point at the back of the rim, the shooter should aim to project the ball up and over the front rim to hit the back eyelet and drop in with backspin. This is the focus point suitable for the majority of goalers. Goalers should give it a fair trial before considering switching. For shooters who consistently overshoot despite technical corrections (they miss by putting too much on the ball with their natural shooting action), a focus point on the front rim may suit them better. With this focus point, they should aim to clear the rim with the ball, as a high jumper would clear the bar. Once a focus point has been incorporated into the shooting routine, a player should not deviate from it. Training the eyes and body to work together to produce a consistent, smooth action requires delicate blending of gross- and fine-motor coordination. To mess with the focus point plays havoc with accuracy as the body needs to recoordinate a completely new set of variables with brain messages, flight paths and projection adjustment.

- **Elbows.** Elbow action is the catalyst for straight shooting. In the set-up, once the grip is right, a shooter's arms should be extended high overhead so that he is almost touching his ears (see figure 4.1b). He should be wary of "chicken wings" sticking out; elbows poking out to the side will project the ball off target laterally. A good cue for goalers is to imagine they are shooting between two brick walls, close to each elbow of the shooting arm. This will encourage a front–back lever action, reducing sidespin errors and the chance of skewing the ball right or left.

- **Swish.** Swish is the sound all shooters love to hear at the end of the shot. It means the ball has gone through the ring cleanly. Swish can also describe what occurs at the wrists on release to make that happen. When ready to release, the shooter should slightly bend his knees, elbows, wrists and ankles simultaneously, while transferring momentum forward, and release the ball with a swish (wave goodbye), leaving his hands and fingers up there for two seconds after release. Exaggerating the hands-up segment will prevent the shooter from drawing his hands away straight after the shot and destabilising the release point.

To execute the standard shot, the shooter should look to the post first after receiving the ball. Feet should be shoulder-width apart, with toes, hips and shoulders level and vertically aligned with the post. When on balance, the shooter fixes the eyes solely on the focus point, taking a centering breath and reciting a simple

Figure 4.1 The standard shot as seen from the *(a)* front and *(b)* side angles.

mantra to reinforce cues and assist with timing (e.g., "focus, elbows, swish" at the moment of stillness). The shooter drops the ball behind the head with slight elbow flexion to release, feeling the ball "zing" off the index and middle fingers last. The player should release the ball at the highest point of the extended shooting arm at an angle of around 60 degrees from horizontal for a mid-range shot. To finish the shot, the player shifts weight forward up onto the toes and swishes his wrists to impart pure backspin on the ball. The shooter should follow the shot forwards, moving half a step directly towards the post after release to complete the follow-through and move to rebound if necessary. The shooting action should look and feel smooth and relaxed.

Slight variations in technique are to be expected, and no two actions are identical. Relevant physical as well as mental practice should be employed regularly to optimise technique, fluency, accuracy and confidence. Players should practise using the BEES principle in training to keep technical key points in check. Along with individual technical practice and practice when fatigued, it is essential that shooters get opportunities to practise in game-replicated situations, with full defence and simulated pressure at team training sessions.

Standard Shot Variations

Once a player has reached a fundamental degree of mastery and is executing shots with a reasonable degree of consistency and accuracy, it is time to look at some variations of that standard technique. Although the standard shot should be used wherever practicable, sometimes different situations call for a variation in technique to maximise chances of success. For example, a tall defender with an excellent reach is likely to get a hand very close to the ball on a lean, impeding the shooter's natural action and obscuring her focus point. Therefore, alternatives are needed to give the advantage back to the shooter.

Back-Step

The back-step is an essential skill for a shooter hoping to play at a high level, especially if height is not one of the athlete's major attributes. In the back-step technique, the shooter takes a 30- to 40-centimetre step backwards, away from the post, to give himself space when a defender's arm obscures the shooter's vision or will interfere with his follow-through (see figure 4.2). The back-step is also very useful when a ball is received directly under the post.

To execute the back-step, a shooter should line up and address the post exactly as for the standard shot. The shooter needs to make an early decision to step away from the defender. After balancing and sighting the focus point, the shooter should take the step. A small step is all that is needed to release defensive pressure; stepping more than 40 centimetres will affect balance and timing too much to execute a good shot within the three-second time limit. The step must be taken on the second grounded foot; the lifted foot must remain off the ground in accordance with the rules and remain in line with the hip for optimal balance. After the step, the shooter needs to rebalance and refocus, pause for the moment of stillness, and release as for the standard shot, keeping hips aligned and exaggerating the swish phase of the wrists. To complete the shot, he follows through with the body, coming up higher onto the toes than for the standard shot to retain adequate power to compensate for a one-foot launching base instead of two.

Figure 4.2 The back-step shooting technique.

Side-Step

Identical in principle to the back-step, the side-step is deployed when the opposition defender is positioned to the side of the shooter. The side-step is a 40- centimetre step to the side, away from the defender. The footwork rule is critical in this technique, as the preferable side space to enter may be the grounded foot's side, which must not be lifted and regrounded. If this is the case, a back-step can be used successfully instead, achieving the same objective. The advantage of the side-step is that its lateral movement will not increase the shooter's distance from the post. To execute the side-step, a shooter should line up and address the post exactly as for the standard shot and go through the same steps as for the back-step. The only difference is that the step is to the side.

Jump Shot

The jump shot is another variation of the standard shot. It is sometimes used when a shooter is attempting to score from long range or has overbalanced past the baseline, most likely from pulling in a rebound. The set-up for the long shot is identical to the standard shot technique, but a *slight* jump at the release stage gives the shot extra momentum to counter the extra distance the ball needs to travel. Slightly more flexion at the knees and elbows is also advantageous, ensuring that vertical alignment is maintained. Retaining balance is critical in the success of long-range jump shots. Jump shot techniques carry a high degree of difficulty, and they require excellent dynamic balance, as the shot is taken from an aerial base. In the top netball nations, goalers usually opt to pass out and reposition rather than attempt a long jump shot.

The out-of-court shot is a jump shot taken in the air out of necessity when the shooter's centre of gravity is heading over the baseline, and she is unable to rake the ball back in for a standard shot. To execute an out-of-court shot, the shooter should bring the ball to the midline of the body as quickly as possible. She then turns to align the body with the post as she jumps in the air over the baseline and executes a bent-arm shot on the up phase of the jump. The shooter must strive to maintain balance as best she can. A quick recovery is essential to reground feet on the court, as there will be a strong chance of a rebound.

Running Shot

The running shot, as with the out-of-court jump shot, is an emergency shot that should be taken only when circumstances dictate that the chance of a standard shot is impossible. The running shot is used when a shooter receives a ball at full stretch while moving towards the post with a clear pathway and is unable to pull up safely to shoot in the standard fashion. To execute the running shot, the shooter must bring the ball towards the midline of the body as she takes the first step. The shooter then strides onto the take-off foot (ideally the preferred foot that stepping shots are taken from), striving to maintain balance. The shooter then takes a bent-arm shot at the top of the up phase of her jump towards the post, aiming to slow the momentum of the ball and attempting to finish with a swish of the wrist. A quick recovery and regrounding of the feet on court for rebounds are advisable.

Fake Shot

The fake shot is a handy weapon for a goaler to possess in her shooting armoury. It is executed when a defender uses a jump technique to defend the shot. The fake entices the defender to jump too early, mistiming the leap and giving the shooter the chance to reset the shot with a clear view of the target. The procedure for the fake is very simple. The shooter sets up for a standard shot and begins the shooting motion but stops suddenly at the release point, at which time the defender usually leaps to deflect the ball. The non-shooting hand slides closer to the front to prevent the ball from accidentally slipping out. The shooter then refocusses and executes the regular shot. The only other consideration is the timing. The fake needs to occur early enough in the action to get the real shot away properly within three seconds. However, if the fake is put on too early, the defender might not fall for it, so practice with a defender and a stopwatch is beneficial before this technique is attempted in a match. The fake needs to occur at the one-and-a-half-second mark to allow time to take the real shot within the time limit. An added bonus of the fake shot is that it often draws a contact or obstruction call, resulting in a penalty shot.

Penalty Shot

A penalty shot is awarded as the result of a contact or obstruction infringement by a circle defender in the goal circle, contact or obstruction by a wing defence or centre on a shooter in the shooting circle, or an advancement of an infringement up-court as a result of disciplinary action by the umpire. A penalty can be taken as a standard shot or by stepping in and taking advantage of a decrease in distance to the post (see figure 4.3). The majority of top shooters in the game would endorse the advice of always shooting penalties rather than passing them off, forfeiting a valuable two-on-one scoring opportunity. The only exception to this would be if the remaining in-play defender overcommits to defending the shot and is clearly committed to the shooter, leaving the other goaler free under the post in a more favourable scoring position.

To execute the step-in, the shooter sets up as for the standard shot. She takes a reasonable-size step towards the post on the second grounded foot, keeping both eyes on the target (the step-in can be much larger than the side-step or back-step, up to one metre, as the movement is towards the post). Maintaining balance while keeping hips level, the shooter must refocus, pause, then execute the remainder of the shot as per the back-step and side-step techniques.

The actions of the opposition defender in play will dictate any changes to the step-in penalty. The defender can do three things. The first is to guard the non-shooter to prevent an off-load and easy goal, in which case the shooter is free to step in as far as she likes and make the shot unchallenged. The second option is for the defender to commit to defending the shot (usually for closer-range shots). In this case, the shooting partner should assist by providing a holding lead to the side away from the defender as a decoy, so the defender has to consider covering the lateral off-load. If the defender stays over the shot, the shooter can dish

Figure 4.3 The penalty step-in shot with GK out of play.

off (complete a short, sharp pass) safely to the shooting partner. If the defender moves towards the non-shooter, the shooter can step in for an easy shot. Astute defenders, however, will hover in between, aiming to put the shooter in two minds as to whether to dish off or take the shot (see figure 4.4). Here, the shooter must sense where the defender's weight shift is and take the opposite tack. If the defender's weight is towards the shooter, the off-load option is available; if her weight is on the back foot away from the shooter, it is virtually impossible for the defender to be effective in disrupting the shot for goal, so the shot should always be taken confidently.

Variations in Style

As no two shooting actions are identical, coaches and players have the rather taxing problem of deciding whether to attempt to alter a shooting action. Slight variations in style are inevitable, but the problem that coach and player must solve together is when to modify a shooting action and when to let it refine itself with pertinent practice, confidence and experience. The critical question is "Is it

Figure 4.4 The positioning of players for a mid-range penalty shot with a defender hovering.

a dead-end technique?" It must be determined whether the action, if reasonably accurate at present, will be successful as the level of defensive pressure increases or the player advances up the grades.

Symptoms of a dead-end technique include the following:

- A low or bent arm action—the ball may be deflected with better defence
- Too many moving parts—the more parts that move, the more places the shot can go off track, and the more problems the shooter will have with consistency
- Too much sidespin influence—once the supporting hand also imparts spin, the two forces tend to work against each other, creating more chances for error

The coach needs to work with the shooter to pinpoint and address any problems. This is best done by recording the action and reviewing it together. A mobile phone or digital camera that has recording functions provides instant, time-efficient feedback. For major adjustments, the player should see the action on a larger screen with a remote control for freezing frames and viewing slow-motion replays. Once the faults have been identified and discussed, the coach should develop a program with drills (see drills at the end of this chapter) so the shooter can work on implementing the change off-season.

Changing technique during a season does not allow enough time for such a complex new skill to become concrete, and hybrid versions can be disastrous. Under pressure, the last skills learned are the first ones to come undone. With only two players able to score, it is not fair to the team or the shooter to dramatically change a technique during the season if it means the team's accuracy will suffer. Small technical adjustments in shooting are part of the learning program for the season. Altering fundamental aspects of an entire action should be deferred to the off-season.

The most difficult situation with changing an action is when the shooter has perfected the dead-end technique and is very accurate using it. Changing may result in temporary inaccuracy, but if the decision to change was the correct one, the player will certainly be grateful in future years.

Shooting Partner

A player can do many things to be an effective shooting partner (the other half of the shooting pair not taking the shot). One is to not stand directly under the net waiting for the goal to be scored! The goaler not taking the shot should be contributing and assisting the shooter in one of three effective ways. A handy acronym, ROS, can enhance the effectiveness of the shooting partner.

- R: rebound option
- O: off-load option
- S: screener

- **Rebound option.** The shooting partner should aim to secure the optimal spot for any potential rebounds on an unsuccessful shot. This spot is on the opposite side of the ring to the shooter, one metre out from directly under the ring (see figure 4.5a). If this premium spot is claimed first by the rebounding goaler, she must hold her ground with great strength, as the opposition defender may attempt to hustle her under the ring to claim top spot.

- **Off-load option.** If the shooter is a middle to long distance away from the post, the other goaler should assist by positioning herself as a viable close target so the shooter has the option for an off-load (short-distance pass to get closer to the post, also referred to as a dish). It is critical that the shooting partner set up correctly, minimising the chance for an interception or deflection by the opposition defenders. To be an effective off-load target, an attacker should ensure that she seals off her opponent's feet by positioning both of her feet in front of both the defender's feet, making it impossible for the defender to legally contest the ball as it is passed (see figure 4.5b).

- **Screener.** If the shooter is mid-circle distance or closer to the post, the shooting partner might consider screening her shot. That means protecting the space to shoot in by positioning herself directly in front of the shooter, within the

.9-metre distance (see figure 4.5c). This releases defensive pressure over the shot, as the defender must negotiate the player standing in front of the shooter and take care not to make contact, making a leap or lean over the ball ineffective. The screener must get in position quickly and carefully so that she does not contact the defender's arm or move into a space the defender is taking off into, risking the contact infringement to be called, as it would be up-court.

Figure 4.5 *(a)* Helping the shooter by providing a rebound option. *(b)* Helping the shooter by providing an off-load option, sealing off the defender's feet. *(c)* Helping the shooter by providing a screen option.

Screening is an atypical netball body movement because it involves two attacking players moving towards rather than away from each other, as is the case in nearly every other attacking move. It is worthwhile examining the rules governing protecting of space (refer to contact rules in a copy of the current rule book) so that coaches can implement tactics with confidence and success.

In practical terms screening is legal, providing players who are screening an opponent do not touch, lean on or stand too close to the defender or get in a space that the defender has already committed to, as would be applied anywhere outside the shooting circle. It is legal to stand within .9 metre (three feet) of a team-mate, or opponent for that matter, as long as no attempt is made to defend the ball or impede a player's passing or shooting action.

Rebounding in Attack

Two perspectives must be considered in offensive rebounding, the first from the non-shooting goaler and the second from the shooter. If the non-shooting goaler has decided that R is the most appropriate option in the ROS repertoire, she should aim to secure the optimal rebounding position. If the rebound is reachable from her position, the attacker should attempt to strongly pull in the ball with two hands, snatching it into the chest to secure possession. If contesting the rebound from behind the opposing defender, to take it cleanly the attacker would need to hollow out (make a concave shape with her body at full stretch to avoid knocking the player in front) and get first hands to the ball without drawing a contact call. This is a difficult manoeuvre to pull off, but it is possible for players who are able to outjump their opponents. The second and most appropriate technique for an attacker contesting from behind is a tap-and-collect sequence. This enables the attacker to contest with one hand to gain greater elevation and have a better chance at getting first touch on the ball to tap it clear and gather or guide it to the shooting partner.

Rebounding by the shooter is very simple. After finishing the shot with a swish of the wrist, as soon as the ball is on its way, the shooter should head to the post for first spoils of any shot that pulls up short. If the defender of the shot puts on a good block to prevent the shooter from rebounding, the tap-and-collect sequence should be adopted. It is imperative that the shooter not expect a rebound when she is in the act of taking her shot. If she is thinking about rebounds at this point, she is not expecting the shot to be successful, which indicates a shortcoming in her mental skill proficiency. Beware of shooters who are too quick to rebound!

Performance Points for Shooting

- Develop a technically sound standard shot, and continually service it with practice.
- Follow the BEES principle; go back to it at training and for reference when inaccuracy strikes.
- Develop a range of variation shots so you can be prepared for all circumstances.
- Be prepared to do the extra physical and mental practice that comes with the position.
- Practise isolation shooting, shooting on the move, defensive pressure shooting and shooting with distractions as part of a balanced high-transfer program.
- Look to be a scorer—the main objective is to put goals through for the team.
- Be an asset when your partner is shooting: set for rebounds, set up an off-load option or screen.

Shooting and Goaler Movement Drills

Goalers' drills can be creative and interesting. As shooting is one of the most practiced skills of a goaler's repertoire, there is plenty of opportunity to add some purpose and challenge to maximise shooting effectiveness. Shooting provides immediate feedback, so a goaler can progress rapidly through a shooting skill sequence with confidence and receive a reasonably accurate measure of her shooting proficiency. Drills should be sequential, starting with stationary technical checks, then adding a post, shot variations, movement, feeders, defensive pressure and skill overload.

Individual Shooting Drills

Shooters need to practise their craft in between team trainings as well as at sessions to maintain accuracy, stay in the zone, keep confidence levels high and continually smooth out their technique. If a shooter's game is plagued with inaccuracy, she can go back to her basic individual technical drills, identify errors (ideally with the help from a knowledgeable coach) and adjust her technique accordingly, restoring confidence for the next session or match.

SHOT-CHECK EXERCISE: VIDEO CHECK

OBJECTIVE

To enable the player to gain a better self-concept of her shooting style and make positive adjustments through viewing her entire technique from an observer's perspective. This exercise provides a very powerful visual tool to infuse corrections straight into drills and practice matches, with a lead-up to improvement in technique and accuracy.

REQUIREMENTS

One ball per player, goalpost, visual recording device and operator, visual playback facility, list of shooting activities to be completed

METHOD

The video operator records the player as she performs a shooting sequence as set by the coach.

1. Standard shot from front, back and side perspectives
2. Stepping shots—back-step, side-step, penalty step-ins
3. Receiving a shot from a feeder outside the circle with turning and set-up
4. Shooting over a defender using a variety of leans and jumps
5. Shooting with a feeder and defender

If the video operator can take footage from a range of positions, including an aerial perspective (e.g., from stairs in a stadium), this adds another useful dimension. The player and coach sit down together to view the footage and come up with possible plans of action as soon as practicable.

VARIATION

Include the running and jump shot techniques.

ONE-ARM SHOOTING

OBJECTIVE

To isolate and correct the role of the shooting arm from set-up to release and improve kinaesthetic awareness in relation to the rest of the body. The drill identifies errors with the shooting arm as well as provides positive transfer of cueing, loft and backspin to the regular shot.

REQUIREMENTS

One ball per player, goalpost, coach or recorder

METHOD

This drill is always performed at close range because it limits the strength of the isolated arm. (If done further out, technique would be adversely affected because of overcompensation.)

1. The shooter sets up for the standard shot, then retracts the supporting hand behind the lower back, taking care to keep the shoulders aligned and level.
2. The shooter then completes the shot using the BEES principle without the aid of the supporting hand, aiming to loft the ball slightly higher than normal.

3. She completes 10 attempts from the left side, 10 from the centre and 10 from the right.

4. The coach records the player's accuracy with a score out of 30 on a scorecard.

5. The player tries to better her score next time.

6. Always monitor technique as it should not alter from a standard shot.

This is a great drill for players experiencing inaccuracy caused by sidespin (shot is rebounding out to the side) as well as errors with the ball falling short of the target.

VARIATION

A point is scored only if the goal is "all net".

DOUBLE-FEED SHOOTING

OBJECTIVE

To enhance concentration skills while maintaining technique and timing

REQUIREMENTS

Three players (A, B and C), two balls, goalpost

METHOD

The worker, A, sets up to shoot with a ball at close range, directly in front of the post. Feeder one, B, stands to the left of the post almost underneath the ring with a ball. Feeder two, C, stands to the right of the post almost underneath the ring with no ball. B and C face A.

1. A shoots for goal using a standard shot and the BEES principle. As the ball is released, B simultaneously releases an easy, high, accurate feed into A's hands. (A does not rebound.)

2. Without taking her eyes from the focus point, A receives the incoming ball, resets and executes a shot with gamelike timing.

3. C rebounds the first shot and delivers a feed to A in the same fashion as B's.

4. The sequence is repeated until A has taken 10 shots, counted by B.

5. A is given her score out of 10, and players rotate one position left, so A becomes B, B becomes C and C becomes A.

Repeat the sequence twice, with players aiming to improve their scores. This is a great drill to include on match day, as it gets the "shooting brain" into gear.

VARIATION

Add another feeder under the post to feed in between B and C, and move A back a step. This adds another dimension to the drill and increases perceptual and concentration demands on the shooter.

Pairs or Group Shooting Drills

It is motivating and refreshing for goalers to do shooting drills together, adding a bit of competition to the session. Practising with another goaler not only increases the number of interesting ways to train but also helps a goaler pick up on some successful habits and aspects of other goalers' actions or routines and incorporate them as her own.

SHOOTING ZONES

OBJECTIVE

To practise and be comfortable with taking shots from all parts of the goal circle

REQUIREMENTS

One ball per player, goal circle and post, chalk to mark zones on the floor or ground, a pen and scorecard for recording scores

METHOD

Divide the circle into zones as illustrated in figure 4.6, marking the lines and score values with chalk.

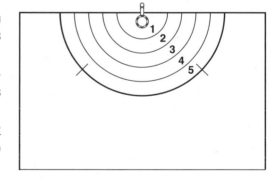

1. The shooter takes a shot from anywhere in zone 1, rebounds and moves to anywhere in zone 2.

2. The shooter then rebounds the shot from zone 2 and moves to 3 and so on through to zone 5.

3. This sequence is repeated six times and a score from 30 shots recorded.

Figure 4.6 Shooting zones.

The score of each goal corresponds with the zone from which it was taken. For example, a goal scored from zone 3 is worth 3 points, and a goal from zone 1 is worth 1 point. The maximum score is 90 points. Stepping in as per the technique in penalties is permitted from zone 5 only. A partner to record scores is ideal.

VARIATION

Do the drill immediately after an aerobically demanding exercise as recovery and concentration work, or count the goals scored from zones 1 and 2 (or 1, 2 and 3) only if they are "all net".

CONDITIONING SHOOTING

Goalers must practise shooting not only when they are fresh but also when they are fatigued. It is vital that accuracy not drop because of tiredness, so aside from general netball fitness work, training the body to maintain concentration and technique when the heart rate is up will help prevent fade-out in the goal circle.

OBJECTIVE

To improve stamina and the ability to maintain technique and accuracy late in the game or with the onset of fatigue

REQUIREMENTS

Two balls per player, a netball court or approximate running area and a skipping rope, 10 markers

METHOD

Place one ball under each goal ring, and place markers at five different locations in the goal circle at both ends. The worker starts at a baseline.

1. The player completes five sit-ups, five push-ups and five shuttle runs at top speed (one court length equals one shuttle run), then puts up five shots from the markers, rebounding each shot in between, trying not to let the ball hit the ground.

2. Without recovery, the worker then replaces the ball under the ring and completes the same sequence with four of each activity, finishing with four shots.

3. The player continues with sequences of three, two and one.

If a helper is available, recording accuracy is very motivating, and the player can aim to beat her score next time the drill is set. Fast skipping with a skipping rope can replace shuttle runs if the drill is done away from the court.

VARIATION

Start the drill on 10 repetitions, incorporate step shooting and a few jump shots and increase the distances of the markers from the post. Triceps dips could also be added into the sequence after push-ups to really make those arms work hard.

Group Goaler Movement Drills

It is essential that the goaler blend shooting practice with specific goaler manoeuvres if the aim is to operate fluently and effectively in matches. Quality replication of the finishing moves of an attack completed at game pace will transfer to positive, dynamic, well-coordinated moves in games.

STOP-DEAD MANOEUVRE

OBJECTIVE

To improve the all-important timing of a stop-dead, or dig-in, manoeuvre on a drive to the post

REQUIREMENTS

One ball, two to four players, goal circle, post

METHOD

The workers (A, B, C) line up seven metres out from the 45-degree mark of the goal arc, facing the baseline. The feeder (D) starts with the ball at the top of the circle, outside the arc.

1. D tosses the ball up to herself to initiate the drill.
2. On this cue, A drives to the post in a straight line until she is about three steps away from the post. At this spot, A digs in sharply with the back foot (with respect to D) and lunges towards D with the front foot, arms outstretched to receive a pass.
3. A receives a shoulder pass, lines up and shoots.
4. A then rebounds, passes back to D and runs outside the drill to join the back of the line.
5. D initiates the drill for B and then for C.

Rotate D after a few minutes, and change the starting point of the line to the opposite side.

VARIATIONS

1. Substitute the lunge for a roll. A digs in on the foot nearest the post, turns the body to face the baseline, pivots on the planted foot to roll (blind to D), steps to D with the front foot, receives and shoots. Encourage the player performing a roll to turn her head first to sight the target quickly and reduce disorientation. This extension may need to be performed in slow motion until the mechanics of the roll are sound.
2. Add a defender to the driver to replicate a game situation and challenge the timing.

BEAT THE BLOCKER

When a shooter plans to enter the circle, she frequently faces a mid-court or circle defender at the perimeter with the sole intention of not letting her enter the goal circle easily. The goaler can use a range of options to beat the blocker while being delayed only momentarily, as well as avoiding contact.

OBJECTIVE

To equip the goaler with a range of workable options to use when faced with a defender blocking her entry to the circle

REQUIREMENTS

One ball, two to five players, markers, goal third, post

METHOD

The goalers (A to D) line up on the right side facing the post, five metres back from the 45 mark. A marker is set up on the circle at the 45 mark in line with the goalers' queue. A feeder (E) with the ball sets up facing the goalpost three metres back from the perimeter at the top of the arc, slightly to the left of centre.

1. E tosses the ball to herself to initiate start of movement for A, who drives forwards to the marker on the arc.
2. A dodges past the blocker (marker) one way, drives to the post, receives a pass from E, shoots and rebounds.
3. A passes back to E and joins the back of the queue. E starts the drill for B.
4. When all players have had a few attempts, replace the dodge with a double dodge.
5. After the double dodge is mastered, the workers progress to a cut-around and then a roll-around.

For the cut-around, workers drive right up to the marker, plant the feet in a wide base and step back with the foot nearest the feeder. With a quick change of momentum, they cut forwards around the marker with the inside leg and drive past.

For the roll-around, players set up the same wide plant as for the cut-around, then without backing off, roll the right shoulder around an imaginary defender's left shoulder (turning off the ball), keeping the body upright, and drive past. Ensure that dodges, cuts and rolls are practised on both sides, the feeder is rotated, and the queue and the feeder change sides halfway through.

VARIATIONS

1. Substitute real defenders for markers, static to begin with and building up to dynamic defence.
2. Start the drill up-court, setting up a series of markers (progressing to actual defenders) such that the worker must pass several blocks on her way to the post, using a variety of techniques.

CROSS AND DROP

OBJECTIVE

To improve the goaler's reaction to a change of orientation on the crossed ball and to fine-tune passing around the arc

REQUIREMENTS

One ball, three to six players, goal third, post

METHOD

The goaler (A) starts in the circle near the post. Feeders form two equal queues: B and C in queue 1, D and E in queue 2. Queue 1 lines up at the attacking transverse line on one side of the court, queue 2 at three steps towards the goal from the transverse line, level with the opposite side's 45 mark. B starts with the ball (see figure 4.7).

1. D leads forwards and is immediately passed to by B. D should receive the ball a few steps before the arc.

2. A makes a preliminary move and times a lead out of the circle on the ball side to receive a pass from D.

3. A then turns and directs a long pass to B, who is driving down the arc on the opposite side, following the pass.

4. B crosses the ball back across the arc to D, who has driven onto the circle at the 45 mark.

5. D feeds the ball into A, who has rolled back to the post from B at the arc.

6. A receives, shoots, and passes the ball back to C at the transverse line, and the drill repeats with C, E and A.

Roles need to be rotated regularly and the drill reset from the opposite side halfway through.

VARIATION

When B and D are both on the arc, they pass to each other three more times before the ball is fed in to A, while A continues to follow the ball, dig in, roll and drive to the post.

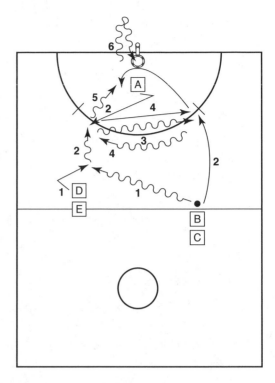

Figure 4.7 Cross and drop.

CONE WORK

OBJECTIVE

To improve agility, turning speed, footwork patterns, circle familiarity and fitness in the circle using goaler-specific moves

REQUIREMENTS

Two balls, two to four players, five markers (cones), goal circle, post

METHOD

Place cones in the shooting circle as shown in figure 4.8. Three should be near the arc, interspersed with two closer to the post. The worker (A) positions herself at the post facing up-court. A feeder (C) sets up on the goal arc, ready to move between the 45 marks. The remaining workers line up behind A.

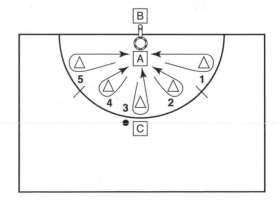

Figure 4.8 Cone work.

1. C side-steps around the arc between the 45 marks as A drives at full speed to the cone on her far left and quicksteps around it, with chest oriented to C at all times.

2. After rounding the first cone, A moves quickly back to the post, again with the chest facing C at all times.

3. A proceeds to go around all cones from left to right and back to the post at full speed, ending the sequence with the final drive to the post from the last cone.

4. A tags B, the next worker, and B begins the drill.

5. After a few turns each, roles are rotated and the workers move in the opposite direction, starting with the far right cone.

Build up to two workers operating simultaneously in opposite directions, which simulates the congestion of a game situation. Each worker must read where the other person is going and time her moves so the space remains balanced and open at all times. At this stage, the worker is turning on the ball (i.e., she faces the ball throughout the turns).

VARIATIONS

1. Increasing the difficulty of body movement by turning off the ball when rounding the cones will further challenge the workers. To execute a turn off the ball, A advances to the cone with shoulders facing C. A passes by the cone on the inside with respect to C, pivots away from C, turning blind (with back to C), and sprints towards the post, turning the head quickly to resight the feeder as soon as possible.

2. Add a ball to be fed in by C, who ceases to side-step and remains still at the top of the arc. C calls one of the workers' names and simultaneously delivers a pass to that player. The receiver must stop, balance, line up with the post to shoot, hold for a second, then pass back out to C and restart movement. The other worker positions herself for a rebound while the shooter lines up. After the pass out, both players recommence movement. A shot is taken after six passes in.

ROTATIONS

Running floor patterns is vital for the slick movement of goalers in the circle. The goaling pair's driving and clearing movements need to complement each other to maintain flow and balance of goal circle movement. The body needs to be trained to automatically drive when moving towards the post and directly away from it to the ball, as well as when mixing up the pace by clearing from a wide position to open up space for a partner in a game situation. It takes a lot of practice as a goaling pair to synchronise these movements well. We will look at two basic movement patterns that promote good rotation: triangles and figure eights.

OBJECTIVE

To establish movement patterns in the goal circle to maximise the ideal flow of momentum between shooters during a game so that one of them is open for a pass and receiving in a good scoring position as much as possible. The drill also promotes awareness of the goaling partner so that the goaling pair can function as a unit rather than as two individuals.

REQUIREMENTS

Two players in the goal circle

METHOD

Rotation Pattern 1: Triangles

Simple in design, triangles are great for short, sharp changes of direction. Workers need to stay in a smaller area and not cross sides of the goal circle.

A starts on court at the baseline, facing up-court slightly to the left of the post (her left as facing the centre circle), and moves only in that half of the goal circle. B starts on court at the baseline in the far right corner of the goal circle, facing the post (her right as facing the centre circle), and works only in that half of the goal circle.

1. On "go", they both begin a triangle movement pattern using the whole of their designated area, running in the pattern "drive, clear, drive" for A and "drive, drive, clear" for B. The drives are a sprint along the baseline from perimeter to post and a sprint from the post straight up to the top of the goal arc. The clear is a slower-paced curved lead from the top of the circle just inside the perimeter to the corner of the goal circle where it meets the baseline (directions detailed in figure 4.9).

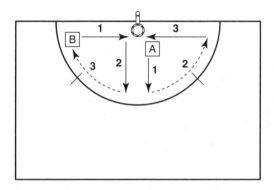

Figure 4.9 Rotations: Triangles.

2. Players complete the rotations for 30 seconds then rest for 30 seconds, performing the drill five more times.

The clearing lead takes the same time as two driving leads, so the rotation should be fluent if both workers are moving at a similar pace. The timing of the workers' moves must be synchronised so they never catch up to one another. If this begins to happen, the faster mover delays slightly until the timing is back in synch.

VARIATION

On driving to the post at any time in the rotation, A or B can call, "Switch," and drive along the baseline to the other triangle (to the post starting position). The partner responds by reversing her own clearing lead to the opposite side, and they repeat their sequences on the opposite sides of the circle. In essence, the two workers swap sides and continue the pattern in the other circle half.

METHOD

Rotation Pattern 2: Figure Eights

Figure eights challenge timing skills, involve constant crossing over and require players to cooperate with each other more by holding their movement on the spot (delaying) and defining their drives more succinctly. It is a good drill to run when triangles are mastered. The movements in figure eights are more gamelike.

A starts at the baseline close to the perimeter of the circle. B starts at the top 45 mark on the opposite side of the circle near the perimeter (see figure 4.10). Both workers face the top of the circle at all times.

1. On "go", A drives diagonally to B's original position while B clears in an arc pattern to her same-side base.

2. When B hits the baseline, she drives diagonally across to the opposite top 45 mark as A clears to her same-side base.

3. Both workers follow each other in a giant figure-eight pattern, sprinting through the diagonals and clearing the "loops".

4. Players complete the rotations for 30 seconds, then rest for 30 seconds, performing the drill four more times.

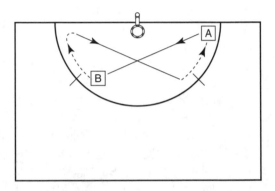

Figure 4.10 Rotations: Figure eights.

One worker is always driving while the other clears. If the driver is catching up, she moves on the spot and delays her run until her partner has finished driving. As with all rotation work, the timing is critical to maintain the flow of movement.

VARIATION

Add a feeder at the top of the circle to feed the ball in randomly. The receiver must gather, balance and look to shoot as her partner moves to a rebounding position. The receiver then passes back out to the feeder at the top, and movement is restarted.

CHAPTER 5

Creative Attacking

Obtaining and keeping possession of the ball until the team scores is the basis of the game of netball, and how well a team does this constitutes the effectiveness of the team's attacking skills. Netball has often been described as an attacker's game, mainly because the contact and obstruction rules originating from the early versions of the game in the late 1890s restrict a defender's natural inclinations of access to the ball. Examining the combined strengths of the players in the attack line can assist in tailoring a blueprint to maximise the team's offensive potency. It is important that the members in the attacking unit (centre, wing attack, goal attack and goal shooter) identify themselves as such and work as a distinct unit in team training sessions. The attacking unit needs to combine their skills and develop an appreciation of what each member's skill set brings to the unit.

This chapter explores relationships, patterns and concepts about the four players who operate together in the team's frontcourt (attacking half) through to the goalmouth. It explains the principles of attack, how to divide the space, systematic and read-off styles of play, the importance of adaptability and the use of floor patterns.

Principles of Attack

Netball is played in a small area per number of players as compared with other team sports, so some principles take on heightened importance. Principles of attack in invasion games such as netball are width, depth, improvisation and mobility.

- **Width.** Width in attack refers to the placement of a team's attacking players with respect to the breadth of the court. Width is important in team attack to split the opposition defence and prevent their working together. If the attack is spread out, the defence is spread out, creating more space for the attackers, which is a precious commodity in netball. Staggered court spacing in attack is critical because the court is only 15.25 metres wide. Attackers positioned too adjacently in a line with other team-mates increase the presence of defenders in the vicinity.

- **Depth.** Depth in attack refers to the placement of a team's attacking players with respect to the length of the court. Depth is a major concept for frontcourt players to grasp. The theory of first looking down towards the goal when selecting a passing target is not practical if there is no depth down-court. If the court spacing is too wide and close to the feeder, it enables the defence to close in and restrict space for offensive moves. This means there are fewer passing options, and the ball tends to move sideways and backwards rather than directly down-court. The fast-moving direct down-court pass puts the defenders under the most pressure as it increases the passing corridors available and the number of attacking leads to cover.

- **Improvisation.** Improvisation in a team attack means being adaptable and able to switch to plan B reasonably effortlessly. Because the ball handler must pass or shoot the ball within three seconds, any move made without precision timing creates doubt for the thrower, and other options need to become available very quickly. The attacking unit also needs to improvise when defensive tactics are changed during a quarter, such as the defence's converting to a zone or offline style. A well-drilled team will have coping strategies rehearsed in order to survive the onslaught, then look to take advantage of any newly created weak spots in the defence.

- **Mobility.** Mobility in netball translates to keeping both players and the ball on the move. A dynamic attack keeps opposition defenders guessing as the ball swings quickly to new destinations and their opponents' locations are transient. Mobility also significantly reduces opposition defenders' reaction times and their ability to join forces and work together.

Attacking play must be coordinated with player movements, so the learning progress of new skills is slower than for defensive skill development, which is largely reactionary. Coaches should ensure training time is allocated accordingly, with more time designated to attacking, so coordinated attacking play can develop.

Dividing Up the Space

On the netball court, space is precious. It can be manipulated by attacking units and defence lines alike to their own advantages. Attackers try to create space and open up the court, while defenders try to shut down space to effect a turnover. To apply the attacking principles of width, depth and mobility, players must have space. The concept of balancing the court revolves around dividing the space fairly so that each attacker has room to make her move.

When a team is making the transition into attack, overzealous team defenders who instantly drive down to patrol the attacking transverse line with good intentions of helping out may be doing a great deal of damage. Their presence near the attacking transverse line often undermines the attack's chances of scoring, as they can be taking up the space that the wing attack and goal attack need for their forward leads. A team's own defenders can actually help the opposition defence shut down space by closing off room at the transverse line if they drive as far as they can before the mid-court players have progressed deep into the goal third. If attackers are struggling to find space, coaches need to get their defenders to stay in their own half. If the attackers have moved too early and are not available, then the backcourt players should time their run as a back-up lead. The skill of holding back in this situation makes the backcourt players a huge asset to the attacking unit and an integral part of frontcourt fluency and success. The reverse applies to when the opposition is in attack: having the wing attack and goal attack at the teeth of the team's defence near the defensive transverse line (see Flooding, chapter 6) is an asset to crowd opposition attackers and restrict space.

Play in the Attacking Half

In netball, there are two basic methods of play in the attacking half: systems and read-off. Elite teams have operated their forward lines successfully using both methods, as well as a combination of the two. It is up to the coach to fully examine the advantages of both with the attacking unit and set a formula for execution that best suits the playing personnel. An important concept to keep in mind when implementing any type of structured play is adaptability. In a game where decisions must be made so rapidly and the ball moved on so quickly, being adaptable when things do not go exactly to plan is a vital element in any team's playbook.

Systems

Attacking units use the systems (or leads) method of play through the goaling pair to add structure to an attack line, with the aim of making play flow better and reducing crowding and indecision. Goalers know the primary target in advance when the ball crosses the halfway mark into the frontcourt. When the ball enters the attacking half, systems commence according to which side the ball enters. An alternative cue for the start of the system is which feeder takes the first attacking-half possession. When the pressure is on, systems give forward lines direction, confidence, the chance to be one step ahead and a foundation to fall back on. Systems provide a good base plan for movement of players and the ball in the frontcourt, to which alternatives and variations can be added for variety and individual player strengths.

There are six basic leads for goaling pairs when using the side the ball enters the attacking half as the cue for starting. Countless variations and overrides can be added with a little imagination and knowledge of attacking principles. An example of a six-system set follows:

- One = closed circle: both goalers start in the circle (the centre-court players play deep).
- Two = open circle: both goalers start out of the circle and cut in simultaneously.
- Three = GS makes the leads on the left side of the court, GA the right.
- Four = GA makes the leads on the left side of the court, GS the right.
- Five = GS stays in the circle; GA makes the leads on both sides.
- Six = GA stays in the circle; GS makes the leads on both sides.

It is usually the goal shooter's call as to which system to run, when to change and when to use read-off, playing spontaneously. When making the call, the goal shooter needs to consider the workload of both goalers plus the centre-court players, as well as the strengths of the opposition. Some teams use systems only from a defensive throw-in or off centre passes, and others run them off every play. Purposeful practice develops the ability to execute systems under pressure at game speed to enhance understanding, timing and flow between forward-line members. Systems can be a saviour for a floundering attack line high in error rate or lacking cohesion and creativity, as well as instill confidence and direction to the team as a whole.

Systems dictate which goaler will lead for the ball, and space is divided up accordingly. When a goaler is on the lead, she knows she will be considered as the first option and will put everything into that lead. The players around her clear space to assist her and provide back-up leads. If the primary target does not become available (because of bad timing or because the attacker cannot shake the defender), the ball switches to the second option—a complementary or back-up lead—and play continues as normal. The goalers are the only two players in the frontcourt who run the leads; the centre and wing attack play more instinctively around them, seeking primary targets when they have possession. It is too rigid and difficult for the feeders to delegate leads and sides for themselves as well (and far too predictable), so half the unit is systematic, and the other half is instinctive in live play.

Systems play has some key faults. Goalers can stay on the same system for too long and become predictable or choose an inappropriate system for their current game situation. Systems can allow defenders and opposition coaches to read the play more easily (especially with the assistance of video replays), and defenders can combine efforts to intercept nominated balls or block certain pathways. Practising using the complementary and back-up leads is therefore important. If not operated with flexibility and variation, systems play can become too rigid. Too much rigidity in the forward line can cause attackers to lose their instinct. It is a fine line to tread and a challenge to strike the right balance between systems, read-off and combinations of both.

Read-Off

In read-off, a less sophisticated form of attack than systems, every lead is spontaneous as players read off the team-mate in front of them and react with a suitable lead. Coaches have the option of blending the two methods, where read-off becomes one of the options within the systems set. Athletes who have been playing together a long time can afford to play read-off style more often because they know their team-mates' moves very well and can predict and time their own moves easier. Teams who play read-off maintain spontaneity and unpredictability and are often very adaptable. They are difficult to defend, as the ball switches lanes all the time and attackers lead more. There is no second option; they all lead, keeping their opponents in constant motion.

> *"To keep the upper hand, creative attackers need to be quick and assertive in decision making and have an instinctive personality to challenge and outwit their opponent."*
>
> ~ Donna Loffhagen, Former Silver Ferns' Goal Attack and Goal Shooter, Two-Time International Netball and Basketball Representative, Two-Time Olympian, Commonwealth Games Silver Medallist

Although the spontaneity of read-off can be exciting to watch, it takes away the advantage of being one step ahead, as players are improvising the whole time. The ball can move on very quickly, but passes often go to who is free first and not to who is the best option, catching players out of position and jamming the ball up with too much width. Key faults in the read-off style of play include a high error rate because of duplication of moves, crowding, congestion and hesitation if players are not sure who is going where. In read-off the passer tends to look at everyone, taking in too many cues instead of having a target in mind and zeroing in on it rapidly, getting a fast release underway. Read-off is less likely to place receivers in prime feeding or shooting spots, and when play is too erratic there is no base plan to fall back on to steady up and regain confidence. Read-off can be far less energy efficient than systems because often every player leads for every ball instead of balancing primary, secondary and back-up leading.

Adaptability

Circumstances can change quickly on the netball court, and highly developed improvisation skills are needed to cope and thrive. Situations that call for adaptability in forward lines are chiefly changes in personal opponent defensive styles or tactics (including player substitutions), changes in team defensive styles (e.g., one on one to zone) and changes in their own team's tactics (e.g., systems to read-off). To be adaptable and resilient, attackers must possess a good range of preliminary moves, be able to think on their feet and communicate, and have well-rehearsed responsive change-ups to opposition tactical variations. The attacking unit must always be thinking in terms of taking advantage.

Floor Patterns

Identifying common floor patterns, or pathways, favoured by the attacking unit helps cement familiarity in basic movement patterns. This can instill flow and timing into attacking play. Floor patterns provide a base for drill design for the team. Floor patterns common to sound attacking plans include the three-option strategy and two- and four-player patterns including screens, double plays, systems and set plays.

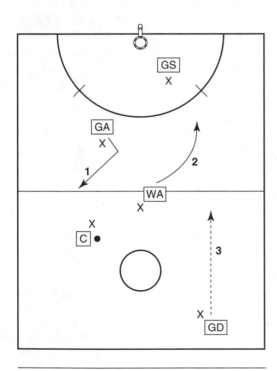

Figure 5.1   Three-option strategy: GA primary, WA complementary, GD back-up.

Basic Attacking Strategy: Three Options

The three-option strategy is a common basic attacking approach. When a player has possession in attack, she should have a choice of three players to use as a target. When playing read-off, she chooses the best of the three options, following the principles of looking down-court first and choosing the best option rather than who is free. When playing systems, teams have a primary target, a complementary lead (the eyes or back player in the forward pair of attackers) and a back-up lead, either to the side or slightly behind the passer. The primary target should be the first choice, the complementary lead the second choice (to keep the ball moving forward) and the back-up lead the last choice if options one and two are unavailable (see figure 5.1).

Combined Attacking Strategy: Two Players

Certain attacking plays involve the work of two players. It could be argued that these plays involve all four players, but two players complete the main task. Prime examples are screening and the double play. Screening can be employed chiefly in two situations: screening the shot for goal (see Shooting Partner, chapter 4) and screening in general attacking play (see Preliminary Moves, chapter 3). Adopted from basketball, screening in netball has the same principle, which is fundamentally for one player to give up her chance to get the ball to protect a space for a team-mate to move into, creating an unopposed target (see figure 5.2, *a* and *b*). Attackers need a lot of practice to get this right in both the timing

Figure 5.2 *(a)* Players in formation for a screen on a crossed ball. GS is setting the screen on GD. *(b)* GA cuts past the screen set by GS to receive the ball.

and execution. Communication is also essential, whether it be verbal or through eye contact.

In a double play (also called a give and go or a pass and cut), the passer delivers to a receiver then takes off down-court to receive the ball back again. The key cue to identify the best situation for a double play is when an opposition defender overruns her opponent when trying to intercept and leaves the passer free with a vacant space to run into unopposed. The double play can also be used to successfully bring the ball out of defence, again when an opponent has overrun and left the passer unattended.

When negotiating the double play, the runner must look ahead to avoid running into a team-mate's opponent. Misuse of the double play can cut off down-court leads and leave attackers stranded and frustrated (e.g., a wing attack sprinting to the ball being cut off by her own team's goal defence, who cuts right in on the lead). This not only costs the team by preventing the deeper option from being used but also enables the wing attack to be blocked from re-entering prime feeding positions. If a player does cut in on a team-mate's lead, the player on the original lead must clear out to take the defender away from the ball's path and balance up the court space.

Combined Attacking Strategy: Four Players

Some attacking plays involve all four members of the attacking unit in the same play. These types of plays highlight the need for the unit to work as a team within the team, as some of the more sophisticated and elaborate moves cannot succeed without all four players contributing. The two most obvious four-player moves are systems and set plays.

Systems involve all four attackers in general down-court play. When the ball hits the frontcourt, all four players must carry out simultaneous movements for a system to work (see Systems section of this chapter). One player acts as the primary target, the player immediately behind provides the complementary lead ready to convert to the target if the primary one is unsuccessful, another provides the back-up lead, and the remaining attacker is either the passer or moves to balance up the court space. If one team-mate does not play her role, the whole play can self-destruct, and possession may be in jeopardy.

Set plays involve designated player and ball movement from a throw-in or penalty pass (refer to chapter 8). The stoppage after the umpire's whistle enables the attacking unit time to position itself for maximum impact. Any player allowed in the area can take the throw-in or penalty, so the first decision to be made is assigning the passer. While the passer moves into position with the ball, the other three set up simultaneously in the pre-determined spatial arrangement that the particular play dictates. Penalty set-ups and throw-in tactics should be pre-planned and well rehearsed. The improvisation principle should come into play should the opposition defenders prevent attackers from positioning themselves exactly as they would like. Sometimes the best person to take a penalty is the closest person if she has the chance to take it quickly and catch the opposition out of position.

Linking the Attack Together

The players running the floor patterns run through specific phases during the transportation of the ball through the mid-court to the goal circle. Linking the attack is essential for the smooth and efficient movement of the ball down-court to the goal. When a team makes the transition into attack, the centre-court players run the show and must ignite the attack with fast-breaking, quick-response leads to move the ball down-court quickly. This style of fast-breaking play in open flanks alters dramatically when the ball reaches the goal circle, where the runners link the play by transforming into static feeders. Players must adjust their tempo so that they become less mobile and their passes become more precise and instantaneous over short distances in a confined space. The goalers play their part in linking the play by executing moves that finish the play with a shot for goal, as opposed to longer leads away from the post when the ball is off the goal circle. To maximise attacking potency, both groups of attacking players—the centre-courters and the goalers—must understand the broad dynamics of linking the attack by making movement and passing adjustments as the ball traverses court areas.

Courtesy of The Advertiser.

As the wing attack gathers the ball, the goal shooter links the play by timing a finishing move on the ball side.

Engine-Room Moves

The centre-court players are the engine room, or prime movers, of full-court attacks. They are the catalysts for successful flow of attack between the extreme areas of the court, and the ball must pass through the centre third when traversing between ends. Skilled mid-court players direct and redirect play, look for over-runs and fast breaks, know when to clear out and rebalance the court and seek out the long target in goals. The engine room can exploit its collective strengths by designing play around the physical attributes and special skills of the three mid-court players. For example, a team may have a very fast centre, a tall wing attack and a wing defence with brilliant ball-handling skills. Dominant team plays may hinge on the wing defence's ability to take all penalty passes and throw-ins in the mid-court, the wing attack's ability to use a lot of hold-and-drop moves to get into the goal circle on a deep coverage, and the centre's ability to run the flanks and cut into the middle. A team with a tall wing defence and a fast centre and wing attack may play entirely differently.

The engine-room players need to monitor the three-option attacking strategy constantly, as it will involve one of those players every pass. The wing defence needs to consider keeping the frontcourt space free for the attacking unit to use but also needs to be available to back up. It is a fine line to tread and an off-the-ball skill of great importance. Allocating adequate space for the attackers has a big influence on attacking fluency. The centre and wing attack also need to be mindful that one of them must be available in the goalmouth vicinity to deliver the ball to the goalers. If both feeders spend excessive time up-court, the goalers will be drawn too far out from the goals and the team starved of shooting opportunities. The pass in to the goal circle is as important as the shot itself, and determination to be in the best positions for the feed as well as to execute the best possible delivery is critical.

Delivery to the Goal Circle

The fundamental objective for feeders in the frontcourt is to deliver the ball to the goalers so they can gather it with minimal effort and set up to shoot. The best place to feed the ball in to the goalers is from the edge of the circle between the two 45 marks. Balls fed in from off the circle are usually under extreme pressure from the opposition over the ball, and balls fed in from the deep pockets cut half the space off because of the baseline. An elite-level feeder can deliver high-quality passes from any angle but would still prefer the luxury of a central angle and close proximity. Every reception in the frontcourt should warrant a quick scan of the goal area to check for goalers on a post move or an opportunity for a direct feed (e.g., an opposition defender with her head down). The only exceptions are when the receiver is off balance and needs to off-load to the nearest team-mate to maintain possession or when an opponent has clearly overrun a team-mate, and the team-mate sets for the double play to land on the circle's edge.

When both goalers are in the circle, feeders need split-second decision-making ability to scan goalers' positions, orientation and defensive coverage and be able to hit the one in the best position the instant she becomes open. This requires depth in vision to track the back goaler, who is usually obscured. The feeder must also decide whether to make a quick pass to the goaler in front at the expense of the back lead. If a goaler charging forward is not used, she usually receives heavy blocking attention from her opponent, who has her where she wants her, away from the post without the ball. Feeding is instinctive, and the art of feeding needs plenty of opportunity to develop and flourish so that smooth connections between feeders and goalers can be made. The more the feeders practise connecting with the goalers, the less hesitation the feeders will have on release. Feeders familiarise themselves with the goalers' body movements and can predict movement in advance with a trained eye.

Well-developed fake passing is an asset to any attacking unit, particularly fakes from feeders to goalers. It is tough enough for defenders, with the ball swinging rapidly and goalers spinning, sprinting and dodging, let alone when the feeders use fakes, taking away another cue for them. Faking from penalties where the defence starts from a stationary set-up is an essential skill in the feeders' checklist.

Around the goal circle, the wing attack and centre should always anticipate a pass out from a goaler set up to shoot. Once a goaler takes aim, her opponent will invariably set up to defend the shot. When the defender is in position, the shooter may elect to swing the ball out for a double play and reposition for a closer shot. The feeder must try to position herself on the side most advantageous for the shooter to pass out (see figure 5.3). On most occasions, this will be the ball side (or the side where the ball does not have to cross the feeder's opponent), but the position of the other shooter and the other feeder as well as the defenders will determine the best side to protect. Making a hand signal in the ideal space to provide a cue for the shooter as well as placing one foot off the circle to block off a target side (making a perpendicular stance with the arc) are useful procedures that maximise accuracy for the pass out. To minimise defensive recovery chances, wing attacks and centres should develop control in their passing to be able to accurately bat the ball back to the repositioning shooter. The feeder should also note the position of the non-shooting goaler before receiving, as the best pass back in might be to that player. A cue to check is the positioning of the non-shooter's feet in relation to the defender's feet. If the goaler has secured the space by cutting off both the defender's feet, it will be difficult for the defender to reach the ball as she has to get around the body first, and a quick pass in will beat her.

Figure 5.3 Positioning for the pass out.

Feeders should constantly fine-tune their range of deliveries and be prepared to practise their weakest ones the most. They should aim to be able to deliver the ball equally well from both sides of the body, from low and high angles and with one or both hands. Feeders should also know which feeds each goaler prefers. Techniques in the essential feeding repertoire include fakes (ball and eye fakes), low bounce passes, short and long lobs, underarm slings, overhead passes from off the circle, chest passes, shoulder passes and side passes. Often a goaler will become open for a split second only, and the feeder must thread the ball through instantly, aiming to make it as easy as possible for the receiver to collect, balance and line up to shoot.

Finishing Moves

A finishing move is a move by a goaler that results in a reception near the post concluding with a shot for goal. Goalers need to recognise when the opportunity presents for a finishing move and coordinate a manoeuvre that will complete the team attack. The most obvious circumstance for a finishing move is when the attacking team is on a fast break and there are no other players between the ball and the goal shooter (except for her opponent). The goal shooter has to beat only one player and has the vacant space available near the post. Finishing moves include up-and-back leads (the drop-back), roll-and-drop combinations, hold-and-drop moves and dodging back to the post.

The shooter must complete a fast break with a finishing move to take advantage of the momentum, positioning and space available. If the fast break is greeted by an out-lead from the shooter, all advantages of the fast break will be lost as the opposition has time to catch up and congest premium space. A well-timed, successful finishing move completes a clean, exciting passage of play for the team. It looks great and gives the whole team a boost.

Performance Points for Successful Attacking-Unit Play

- Move with a purpose. Do not be a passenger!
- Move the ball quickly without rushing or forcing passes through.
- Share space; support and cover team-mates and maintain court balance.
- Play without hesitation or fear, and learn from mistakes.
- Be adaptable, flexible and resilient.
- Maintain possession in tough passing situations.
- Strive to put the team first; be prepared to sacrifice personal possessions for the chance to set up a better possession or scoring opportunity for a team-mate.
- Stick to the team systems, working individual play and flair within the team context.

Attacking Drills

The following drills are designed to develop understanding and skills in the attacking unit. They are completed largely in an on-court, attacking-half situation, moving from single-skill tasks to individual multi-tasking and combining as a complete attack line. Individual drills for building personal skills as a base for team attacking skills are featured in chapters 2 and 3.

Small-Group Attacking Drills

Although these drills are designed for players in the attack line, the whole team can benefit from understanding how the scoring half of the court operates by transferring concepts to the defensive and mid-court areas. The drill set features the development of floor patterns and systematic play, as well as the integration of individual player movement into slick team plays. The drills challenge the cohesion and timing of group movement against time and introduce mobile screening as a four-person collaboration.

FLOOR PATTERNS

OBJECTIVE

For each player to increase her awareness of court coverage patterns and preferred individual pathways of attack. Also by being aware of preferred individual movement patterns, players can attempt to add new pathways to their range, blending with the rest of the unit, to avoid predictability.

REQUIREMENTS

Four attacking-unit players, six markers, half a netball court

METHOD

Players set themselves up in their preferred starting positions for a central down-court attack.

1. On "go", players move simultaneously through the court spaces without the ball, simulating a down-court attack, moving individually from their own imaginary ball location. Players jog through the drill at first.

2. Increase drill speed, ensuring players take care to preserve court balance and open spaces. Emphasis should be on footwork and smooth movement.

3. Add replications of throwing, catching, preliminary moves, leading and defending.

4. Players work for 90 seconds, rest for 30 seconds, repeat.

Players need to have reasonable visualisation skills and be able to work hard independently to gain maximum benefit from the drill.

VARIATION

After two blocks of 90 seconds, increase the movement to full speed. Players work for 30 seconds, break for 30 seconds, repeat. To increase perceptual demands, markers (approximately six) representing opponents can be added to the court randomly for players to avoid. The coach can move the markers during the drill.

90-SECOND TIME TRIAL

OBJECTIVE

To score as many goals as possible in 90 seconds in a concentrated three-point attack situation. The drill aims to fine-tune one-on-one goaler leads and works towards perfecting direct feeds to the goaler.

REQUIREMENTS

Four players (three attacking-unit players plus a goal keeper with a bib), one ball, half a court

METHOD

Three players set up as centre (C), wing attack (WA) and goal shooter (GS) in a three-on-one situation. The remaining player acts as goal keeper, wearing the bib and defending the shooter one on one. The centre starts with the ball behind the centre circle facing the goal.

1. As C steps into the circle, WA completes a preliminary move and lead.
2. C passes to WA and drives down the opposite side of the court to position herself for the next lead.
3. The three attackers work together using full netball rules to score a goal, with the goal keeper applying as much defensive pressure as possible within the rules.
4. After the goal is scored, GS passes the ball to C, who is sprinting back to the start to begin play again.
5. Players rest for two minutes and repeat, trying to beat the score from last time.

WA must vary centre-pass leads, and C and WA must not be still at any time except when the goaler is shooting (they can side-step, back off, drive onto the goal circle, switch positions, and so on). The three attackers must determine the most efficient methods of play as well as how to reduce dead ball time after the goal. If more players are available, groups can compete against each other, rotating the defender after every 90-second trial.

VARIATION

Add a floating defender that can play a wing defence role, then switch the defender to a goal defence role, creating a one-on-two situation in the goal circle.

MOBILE SCREENING

OBJECTIVE

To teach players the principles, techniques and applications of screening in the goal circle within the framework of the rules. The drill exposes players to the fundamental concepts of moving away from the ball to help a team-mate receive rather than moving to the ball as an individual.

REQUIREMENTS

Six players; one ball; bibs of the same colour for goal shooter (GS), goal attack (GA), wing attack (WA) and centre (C); bibs of a different colour for goal defence (GD) and goal keeper (GK)

METHOD

C and WA start on the edge of the circle at the 45 marks, C with the ball. GA and GS start close together at mid-circle, with GD and GK defending their respective opponents one-on-one style.

1. C passes a high, loopy ball to WA while GS (the nominated screener at this point) turns to defend GD, protecting a space for GA (see figure 5.4).

2. GA cuts "razor close" to GS into the space protected to receive the pass from WA.

3. GA lines up to shoot, fakes the shot and off-loads the ball to a feeder.

4. The play is reset and repeated five times.

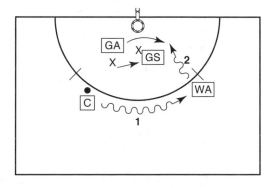

Figure 5.4   Mobile screening.

5. WA counts the number of fake shots for the goaling pair and calls the goaler to shoot on the sixth attempt while the non-shooter screens the shot and all players contest the rebound.

Mobile screening is an advanced skill, so the speed of the drill should be at walking pace to begin with. The screener must be visible to the defender she is "defending", and the shooting partner must be able to identify exactly which space she needs to move into such that her opponent cannot contest the ball. After 10 attempts, the GA and GS swap roles. Feeds should come in from both sides of the goal circle.

VARIATION

Move the drill to game pace, starting from the transverse line; add defenders around the edge of the circle (WD and opposing C). Play without a nominated screener. The screener is decided spontaneously in the course of play. If a screen does not work, then the ball is crossed from feeder to feeder, and the goalers keep attempting to screen on the crossed ball until successful.

FRONTCOURT THREE-POINT COMBINATION

OBJECTIVE

To improve passing in a gamelike situation by simulating centre-court and goaler movement and passing connections. The drill provides the opportunity to combine position-specific moves and taxes timing, good placement and technical combination work.

REQUIREMENTS

Six players (minimum), two balls, half a court

METHOD

Set up in three queues for the centres (C), wing attacks (WA) and goal shooters (GS) as per figure 5.5. The drill starts with the first worker in the C queue tossing the ball to herself to set the timing of the possession.

1. WA cuts towards goal in a V-lead, digs in, then drives towards C.

2. C shoulder passes to WA, then drives onto the 45 mark, on the opposite side of WA.

3. WA turns to hit GS on an out-lead with a shoulder pass or reverse shoulder pass.

4. GS receives and swings a loopy ball to C at the opposite 45 mark and follows the pass.

5. C passes a lob back in to GS on an up-and-back (to the ball, dig in and drop back) move to the post.

6. GS shoots, rebounds, then returns the ball back to the new C, who restarts the sequence for the next wave of workers.

Reverse the drill after five minutes, with WA working from the opposite side, and substitute a roll-and-drop move for the up and back. Players performing the C and WA roles should change queues alternately throughout the drill.

VARIATION

Add one defender and build up to three. Defenders should pressure the passes and delay the attackers from driving exactly where they want to go but should allow them to receive, as it is a set movement drill.

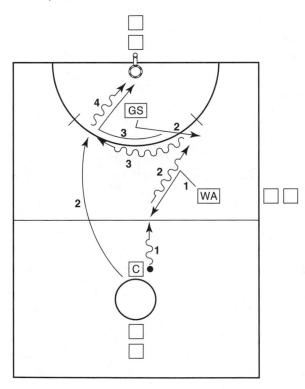

Figure 5.5 Frontcourt three-point combination.

ATTACKING-UNIT SPLIT CONDITIONING

Conditioning drills develop players' fitness systems. Drills that replicate position-specific skills and movement patterns double up on training time efficiency.

OBJECTIVE

For goalers and centre-court feeders to develop stamina while maintaining movement quality in games. The drill promotes working with concentration and accuracy through fatigue.

REQUIREMENTS

Four attacking-unit players, two markers, full court

METHOD

The drill is run independently and simultaneously in the centre third and defensive third for the feeders and in the goal third for the goalers. The defensive third acts as the goal third for the feeders.

Goalers' circuit:
Set the two markers three metres out from each 45 mark of the goal circle. The goalers complete a five-lead sequence, with one working while the other rests. The sequence starts mid-circle (see figure 5.6a).

1. The first goaler rolls left around an imaginary defender and sprints on a 45-degree-angle lead to the left marker.

2. She slip-steps around the marker as fast as possible and drives back to the starting point.

3. She sprints to the right marker and rolls and drops back to the post.

4. The goaler slip-steps back to the starting point and completes a triple dodge.

5. She sprints through the top of the circle on a slight angle to the transverse line, turns and sprints back to the post.

6. She jumps to touch the net twice to end the drill and tags the next worker. Players repeat the sequence five times, with a 1:1 work to rest ratio.

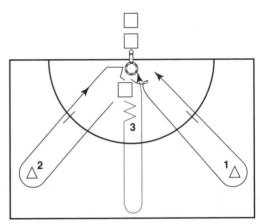

a

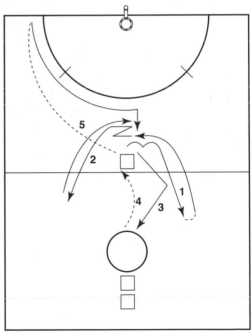

b

Figure 5.6 Attacking-unit split conditioning: *(a)* goalers' circuit and *(b)* feeders' circuit.

Feeders' circuit:

At the opposite end of the court to the goalers, the feeders simultaneously complete their conditioning sequence. The sequence starts behind the transverse line where the wing attack would set up to receive a centre pass (see figure 5.6b on previous page).

1. The first feeder half rolls and drives out on an angle as for the centre-pass action.
2. She digs in, pivots towards the goal, fakes a pass and returns to the starting point.
3. She double dodges and drives out to the opposite side to the first lead.
4. The feeder runs back to the start, drives forwards four steps, then breaks for the centre circle in a V-lead, touches the circle with a foot and shifts to a fast backwards slip-step to the starting point.
5. She runs a clearing lead to the baseline on the nearest side of the circle and cuts to the top.
6. She tags the next worker at the transverse line. Players repeat the sequence five times, with a 1:1 work to rest ratio.

VARIATION

One worker performs the sequence twice in a row, the second time reversing directions for each movement. Build up to five times in a row, emphasising technique.

Attacking Team Drills

All players are attackers when the team has possession of the ball. The better the team's defenders are at attacking, the smoother and more successful the delivery to the goal third will be. Many of the following drills are suitable as part of the pre-game warm-up routine.

MULTI-SKILL ATTACKING

OBJECTIVE

For each player to blend together attacking movements such as cutting, driving, taking a high ball, transitioning, pivoting, passing, refocussing and timing

REQUIREMENTS

Four workers (A, B, C and D) and two feeders (E and F), two balls, four markers, half a court

METHOD

Set a marker on both sides of the post on the baseline, halfway between the goal arc and the sideline. Set the other pair of markers eight metres down-court from the first two. E stands at one marker, and F stands at the other; they each have a ball (see figure 5.7). The rest of the group (the workers, A to D) form two equal queues (Q1 and Q2) behind and slightly to the right of the baseline markers facing the feeders.

1. On "go", the two workers at the front of each queue (A and C) cut hard around the marker to their left to receive a high ball from their respective same-side feeder.

2. They simultaneously shoulder pass the ball across to the opposite feeder and drive around their original feeder.

3. The original feeders release a lob to their own side's worker as the worker cuts sharply around them to snap the ball in and pivot to the other worker.

4. The workers cross balls. Q1 workers always use a shoulder pass, and Q2 workers always use a bounce.

5. They pivot, return the ball to the start of their original queue and replace the feeder on their side as the feeders join the end of the queues.

6. The new workers (B and D) pass to the new feeders (A and C) on their respective sides, and the drill repeats.

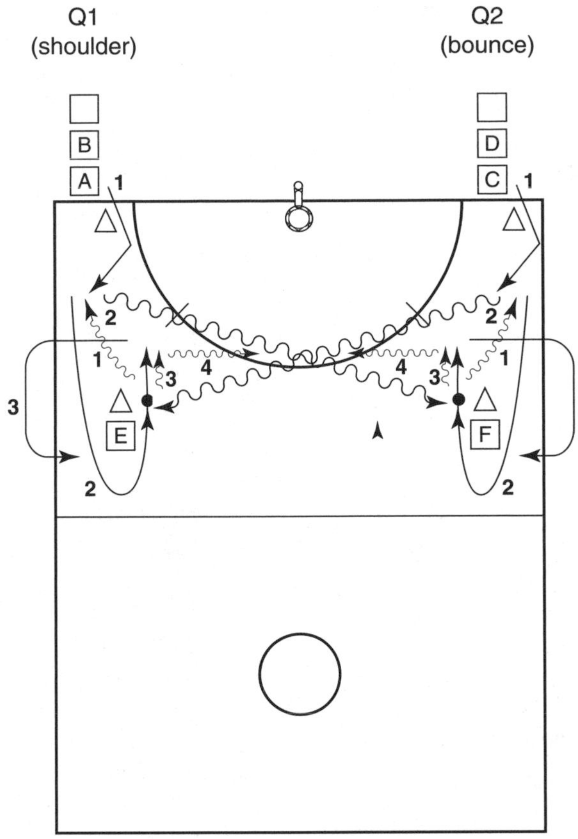

Figure 5.7   Multi-skill attacking.

Players should change queues at every return to work both sides.

RUNNING SHOT SEQUENCE

OBJECTIVE

For each player to develop the skills of precision passing, setting mobile screens and shooting on the run

REQUIREMENTS

Six players (minimum), two balls, two markers, half a court

METHOD

Set up a marker two metres in from each sideline on the attacking transverse line. Form

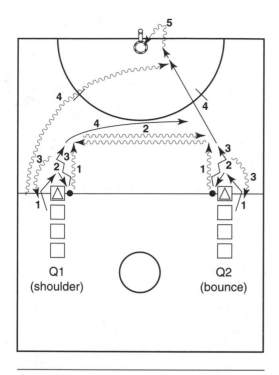

Figure 5.8 Running shot sequence.

two equal queues (Q1 and Q2) behind each marker. The player at the start of each queue (the feeders) faces the baseline holding a ball (see figure 5.8). Players need to know which queue does what before they take off, as each queue has a different sequence.

1. On "go", the second player in each queue (the workers) cuts fast around the first and adopts the defensive hands-over position.

2. After holding the position on balance for one second, the workers lunge forward with their preferred foot, touch the ball, back-step diagonally and receive a short lob from their same-side feeder.

3. The workers then cross their balls, with Q1 workers always using a shoulder pass and Q2 workers always using a bounce.

4. The workers return pass to their same-side feeder, then both drive to the goal arc to screen and drive, respectively.

5. The Q1 worker sprints to the arc (slightly to Q2's side) and sets a screen on the goal circle.

6. The Q2 worker cuts by the screen as close as possible and drives to the post as the Q1 feeder lobs a ball just past the screen for the Q2 worker to receive and complete a running shot at goal.

The shooter returns the ball to the feeder at Q1, and the workers join the back of the opposite queue as the new feeders currently second in the queue take their position at the front of the queue with the ball to reset the drill.

FAKE PASSING

OBJECTIVE

For each player to enhance her proficiency at using ball and eye fakes in the context of general play

REQUIREMENTS

Four players (minimum), one ball, one goal third

METHOD

Players spread out in the goal third, one with the ball.

1. The player with the ball tosses it to herself to initiate the drill, and the other three complete a preliminary move and break for the ball within the goal third, reading off each other to maintain court spacing.

2. The player with the ball executes a fake pass (ball or eye fake) and releases to the target lead, aiming for accuracy while maintaining balance.

3. The receiver performs a fake pass and releases to another target, and the drill repeats in this fashion for two minutes. A recorder (can be one of the group) counts the number of errors.

4. The group rests for a minute then repeats, trying to reduce the error count.

Each player without the ball must change her lead or begin a new one on every catch. Players must obey all netball rules at all times. If there are enough players for two groups, they can compete against each other, each group striving for an error-free set.

VARIATION

Add a floating defender with a bib to increase perceptual demands of the throwers and challenge the thinking of the leaders. Add another defender in the next set, and increase the boundary length to half a court.

TRAFFIC

OBJECTIVE

For each player to improve her ability to drive through congestion and use quick hand skills in "traffic". This drill provides the opportunity to fine-tune speed off the mark, timing, agility and quick passing under pressure. It has direct transfer to attacking purposefully through congestion around the transverse line and the goal arc.

REQUIREMENTS

Ten players (minimum), two balls, four markers, one-third of the court

METHOD

Set the markers in square formation 10 metres apart. Two workers set up at each corner (A, B, C and D start the queues), and two feeders (E and F) position themselves outside the square on opposite sides, 5 metres back from the imaginary "sides" of the square (see figure 5.9).

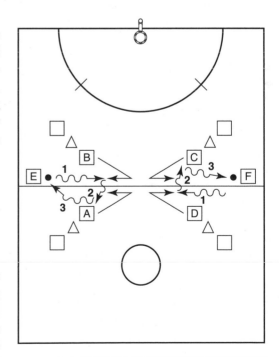

Figure 5.9   Traffic.

1. On "go", all workers at the front of a queue sprint towards the centre of the square.
2. When nearing the middle (stopping a safe distance from the other workers), A and B dig in and break towards E, who passes to either option. C and D dig in and break towards F, who chooses one player and makes a pass.
3. The receivers pass off with "quick hands" to the other worker in their pair (A and B work together, C and D work together), who returns a pass with similar speed to the feeder.
4. The next lot of four workers go in the next wave as soon as the balls are back with the feeders, while A, B, C and D join the back of a different queue.

Players should be sure to rotate queues to work both sides; rotate the feeders regularly.

CHAPTER 6

Dominant Defence

Defence is one of the most concrete elements in the game of netball. It can be the backbone of the team, as it can remain rock-steady when the flair and unpredictability of attack peak and trough. A team that consistently shuts down its opponent's scoring opportunities is always tough to beat. Defence has been considered largely reactive in the past, but the great teams of today play defence very much proactively. Defence in netball is often a thankless task, and the defensive unit has been the less glamorous sister of the attacking unit, which enjoys its fair share of the glory when the team scores. A huge part of defence is attitude. Every player is a defender when her team does not have possession of the ball, and teams that work together enjoy the challenge of setting traps and effecting a turnover. Good defenders understand the effect of combined pressure and relish the chance to pull off a team interception, knowing that their role off the ball enabled a team-mate to fly through and steal it.

This chapter embraces the principles of defence: one-on-one defence and its variations (such as sagging and offline), zone defence (area defence, or space marking) and options for defensive systems. It also details the last chance a team has to stop an opposition score (defence of the shot for goal) and the importance of defensive rebounding.

Principles of Defence

Principles of defence in team invasion games that apply to netball are pressure, help, depth and concentration. These principles apply to all the team's defensive efforts and are critical in a full-court defensive situation.

- **Pressure.** A defender in any situation should aim to apply maximum individual physical and mental pressure on her opponent. In one-on-one defence, four phases of defensive pressure (see the four-chances strategy outlined later in this chapter for more details) should be applied to an opponent. First, the defender should stand very close to an opponent, making her presence felt. Second, if the passed ball is in range, the defender should contest the ball, applying pressure to the catch. Third, when her opponent has taken the ball, the defender should apply hands-over pressure over the ball, cutting into appropriate passing lanes and restricting field of vision down-court. Finally, after release, the defender should apply further pressure by blocking the opponent's drive. If the defender has executed all these phases to the best of her ability, she has done her job (and ideally contributed to a turnover by the attacking team). Applying pressure in any offline situation where the defender patrols a space rather than a player requires the defender to perfect positioning (to confuse or upset the timing of the attack) and to cover her assigned area, ready to pounce on any ball in her range.

- **Help.** Help is the cornerstone of every successful defensive unit. The ability to back up a team-mate, do the hard work off the ball and support or cover a team-mate who has been exposed is what galvanises the defence. Knowing individual efforts are magnified with the help of the defensive unit gives defenders the confidence to play aggressively and proactively, to seek out and hunt down the interception. Any type of zone defence where the objective is to defend an area is useless without constant help from all team-mates.

- **Depth.** As with attacking, depth is critical for a solid defence line. Opposition attackers need to know that if they penetrate the first line of defence, there are plenty more hurdles to clear before the goal is reached. Defence configurations need to have depth so that players can take risks and collectively apply more pressure. If the defensive court spacing is too wide, attacks on goal open up more easily, and opposition attacking momentum and scoring rates increase.

- **Concentration.** As the defence configuration nears the opposition goal, good teams will have a concentration of players around the goals (i.e., the concentration of player positioning is strongest around the goal area). This reflects the basic concept of protecting the goal and guarding the most dangerous areas more heavily. As the destination is obvious and very narrow, defenders should be clustered near the chief scoring areas to shut down space.

From time to time, or if there is a problem with the team's defence, coaches should go back to the principles of defence to checklist the four principles and critically examine if their team is proficient in applying sufficient pressure, adequate help and enough depth, as well as checking the defensive configuration for concentration around the opposition goal circle. Pressure needs to be applied to the body and mind of opponents in one-on-one defending and to the spatial judgment and timing of opposition throwers in zones by correct body positioning and adherence to the rules. The team needs to be operating with the belief that combined pressure, with every player chipping away at their task, amounts to significant pressure applied to the opposition as a team. The team also needs to be active with their help. Defence is not a rest period, and every player should be either helping by shutting down lateral options, applying hands over the ball to help with the team interception down-court, or supplying vocal cues for team-mates near the ball. The game is too fast and weighted in the attackers' favour for individual defensive efforts to be successful without help.

> *"With each team having the same number of centre passes, whole team defence is vital for creating the intercepts and turnovers that make the winning margin. All seven players must work towards this—not just the ones with a 'D' on their bib."*
>
> ~ Naomi Siddall, England Defender, Commonwealth Games and World Championship Medallist

Coaches must check the depth of the team defence and ensure that the positioning of players in team defence is not too wide and high so that there are easy gaps for the opposition to charge through central attacking pathways. Whilst pressure is paramount all over the court, there is nowhere more important for pressure to be impacted than in a concentrated effort in the last line of defence, the opposition goal circle. The opposition crave a one-on-one situation in their goal circle as there is only one defender to beat, so by ensuring that there is a concentrated presence of defenders in the major threat area, teams can minimise the occurrence of this situation.

One-on-One Defence

One-on-one, or player-on-player, defence is the first type of defence a player should learn and master. It is the staple method of the majority of teams and the exclusive method of many teams (see table 6.1 for a summary of the most commonly used types of defence). Each player is responsible for shutting down her positional opponent and minimising that player's impact on the game, whether it be by restricting her scoring, keeping her away from the action or denying her as much effective possession as possible. One-on-one play aims to wear an opponent down with the constant presence of a body close by, restricting an attacker's vision and freedom by applying pressure to every movement and pass. An accomplished defender aims to dictate the terms, gain psychological edges and force opponents to play their second-string moves by taking away their strengths. In one on one, defenders should seek to operate in restricted space,

Table 6.1 Characteristics of Various Types of Defence

Type of defence	Aims	Defensive type	Players involved	Features
One-on-one defence	To exert maximum physical pressure on a positional opponent	One-on-one tight	All	Simplicity, individual accountability and responsibility; very physically tough to play against all match, if executed well; can be the total defence system for the team or makes an excellent primary system; used on a switch and as a "go to" system if more complex systems break down
Double defence	To eliminate a player as a passing target by placing two defenders on one opponent	Two-on-one tight	Circle defenders or centre and wing defence	Simple to execute; can cut a player right out of the play; can effectively shut down a dominant player and upset an attacking unit's rhythm by taking away strengths and forcing attackers to play through their second options
Sagging defence	To cut out the primary target by running back onto a teammate's opponent to create a floating two-on-one situation	Two-on-one tight, spatial combination	All can apply it, but mainly wing defence, centre and goal defence	Forces fluent attacking teams to restructure their play patterns; exploits teams that are inflexible in their attack line; any lead to the ball can be cut into by a sagging defender, but it is particularly effective on a goaler leading out of the goal circle or on set plays bringing the ball out of defence

Type of defence	Aims	Defensive type	Players involved	Features
Offline defence	To upset an opposition attack line's rhythm and timing by defending in spaces rather than on the player	One-on-one spatial, entire unit on system simultaneously	Mainly the defensive unit plus wing attack and goal attack at the front, but it can work as a full-court team defence	Forces attacking units to alter tracking and timing skills and make continual spatial adjustments; useful any time a change-up in defensive style is appropriate to combat dominating opposition attacking patterns or to try to slow down the scoring rate
Flooding defence	To crowd and restrict the opposition's attacking space and occupy the premium attacking pathways	Team spatial	All players except goal shooter	Overloads opposition with visual cues and spatial adjustment; can stall an opposition attack and slow scoring rate; can run off any centre pass or defensive throw-in where there is time for own team's attacking players to set up at the defensive transverse line
Zone defence	To effect turnovers by defending an area rather than a player	Team or unit spatial	All players in a centre-court block, defensive unit in defensive-third zones; wing attack and goal attack are included in the unit in some zones	Can stall dominating players and be an excellent option against fast-attacking teams and if members of a defensive unit are matched up poorly for speed against a wing attack or goaler; can be a very effective tactic to change the pace of an opposition attack; excellent to use against fluent attacks that favour attacking through the middle corridors

working boundary lines and other team-mates' positioning to their advantage. They should quickly assess their opponents' strengths and weaknesses. Effective defensive players apply collective pressure to force opposition attackers to turn the ball over through smart configurations, patience and playing hard.

When playing one on one, a defender has four opportunities to break down each attack; this is called the four-chances strategy. Chance 1 is to apply intense shadowing pressure and force opponents into a poorly timed lead, railroading the attacker into a boundary line or another player's space. This can lead to an interception as the attacker slows down towards the line or can result in a pass that flies over the line and out of court. Chance 2 is to contest the ball, intercepting, deflecting or putting pressure on the receiver to take the ball cleanly. Chance 3 is to execute a recovery step as quickly as possible to clear the required three-foot (.9-metre) distance and then pressure the pass with hands-over intensity on the ball to effect a turnover. If the defender gets a tip on the ball, she must react quickly and chase down the loose ball. If the pass clears, the defender should adopt the ready stance and block the opponent's run down-court by delaying the run or directing the attacker to the sideline, away from the action (chance 4). This effectively reduces the opposition's passing options, adding pressure and possibly forcing an error.

Defensive stance positions and defending preliminary moves are used to shadow and pressure the opponent. Intercepting applies to pressuring the reception, and pressuring the pass is chance 3. Switching, sagging, flooding, offline and double defence are viable alternatives if none of the four chances are working. All these concepts are discussed in this section.

Defensive Stance Positions

A defender playing one on one has four basic choices of stance when positioning on an opponent: defending from the front, side or behind or while facing the opponent. Each attacking situation calls for a different response, and defenders should be adept at switching between all forms of one on one. A shrewd defender will test out a variety of stances early in the game, determine the one her opponent has the most trouble with and use that stance for the majority of the match (chance 1 of the four-option strategy: shadowing pressure).

Figure 6.1 One-on-one defending using the front stance.

• **Defending from the front.** The front stance is the one that will most likely net the defender an interception or deflection. It is easy to move to the ball from this position because the body is oriented towards the ball, and arms and legs are less likely to be tangled, as they are clear of the attacker. The defender stands in front of her opponent, facing the ball about two-thirds of the way across the body, as close as possible without contacting. The defender adopts a ready position, with knees and hips flexed, weight forward over toes, shoulders level and head up, vision wide enough to take in both opponent and ball (see figure 6.1). The defender should be moving in the ready stance by bouncing quickly on the balls of the toes or tapping feet quickly up and down, ready to transfer momentum from a moving start rather than a static start, which is a much slower process. Whenever the attacker moves, the defender shadows her with fast footwork, maintaining the correct front position with every step until the ball comes into range and can be contested.

- **Defending from the side.** In the side stance, a defender positions herself to the side of an opponent, aiming to direct her to a particular side, usually the non-ball side away from the action. This forces the attacking team to use a cross-court pass to be able to use this attacker and gives the defender a better chance of intercepting because of the length and angle of the pass. The defender sets up on the preferred side of her opponent (the side she wishes to prevent the attacker from leading into) in the ready position, bouncing or tapping (see figure 6.2). Some players prefer to stand squarely to the side of the attacker, with one foot in front and one behind, and others adopt a more side–front position, with the back foot slightly in front of the attacker but the body closed off. This allows more movement for the defender and a better chance of an interception, but it also frees up the attacker more to cut back to the closed-off side. The defender must be vigilant about maintaining the side position with quick reactive foot adjustments, or the opponent can slip past on a backwards V-cut and leave her stranded.

- **Defending from behind.** Defending from behind (see figure 6.3) reflects other team-game concepts of keeping between the opponent and the goal. As netball is played in such a restricted area and goals are scored aerially, it is not always a successful concept to employ. However, there are some exceptions, the most obvious being a goal keeper facing a very tall goal shooter who is scoring easily by dropping to the post. If the defender can keep the shooter towards the edge of the circle and

Figure 6.2 One-on-one defending using the side stance.

Figure 6.3 One-on-one defending from behind.

play from behind, this forces the shooter to either shoot long or off-load to another player, giving the team another chance of gaining possession. To defend from behind, the defender positions herself immediately behind the shooter such that both feet are behind the attacker's two feet. The defender can afford to stand a little straighter (but still in the mobile ready position) from behind so that reach will not be too severely compromised. The defender can still contest the ball (especially a high one) with the outside arm so contact is easier avoided.

• **Defending while facing the opponent.** On occasions where an opponent is dominating play with concise preliminary moves and easy receptions, one tactic that may be considered is facing the attacker in a basic tag. This forfeits the defender's chances of intercepting the ball, but it can upset the attacker's rhythm and shut down her attacking dominance. The defender adopts the ready position from the front but faces the opponent rather than the ball. The defender focusses purely on her opponent and shadows her every move, shutting down the attacker's personal space and vision to the ball. This type of defending can incur many contact calls as two sets of arms and legs compete for the same moving space. Defenders should take care to stay out of spaces that attackers have committed to moving into, which not only causes contact but also increases the likelihood of injury. Done safely and properly, face-on defending can be very successful in changing the dynamics of an opposition forward line that has a dominant attacker, by applying the strategy in short bursts. The downside of prolonged face-on defending is that it can invite tension between the attacker and the defender and low-quality play, as well as take away from the spectacle of the game.

Defending Preliminary Moves

Different preliminary moves put on by an opponent call for some variation in defensive technique. To defend an opponent on a straight lead, a stop-dead move, a dodge or any mobile lead where the attacker is facing the thrower, the defender moves with the attacker, striving to shadow her with fast, balanced footwork (chance 1 of the four-chances strategy). The defender continually moves to keep in her ready stance while maintaining a dual ball–opponent focus. If the ball comes into reach, the defender leaves the player and directs her entire focus on the ball. If unsuccessful, the defender must dig in, try not to overrun and pick up her opponent again as quickly as possible.

To defend a half roll or roll-off, the defender must pick the turn of the shoulders and jump sideways quickly to the rolling side, briefly focussing on the opponent to resight her. The loss of temporary ball focus does not matter because the attacker has her back to the ball during the manoeuvre and cannot receive a pass. As soon as the attacker rolls back to face the play, the defender should resume the regular ready stance.

To prevent an opponent from cutting off and entering the front space, a defender should keep her feet moving and move off the player slightly as an attacker steps up to set the cut. Most of the time when an attacking opponent steps towards a defender, she is setting something up, whether it be space, a cut-off, a hold, a roll-around or a screen. This strategy can be foiled by never letting the attacker get close enough to set her own moves. Being proactive may prevent set-ups and frustrate attackers who like to set their moves from a tangible spot. An opponent cannot cut off from any further back than directly behind the defender.

When defending a hold, screen, or roll-around, players should be proactive rather than stand there and wait for it to happen—because if they do, it will! The best advice for avoiding being used as a launching dock for holders and screeners is for defenders to move out of a set-up straightaway and avoid putting themselves into positions where they can be set up. The ball is unlikely to be passed to an attacker who has set up too early or is not in the exact position for a stationary reception, so defenders must take advantage of attackers who telegraph their plays. When an attacker does manage to slip past, defenders should recover quickly to exert maximum pressure on the next pass. Attackers with possession clearly have the advantage, and defenders must keep chipping away to break the attack down.

Intercepting

Making an interception (chance 2 of the four-chances strategy) is the defensive equivalent of scoring about three goals. Anticipation, alertness, being in position ready to pounce and moving to intercept with the feet first, then torso, then hands are the keys to making an interception. More often than not, an interception is the result of pressure being applied by teammates up-court, and experienced defensive units plan together to make it happen. Intercepting requires great mobility skills and determination from the player making the steal. The player must initially assess whether the ball is in reasonable reach. If a player tries to intercept every ball, she will waste energy and become very predictable to the opposition and get peppered with fakes. Once the player has decided that the ball is in range, she must do everything she can within the rules to get her hands on it. The principles for intercepting are the same as for catching (as detailed in chapter 2); intercepting is just catching a ball that is intended for someone else! Taking the ball with two hands is ideal (see figure 6.4) but

Figure 6.4 Intercepting from behind. The defender hollows out and takes the ball early.

not always possible. Deflecting a ball to a team-mate or tapping to collect it are sometimes more realistic options. Defenders must be mindful of the contact rule at all times when attempting to intercept. Front-stance defence is the cleanest way to intercept, as there isn't a body to negotiate. If intercepting from behind or the side, defenders must hollow out their bodies (by making a concave shape) to pass close to an opponent to avoid full-body contact, aiming to take the ball early to avoid contact with the arms. They must also remember to extend their arms across an opponent's path to reach the ball only as the ball is about to be caught. Any earlier and a penalty for obstruction may be called.

Pressuring the Pass

A vital part of effective one-on-one defence is the ability to apply pressure to an opponent's pass (chance 3 of the four-chances strategy) upon gaining possession. The defender should position herself for hands-over pressure in line with the primary target, usually directly down-court between the ball and the opposition goalpost. Sometimes this is not possible near court markings, so positioning on the side is the next best option. The defender should crouch in a balanced, coiled position with knees and hips flexed, weight forward on balls of toes, ready to spring to the ball on release. She should be watching for the opponent's target selection and zoning in on the release point. Arms and fingers should be extended over the ball to exert pressure on the pass or should be in a passing lane to dictate where the pass is more likely to go. Arms placed vertically clear lateral passing corridors and shut down the direct path down-court (see figure 6.5a); arms placed wide open the down-court passing corridors but restrict lateral options (see figure 6.5b). As the ball is released, a player needs to decide whether to have a go at deflecting the pass from close range by exploding to the ball or forgo the pass for a block and delay on the thrower.

Players must be able to position themselves instinctively without looking at their feet. An imperative skill for defenders is a fast, balanced recovery step. They need fast footwork to back off, clear the required distance for hands-over defence (.9 metre) and apply pressure before the opponent selects her passing target. If players are having difficulty with distance, they can practise hands-over defence using the centre circle, which has a diameter of .9 metre, or cut some dowel or scrap wood to the exact length and use it randomly to check distances at training.

Switching

When a positional match-up is not working defensively (four chances are not yielding results) and an opposition attacker is beginning to dominate a defender one on one, defenders can call a switch. This is a way of changing up the defence and releasing pressure on the defender who is being beaten without making an official position change. Members of a defensive pair simply switch opponents and continue playing one on one when the ball approaches the area, giving the two opposition attackers new opponents to combat. Examples of switching that work well are the goal keeper with the goal defence as well as the centre with

Figure 6.5 Pressuring the pass with hands over the ball: *(a)* the defender is dictating the passing options by shutting down the direct ball with arms high; *(b)* the defender is dictating the passing options by shutting down the lateral options with arms wide.

the wing defence. The timing of the switch is important so that anomalies with newly matched players are not detrimental to the cause. For example, a goal keeper and goal defence switch can be timed to run only when the ball is in the defensive half. If a switch is made too early, the opposition goal attack can take easy possession and have open vision down-court, as the goal keeper (the new opponent) cannot move over the transverse line to apply pressure. Switching can also work well when an opponent is not dominating play and should be seen as another weapon in the team's armoury rather than a default option if a player is being beaten.

Variations of One-on-One Defence

Standard one-on-one defence has several variations. A subtle change of altering the placement of defenders can upset the rhythm and flow of the opposition. One-on-one variations include double defence, sagging, offline and flooding.

Double Defence

When a defensive unit places two defenders against one attacker, this is known as double defence. The purpose of double defending is to overload an opponent so that the action will be diverted somewhere else, ideally eliminating a dominating player from the action. To double defend a player, the defenders combine front coverage with side or back coverage. Both defenders adopt the ready stance and adapt quickly when the pass is released. Communication is essential and easy from such a close range. If two players are deployed to combat one player, they need to be intense and make sure that the double-teamed opponent is eliminated as a target; otherwise it is a complete waste of resources.

The two most common situations to run a double defence are (1) both circle defenders against a dominant goal shooter and (2) a centre–wing defence double on the opposition wing attack at the centre pass. To double defend a shooter, the defensive pair should be reasonably confident that the unguarded shooting partner will not take over and lift the overall scoring rate. Sometimes, in a one-prong attack where a team has a dominant shooter paired with a feeder shooter, double defence can be a match-winning move. At the centre pass, double defending a wing attack often makes a team play its second option right from the start. If the wing attack is covered, the centre must go through the goal attack, dragging a goaler away from the target, or pass backwards. Using a back defender for the centre pass is fine if the receiver takes the pass in the front-court, but this can result in traffic in premium attacking space. The risk of double defending the opposition wing attack is that the centre taking the pass can break for an unopposed drive down-court after disposal if her opponent is dragged too wide on the double. Combination defences (double defence switching to one-on-one defence at a certain point in the play) can work well and avoid problems with extreme applications of the technique.

Figure 6.6 The wing defence sags back to cover the goal shooter on an out-lead.

Sagging

Sagging is a variation of one-on-one defence involving a fast change of orientation for the defender when her opponent receives the ball. The defender forgoes the chance to apply pressure over the ball to sag, or drift back, onto the next lead to cut out the primary target (see figure 6.6). This forces the attacking team to play its second option and usually throw cross-court, decreasing the passing angle and increasing the chances for interception. To effect a sag, the defender digs in and backs off as soon as it is clear that a contest for the ball is not viable. With verbal assistance from team-mates, the sagging defender cuts back into the pathway of the perceived primary target to create a floating double defence. If executed well, the passer then must choose a less favourable target. As soon as the pass is released, the sagging defender must recover to pick up her original opponent or call a switch with a team-mate to pick up the closest appropriate player.

Offline

Defending offline is a variation of one on one in which a defender is still responsible for guarding her positional opponent but plays in the space in front or to the side of the opponent (about three steps away; see figure 6.7). The chief purpose of this style is to give the attacking opponent the illusion of space so that she leads into the space at a reduced pace because she feels she is already clear. The defender then accelerates in a late run to try to beat the attacker to the ball at the last second. Defenders in the offline formation are also responsible for picking off any ball that is lobbed to a team-mate's opponent directly up-court from them, should that player elect to drop back in a perceived free space. Defenders should adjust their offline position between opponent and ball with every pass. Eyes-up netball (keeping vision on the play) is essential in offline. Offline positioning also requires visual adjustment from the thrower, so passing errors can originate from the thrower's misjudged pass as well as a soft lead. The advantage of offline is that it can upset the rhythm of the attack by taking away opposition attackers' starting points from which they calculate and begin leads and passes. Offline defence can be a great defensive trap for opposition attackers with suspect spatial skills. The most difficult thing about executing offline is that everyone in the defensive unit needs to be performing proficiently at the same time, or the defence can be cut to shreds by shrewd attackers spotting holes and zipping quick passes through.

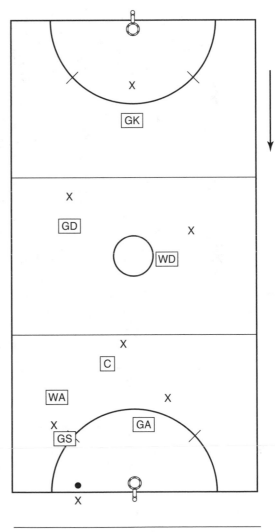

Figure 6.7 Offline defensive set-up.

Flooding

A popular defensive concept across a range of invasion games today is flooding (see table 6.1). Flooding involves crowding the opposition attack end to shut down space available in which opposition attackers can operate. As there is little space available in netball anyway, flooding can cause a number of headaches for attack lines. If a defensive team can space the flooding well, the opposition's scoring rate can be slowed down greatly. When a team calls for the flood, the defenders cluster themselves back around the goal area, and the goal attack and wing attack retreat to the defensive transverse line, placing six players near or in the opposition's goal third (see figure 6.8). As the goal attack and wing attack are not permitted in the opposition's goal third, they have the responsibility of applying pressure at the teeth of the configuration with tenacious hands-over defence on throwers near the line and can double defend the pass in the central corridor. The wing attack and goal attack also strive to keep the opposition attackers away from the transverse line to force high feeds to the goal third over hands, buying time with the ball in the air for the defensive unit behind to intercept. The centre, wing defence, goal defence and goal keeper patrol the key attacking pathways in the ready stance, moving with every pass, ready to pounce on any indirect ball. The defensive unit in the goal third can play one on one, offline, a basic box or a diamond zone (see Zone Defence). The best time to run the flood is from an opposition back-line throw-in or defensive-third penalty to allow time for the wing attack and goal attack to move into place. To flood at the opposition centre pass, the goal attack and wing attack align themselves to sprint close to the centre circle on their respective sides to congest the premium reception areas on their way to the transverse line.

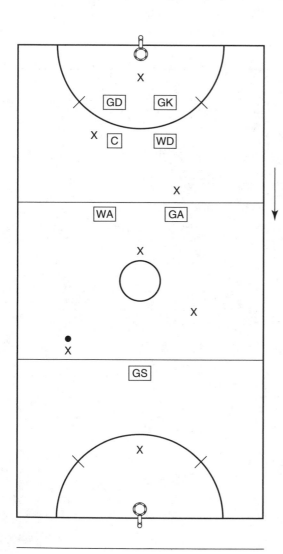

Figure 6.8 Flooding defensive set-up.

Zone Defence

A total structural alternative to one-on-one defensive styles is zone defence. Playing a zone constitutes defending an area rather than a particular player (see table 6.1 for details). Players in a zone protect their assigned areas and aim to keep the ball out of that area. They pick up any opposition player that passes through their zone but do not follow her when she leaves. The responsibility passes on to the next team-mate to pick up the mobile player and make sure she does not become a target in their assigned area. Zones can be an effective change-up from one-on-one defence, challenging the opposition players to alter their playing style to combat it. If the opposition is not prepared, the results of a well-executed zone defence can be outstanding when used as an impact move.

In all zone defences, players remain in formation and adjust the orientation with every pass until the zone is broken (i.e., the ball has cleared the area or the attacking team turns it over). Communication is essential; players at the back of the zone act as the eyes and call the play for their team-mates. It is never more important to act as a unit than when playing a zone. Team-mates who do not play hard and stick to their assignment leave their colleagues high and dry to be totally exposed. Zone defences require trust, experience and commitment from all members for a team to use them effectively as part of its defensive repertoire.

Many zones and variations can be created using the principles of defence and attack and a little experimentation. Some of the more popular zones that have been effective in high-grade netball are the centre-court block, box-and-two zone, diamond-and-two zone, box-out zone and split-circle zone.

Centre-Court Block

Four of the five players allowed access to the centre third set up in a rectangle facing their goal line, covering the extremes of the centre third. The centre positions herself in the middle of the arrangement (see figure 6.9). The goal

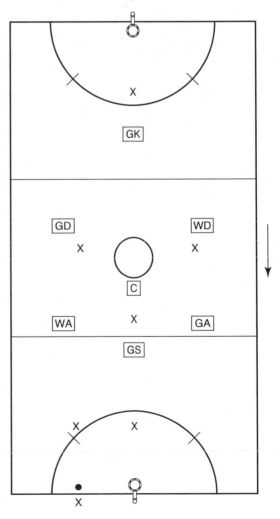

Figure 6.9 Centre-court block.

attack and wing attack take up the front two corners with the help of the goal shooter, who either sets up in front of the transverse line to cover the join in the middle or chases down passes in the opposition's defensive third to apply pressure on feeds to the centre third. The wing defence and goal defence form the back two corners and call for their three team-mates in front. The goal for each player is to prevent opponents from catching a ball in her area. Players are always in the defensive ready position, shifting with every pass, ready to pounce on any pass in their zone. The goal keeper positions herself well back from the zone to act as the safety net should the zone be penetrated. As the rules dictate that a ball must be played in each third, the objective is to break down the opposition attack by eliminating a successful possession in the centre third. The zone aims to force an error by creating a "held ball", an "over a third" call, a misjudged pass that goes to the defenders or out of court, or any other footwork or pressure ball-handling error in the centre third. When a pass is received by the opposition in the centre third, the zone is broken; all players should scramble and retreat to one-on-one defence as fast as possible.

Box-and-Two Zone

Most zones operate in a team's defensive third of the court. The box-and-two defence is one such zone. The four players allowed in the defensive zone set up in a slightly staggered box formation around the middle of the goal circle (see figure 6.10). The goal attack and wing attack position themselves at the teeth of the zone on their respective sides and perform the same role as they do for the flooding defence, pressuring the passes and keeping feeds to the opposition's attacking third long and aerial. Defenders allow opponents to cut through the zone but not receive a pass in it. The zone can be set from a defensive throw-in to the opposition. A centre pass does not allow time for the wing attack and goal attack to position themselves. The zone protects the central feeding pathways to the goal circle, allowing passes (or shots) to be taken on the flanks but not in the premium spaces. The circle defenders have the option of reverting to one on one when the ball enters the goal circle

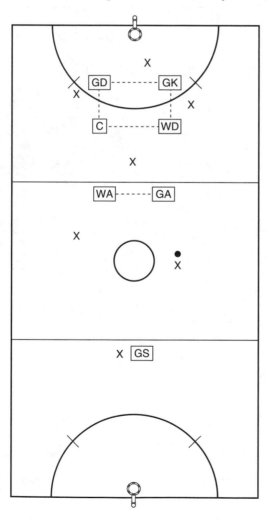

Figure 6.10 Box-and-two zone.

(the centre and wing defence follow suit) or remaining offline and protecting the close shooting spots in the goal circle.

Diamond-and-Two Zone

A diamond-and-two is a variation of the box-and-two with a slightly different orientation in that it places the goal keeper nearer the post and gives the centre more lateral movement, which can be a strength if the opposition goal shooter is very tall and the defensive team has an agile, tenacious centre. The four defensive-third players make a diamond formation at the same place as for the box zone (see figure 6.11). The goal attack's and wing attack's roles are identical to their roles for the box-and-two. Again, the objective is to keep the ball wide and protect premium central feeding spots. Opponents can cut through the zone but not receive a pass in it. When the zone is penetrated, the team reverts to one on one as the safest option.

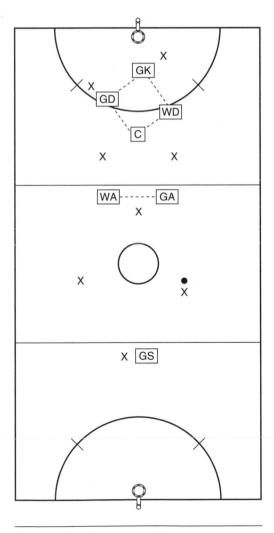

Figure 6.11   Diamond-and-two zone.

Box-Out Zone

A box-out zone uses a box formation with the objective of keeping the attacking players out of the central feeding and moving hot spots. It is similar to the box-and-two but is more compact (see figure 6.12) and involves defenders blocking out any cutter who attempts to enter the zone. This effectively leaves the opposition to attack the goals from wide angles only, taking second-option movement channels and slowing scoring rates. A quick transition to one on one is needed if an opponent breaks the zone or a goaler receives behind it.

Split-Circle Zone

In a split-circle zone, the circle defenders divide the space in the goal circle to patrol. They pick up any goaler that enters the area and try to prevent her from receiving a pass by guarding, blocking and intercepting. The wing defence and

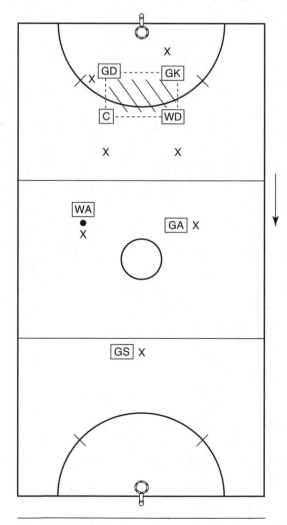

Figure 6.12 Box-out zone.

centre play supporting roles in that they apply pressure to the passes into the goal circle and try very hard to keep the feeders off the goal circle edge so the feeds are longer and over pressure, increasing the chance of an interception. The goal defence and goal keeper can call a split circle during any down-court attack, as it is set so deep in the team's defence that the players have the luxury of set-up time. The circle can be divided in three basic ways (vertically, horizontally or diagonally) according to preference and skills of the defending pair (see figure 6.13). With experienced defensive pairs and excellent communication, the splits themselves can change as the ball swings around the goal arc.

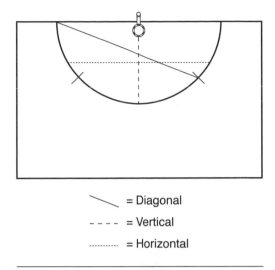

    = Diagonal

---- = Vertical

.... = Horizontal

Figure 6.13   Vertical, horizontal and diagonal splits for split-circle zones.

Defensive Systems

Once a number of alternative defensive options have been established, the team may be ready to develop a set of defensive systems to switch between more frequently, keeping the opposition guessing and keeping concentration levels high. These systems can be called by a nominated member of the defensive unit and communicated to team-mates by signal or verbal means. Following is an example of a one-to-four system from an opposition centre pass:

1. Attack the first pass. Players concentrate full pressure on breaking the centre pass with double defending and side stances.
2. Attack the second pass. Players direct where the opposition can receive the centre pass as the team sets to break the second pass by united predetermined positioning and pressure over the ball.
3. Sag. The defenders sag off to the primary lead when their opponent gets the ball.
4. Flood. Wing attack and goal attack sprint the middle corridors as the defensive unit sets up in the spaces.

The rest of the time, the defence plays one on one. Many more numbered options are available; the degree of difficulty needs to be engineered to the level of the performers. Systems may need to be run off opposition back-line throw-ins to allow more time to set up or the number of changes kept to a minimum to begin with.

Shot Defence

Defence of the shot for goal is often an underestimated, undertrained circle-defence fundamental. A diligent defender can destroy a shooter and make an enormous impact on the game. Defence of the shot can take many forms, and it is up to the defender and coach to practise a range of techniques and select those that are the most effective for that player.

When defending the shot, a sequence of sub-skills should be followed to ensure completeness and maximum pressure application. A simple acronym can act as a reminder for defenders to check periodically for thoroughness in their techniques.

D: distance. Make sure of the .9-metre clearance before hands leave the sides.

A: arms. Arms cause a visual block and exert pressure over the ball, especially low releases.

P: pressure. Apply maximum pressure, whether leaning or jumping to tip the shot.

P: pounce. Explode towards the ball if jumping, or lean into the space to the shooter.

E: eliminate. Eliminate the shooter as a viable rebounder by blocking the path to the post.

R: rebound. Refocus and set up to be first to the post for a rebound.

All circle defenders should aim to be DAPPER defenders. Persistence, resilience and attention to the listed cues will go a long way towards breaking down shooters even if efforts appear to be futile at times.

The goal keeper applies a visual block and maximum pressure over the shot with a two-handed lean.

Successful shot defenders possess certain characteristics. Elite defenders focus on the ball and are well disciplined with respect to the contact and obstruction rules, aiming to keep penalties to a minimum. They treat defending the shot as a challenge to tip the ball or cause a miss rather than something they have no effect on. It is important that circle defenders keep positive, seeing a missed shot without penalty as a success and a successful shot as inevitable some of the time and move on quickly to the next challenge. The two major techniques for shot defence are the lean and the jump. A combination of the two techniques can be effective if the defender can set up with a fast recovery step.

- **The lean.** The lean (or hang) is a tall, static stretch over the ball (see figure 6.14) carried out when a defender has cleared the .9-metre distance from the goaler's first grounded foot. Leaning applies instant pressure over the ball while impeding the shooter's visual clarity and follow-through pathway. A one-hand lean maximises the length of the lean, and a two-hand lean accentuates physical presence and visual distraction to the target. The two-hand lean provides better balance but gives up centimetres in length of the stretch. Some defenders use a swinging-arm technique, starting with one arm and replacing it with the other to aid in balancing as they land to the side of the shooter. Leaning should be practised first in isolation, then at game speed with an opponent and feeder, with the coach timing the lean. Players should

Figure 6.14   The lean from in front.

aim to hold the lean for the full three seconds. Leaning is usually done in front of a shooter, directly between the shooter and the post. Sometimes it is more practical to lean from the side or behind the shooter (e.g., when two defenders are defending the shot or the shooter is almost directly under the post).

- **The jump.** The jump is an attempt to distract the goaler and alter her shot or to tip the ball after the shot is released. Defenders with good elevation often favour the jump (see figure 6.15). A deflected shot can make many shooters second guess their shots for a long while after. Preparation for the jump varies for each defender. Some opt to crouch in a highly flexed position, ready to explode

Figure 6.15   Jumping to deflect the shot.

to the ball; this allows the shooter a great view of the target but is likely to produce a higher, balanced jump more likely to deflect. Others prefer to extend high over the ball with an arm in the shooting path for a second, then crouch and spring to the ball. This technique denies the shooter a clear view of the target but is less likely to result in a deflection because the take-off is more hurried and less powerful. Both techniques should be trained and tried, with the dominant technique being the one that causes greatest inaccuracy from the opposing shooter.

A popular technique that has emerged from the single jump is the double jump. Instead of waiting for the shot, the defender is proactive and jumps approximately on the one-and-a-half- and two-and-a half-second marks of the shooter's (slightly less than) three-second possession. Double jumping can be very distracting for the shooter, upsetting her timing. Defenders should take care to jump vertically up and not in on the first jump so as not to incur an obstruction call on the second one. Jumping can be executed from the side or behind, but it is most successful from the front. When jumping towards the shooter, a defender must land without interfering with the shooting action, or obstruction may be called.

Leaning and jumping techniques can be successfully fused into a combination defence. Most of the time this involves a lean then a jump. The critical aspect of this technique is the timing. To start with, an effective lean and transition into a purposeful jump all within three seconds is quite a feat. Often when attempting to cram too much into one defensive manoeuvre, defence quality is lost.

Defenders also need to be aware of fake shots. Shooters who are adamant about having a clear view of the target will often fake their shot against a jumping defender. A fake can draw the defender into an early jump so the shooter can rebalance and take a clear shot when the defender is in the landing phase. An experienced defender can pick a fake by the movement of the shooter's support hand to the front of the ball to prevent it from falling out with the sudden stop of the motion. The defender can then halt her jump. One way to combat a shooter who fakes a lot is to fake a jump. Using the crouching or the extending, crouching and springing technique, the defender can set for a slightly early jump and pull up just as the feet are about to leave the ground, continuing up with the arms (taking care not to intimidate the shooter and give up a penalty). The goal is to draw the shooter into a fake and then force her into making a rushed shot under pressure when she regathers and set ups for the actual shot only to discover the defender still poised and ready to attack. It can turn into a faking game as both players try to outsmart each other. This is great for the defender, as the shooter would have lost pure focus.

An important aspect of defending the shot is defensive rebounding, which should be utilized by both the defender defending the shot and the defender guarding the non-shooter. If the shot has been launched without deflection, the defender on the shot needs to recover quickly, turn and block out the shooter with a balanced wide base to claim first rights to any rebounds. The defender should adopt the ready position and be eager to spring with two hands if a ball should come her way. She should take the ball early in front of the head with extended arms to prevent a contest from the shooter behind, snapping the ball in strongly to secure possession.

The defender of the non-shooter should try to secure prime front position with respect to the post. This defender has the responsibility of preventing an easy pass-off under the post from goaler to goaler while the shooter has possession, but once the shot is on its way the defender can direct her focus to the rebound. Taking the rebound early in front of the head and snapping the ball in will avoid a possible contest. If the rebound is headed out of court and the defender is not able to take clean possession, it is better to protect the space from her opponent, let the ball bounce out and take the throw-in.

Performance Points for Defending

- Play with intensity, alertness, patience, discipline and resilience. Play hard.
- Develop a strong ready stance, and use fast, balanced footwork.
- Develop a range of one-on-one techniques, and progress in the order of feet, torso, hands when moving to intercept a ball.
- Set aside time to train as a unit to master zone and floating defence systems.
- Know and practise at least two alternative techniques for defending the shot.

Defensive Drills

The following defensive drills have been categorised into three sections: individual, unit and team defence drills. General movement development is intrinsic to basic defensive body movement, so many of the drills in chapter 3 can also be used for the development of sound defensive fundamentals.

Individual and Pairs Defensive Drills

Individual defensive drills can be completed during training as part of a group session or individually to supplement team training. When undertaking defensive drills, players should keep in mind the order in which to attack a defensive assignment—have a plan, use the feet and torso to get to the ball and use the hands last. Players should constantly train their bodies to strive for fast, balanced footwork.

REACTIVE AGILITY

OBJECTIVE

For each player to develop fast multi-directional footwork and recovery, especially in a reactive situation

REQUIREMENTS

One to 10 individual workers, a coach or someone to call commands, the space of half a netball court

METHOD

The workers set up facing the coach, with at least two metres of space in every direction between them and the next worker or a boundary.

1. On "go", the workers begin continuous "fast feet" taps in the defensive ready position, with weight over toes, arms to sides and eyes up.

2. The coach calls a random series of commands (front, back, left, right, up) to which the workers respond as quickly as possible.

3. The workers take three quick steps in the commanded direction (*left* and *right* signal a move diagonally, *up* is an explosive jump), dig in, take a recovery step back, adopt the hands-over defence position, hold for two seconds and recommence fast feet tapping.

4. Repeat several times over.

This is an easy drill to do poorly and a hard drill to do perfectly. Emphasis needs to be on quality, balance, speed and technique. Workers should focus on a smooth transition between accelerating, stopping, backing off, balancing and fast feet tapping.

VARIATION

Change the *left* and *right* commands to translate to diagonally backwards instead of forwards, and have workers complete the fast-feet phase with their arms raised directly in front of them. The coach pauses between commands longer to keep the arms out, challenging balance, stamina and the ability to drop the arms for take-off.

SHADOWING

OBJECTIVE

For each player to develop the skill of shadowing an opponent, crucial for effective one-on-one defending

REQUIREMENTS

Two to 10 workers in pairs, full netball court

METHOD

Workers pair up at one baseline and choose the attacker and the defender. Partners stand .9 metre apart facing each other.

1. The attacker carries out a series of netball movements that must be mirrored by the defender. These movements should include foot and arm movements and whole-body moves, such as dodging, jumping and touching the ground, as well as turning away from the imaginary mirror line between them. Movements should be restricted to a width of two steps.

2. After 30 seconds, partners swap roles.

3. Players repeat with the defender adopting the front stance, starting very close to the attacker but maintaining split-vision focus on the imaginary ball.

4. Players build up to dynamic shadowing, where the attacking worker attempts to make her way to the second transverse line with a series of straight runs, dodges and cuts. The defender faces the attacker about one metre away and attempts to delay her run by mirroring her direction and remaining in her direct path at all times, combining a balanced defensive ready stance with quick footwork.

5. Partners swap roles and repeat the drill.

If the attacker draws level to pass, the defender should turn inside with respect to the side the attacker is passing and continue shadowing from a front stance. If the attacker breaks away, the players should stop and reset.

CHAIR SLIDING

OBJECTIVE

To replicate moving around a body without touching or contacting and to improve agility in moving around a player safely

REQUIREMENTS

Approximately four players, five chairs without sharp edges (people can be substituted if no chairs are available)

METHOD

Set up the chairs randomly in the goal circle.

1. A player starts under the goalpost, runs to a random chair and slip-steps around it (without touching), body facing the goal arc at all times.
2. She returns to the goalpost and moves to a different chair to complete the same movement, returning to the post in between chairs.
3. The player continues the drill until all chairs have been negotiated, then tags the next worker.
4. Repeat sequence 10 times per player.

VARIATIONS

1. Start with two players in the goal circle, one at the goalpost and one at a chair, ready to move in the opposite direction. Both move through the drill using the same patterns as the original set, negotiating each other as well as the chairs.
2. Add a feeder at the top of the circle who occasionally feeds in a ball for the workers to chase down. Emphasis should be on communication and reaction to the ball. Workers return the ball to the feeder after gaining possession and start the drill again.

Defensive-Unit Drills

These drills require operating as part of a unit while performing individual defensive skills. The focus is often switched from a personal defensive effort to reorientation, recovery and second efforts to assist a team-mate. Communication and awareness of the defensive partner or unit should be emphasised.

TANDEM REFLEX BALLS

OBJECTIVE

To react quickly to the ball and combine the skill of coming off an opponent and working with a defensive partner to secure a loose ball

REQUIREMENTS

Two defenders (A and B) and two feeders (C and D), one ball, four markers (cones), a goal circle

METHOD

Randomly spread out the four markers in the goal circle, keeping the two-metre radius around the post clear. C and D set up as feeders on the arc, spaced well apart. A and B act as GD and GK in the goal circle (see figure 6.16).

1. A and B move randomly from marker to marker and from marker to post, using quick footwork and slick changes of direction. They alternate between stepping *to* the marker and going *around* it. Both workers should be well aware of each other's position so they do not clash or overload an area.

2. C and D pass the ball to each other as they move around the goal arc. A and B must reorientate to face the ball during their movement at all times.

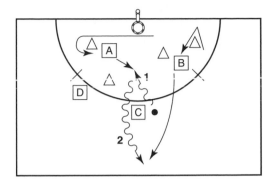

Figure 6.16 Tandem reflex balls.

3. At irregular intervals, C and D throw "loose balls" into the circle for A and B to pounce on, deciding who will go for the ball and who will back up.

4. When the ball is secured, the defender without possession (e.g., B) drives to a space out of the circle (same side as A) and into attack to receive an outlet pass from A.

5. B then returns the ball to C or D, and the drill repeats.

All players must obey the footwork and time-limit rules.

VARIATION

The defender who does not take possession of the loose ball (e.g., B) is picked up by the nearest feeder (e.g., C), who transforms into an opponent that B must break clear from to receive the pass. Meanwhile, D acts as WD to work with A for the next pass. If B cannot shake C within three seconds, the outlet pass diverts to D and the *next* pass goes to B on the drive down-court.

THREE CHANCES

OBJECTIVE

For each player to develop sound fundamentals in three of the four chances she has to create an opposition turnover every time her opponent attempts to play the ball. (The first chance is to shadow so well that the opponent is shut out of the action altogether as a target.)

REQUIREMENTS

Minimum of five players, one ball, five markers, one-third of a court

METHOD

Set two markers two metres apart on the baseline beside the goalpost. Set one marker (the dummy marker) directly in front of these two markers, about two metres out forward of the goal arc. Set the next marker (feeder's marker) at the transverse line directly forward of the dummy marker. The last marker (workers' marker) is set on the same side of the

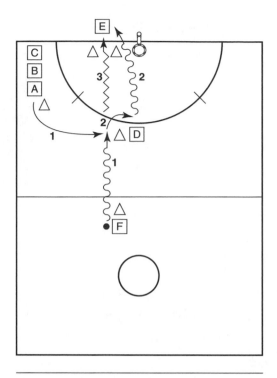

Figure 6.17 Three chances.

court, halfway between the sideline and goal arc, diagonally back from the dummy cone (see figure 6.17 for complete layout). One player acts as the feeder (F) and starts at the feeder's marker with the ball. One player acts as the dummy (D) and stands at the dummy marker. A, B and C move to the workers' marker. A receiver (E) positions herself between the back markers to provide a target for D. All players face the centre of the court except for the feeder, who faces the dummy.

1. On "go" from F, A accelerates towards D with the aim of intercepting a ball right in front of her (first chance). D does not jump but may catch the ball from her stationary position at the marker.

2. F passes a high pass just in front of D and places it such that the ball is just reachable for A at full stretch.

3. If A intercepts, she lands safely, passes back to the feeder and rejoins her queue. If A misses, she digs in, makes a quick recovery step as D pivots to face E down-court, and applies hands-over pressure over the ball (second chance).

4. D fakes the pass to E, and A completes a backwards slip-step delaying sequence to the markers at the baseline.

5. D returns the ball to the feeder, and the next worker takes off.

Rotate roles regularly. When steps 1 to 5 are proficient, D allows A to set up in the hands-over position, then throws to E and attempts to drive towards E as A blocks (third chance.)

FOUR-WAY INTERCEPTING

OBJECTIVE
For each player to improve her judgment and confidence in intercepting a ball from an opponent from the sides, behind and in front

REQUIREMENTS
Minimum of three players, one ball, four markers

METHOD

Set out markers in a diamond formation, with the feeder (B) slightly to her preferred side of the top marker as detailed in figure 6.18. The worker (A) starts behind the back marker facing the feeder. C, who acts as a dummy in the middle of the diamond area, can catch but not jump.

1. A accelerates towards C as B releases a high pass to C that A attempts to intercept. A must hollow out her body to cut close to C without touching her.

2. If successful, A takes the ball, lands safely, passes back to B and jogs to the next clockwise marker. If unsuccessful, A digs in, takes a recovery step, defends the pass from C back to B and then moves to the next marker.

3. A turns around the marker as B releases another high ball to C. A attempts to intercept from the side, taking the ball cleanly with two hands if possible. Step 2 is repeated.

4. A moves clockwise to all markers in turn and repeats the procedure.

Rotate roles after A has completed attempts from all markers.

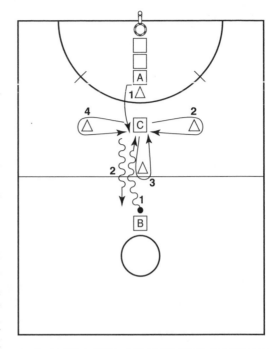

Figure 6.18 Four-way intercepting.

FOUR-SECOND DEFENCE

OBJECTIVE

For each player to successfully defend a mobile opponent one on one for more than three seconds to improve effectiveness in game situations

REQUIREMENTS

Groups of four players, one ball per group, four markers

METHOD

Set the markers in a seven-metre square formation. The defender (A) positions herself with an attacker (B) near the middle of the square. The feeders (C and D) set up outside the square in the middle of two opposite sides (see figure 6.19). A defends B using a front stance. They both face C, who starts with the ball.

1. On "go" from C, B completes a preliminary move and leads anywhere in the square. A must shadow and defend B for four seconds.

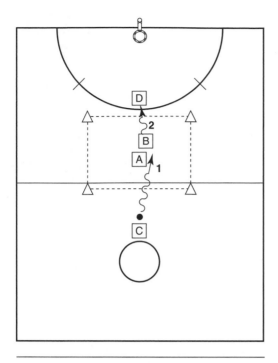

2. C passes to B as soon as she is open. If the pass does not reach B within four seconds, a point is scored for A. If the pass gets through, B passes to D.

3. A and B turn to face D, and the procedure repeats from the opposite direction.

4. A works for 10 passes in and records her score. Players rotate roles.

The dimensions of the square may need to be adjusted to the level of the performers to promote some success for the defender.

Figure 6.19   Four-second defence.

DEFENDERS' CONDITIONING

OBJECTIVE

For defenders to train their bodies for stamina using defence-specific movements

REQUIREMENTS

At least two players, two markers, a goal third of a court

METHOD

Set up the markers at the 45 marks, three metres out from the goal arc. Workers carry out a sequence of the following defensive movements in rapid succession, starting under the goalpost.

1. Sprint to the left 45 marker, then jump to intercept an imaginary ball.

2. Slip-step back two steps, and then run backwards to the post (looking over the shoulder).

3. Jump to touch the net three times, and drive upon landing with a fast transition to the right 45 marker. Complete 20 quick foot taps on the ground (run on the spot).

4. Turn and complete a V-cut back to the post; complete 20 more foot taps.

5. Slip-step two right, return, two left, return, two forwards, return and two backwards, return.

6. Sprint to the top of the arc, take a recovery step to hands-over position, hold for two seconds, and slip-step diagonally (two steps left back, two right back pattern) to the post.

Rest and recover while the second worker completes the routine. Repeat twice more.

Team Defensive Drills

All players regardless of position require team defensive work. For whole-team defence configurations to be successful, every player on the team needs to develop the skills necessary to contribute a range of defensive strategies. The following drill set contains one-on-one work in pairs within a unit, through to area and offline defence work as a team.

CIRCLE PAIRS

OBJECTIVE

For each player to hone the skills of working in tandem to pressure the attack. The drill aims to develop switching, calling, intercepting and recovering.

REQUIREMENTS

Seven to 10 players, one ball, one-third of a court

METHOD

Two players elected as defenders place themselves in the middle of a circle, with the remaining players completing a circle around them. Players forming the circle stand shoulder-pass distance away from each other. One of the players in the circle formation starts with the ball.

1. The player with the ball shoulder or bounce passes to another player in the circle, but not a player adjacent to her, as one defender applies pressure over the ball.
2. The defensive partner adopts the defensive ready stance and attempts to read the play and intercept the pass.
3. After the pass is received, the defensive pair quickly reposition to have the *nearest* defender over the ball and the other defender attempting to intercept.
4. The ball continues to swing around the circle for a 90-second period as the defensive players call and work in tandem, with one applying ball pressure and one attempting the interception.

The defensive pair scores one point for a deflection and three points for an interception. If the players in the circle make any other errors, two points are added to the defensive pair's score. After 90 seconds, two new players enter the circle and are replaced on the circumference by the original defensive pair. The aim is for a pair to score more points than the other pairs. Emphasis should be on communicating, reading the play and recovering.

GRIDS

OBJECTIVE

To improve the concept of defending an area and the players and balls entering it. The drill aims to develop the skills necessary for offline and zone defence.

REQUIREMENTS

Ten players minimum (up to 20), one ball per 2 attacking players, 21 markers (cones), bibs for all defenders. The number of grids depends on the number of players: 10 players need half a court (six grid sections); add two sections per extra 4 players.

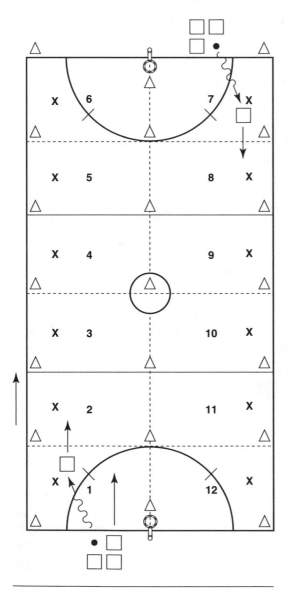

Figure 6.20 Grids.

METHOD

For 20 players: divide each third into quarters, as detailed in figure 6.20, placing markers at the corners of each section of the grid. Place one defender (all wearing bibs) in each section of the grid (1 to 12). The remaining players set up in pairs, with one ball per pair, split evenly at the baseline of grids 1 and 7.

1. The first worker of attacking-pair 1 sets up for a throw-in as the attacking partner sets up in grid 1. The attacking pair at the opposite end mirror this procedure in grid 7.

2. On "go" from the defenders in grids 1 and 7, the attacking pairs attempt to move through the grid using full netball rules, catching at least one pass in each grid.

3. Attacking pairs score a point for each successfully completed grid. If they lose possession or break a rule in a grid, they pick up the ball and move to the next grid, beginning with a throw-in start.

4. Players repeat steps 2 and 3 and try to beat their score the next time through.

5. Rotate everyone down the grid when attacking pairs have completed two circuits each.

6. The maximum score for each pair matches the number of sections in the grid.

The drill works best with an equal number of attackers and defenders so that there is always action close to each player. Emphasis should be on communication in adjacent sections as well as sound defensive fundamentals.

TWO-ON-TWO IN THE CIRCLE

OBJECTIVE

For circle defenders to enhance their one-on-one skills in the goal circle by simulating play and conditions as well as developing communication and cooperation skills

REQUIREMENTS

Six players, one ball, bibs of the same colour for the attackers, bibs of a different colour for the defenders, one-third of a court

METHOD

Divide the players into four attackers (GS, GA, WA and C) wearing bibs of one colour and two defenders (GD and GK) wearing bibs of another colour. The circle players all start in the goal circle, on their respective opponents, WA stands between the transverse line and goal arc. (see figure 6.21).

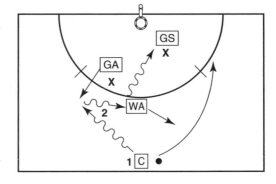

Figure 6.21 Two-on-two in the circle.

1. C tosses the ball to herself at the transverse line as WA and GA break for complementary leads.

2. C passes to one and drives forwards into a space to reoffer.

3. The recipient pivots and chooses from the next pair of complementary leads (GS and either C or the non-receiver of the first pass).

4. Play works its way into the goal circle, where the attackers aim to score a goal. The defenders utilize the four-chances theory of effecting a turnover on every play by their opponents (pressure defence of the lead, contesting the ball, pressuring the pass and delaying the reoffer).

5. Every four repetitions, defenders call a switch in general play or from the initiation of the drill.

6. After the goal is scored, the ball is returned to the wing attack, who restarts the drill (alternating with the centre). Players repeat, trying to beat the last score.

Attackers slow the play slightly, as there is no defence on the feeders, so that defenders can execute their four chances with precision. Tally the number of touches or attacking errors after 10 attempts. If the defenders get a touch, play is stopped and restarted, with a score to the defenders. If the ball is intercepted cleanly, the defenders read off and transition to attack, transporting the ball safely over the transverse line for an extra point (feeders cannot defend, only direct opponents). Full netball rules apply.

VARIATION

Add a WD and a defensive C to defend the feeders to add to the unit, increase pressure, and increase the flow to play at game speed.

CHAPTER 7

Smooth Transitions

An exciting interception deep in defence initiating a smooth transition to a full-court attack that fast breaks, flows and results in a goal is what teams train for. Slick changeovers from one mode to another and smooth, balanced court dynamics that accompany the transition are hallmarks of a well-drilled team. This chapter discusses transitions from defence to attack, when the team gets possession either unexpectedly in a live-ball situation or through a throw-in, missed opposition goal or penalty. Passing lanes, three-option strategies and court spacing are concepts discussed in the transition plays from defence to attack, as well as considerations for playing through zones or floating defences in contrast to one-on-one style. The chapter also considers the reverse situation, transitioning from attack to defence, where the team loses possession, unexpectedly or otherwise, and details best-percentage practices to apply maximum pressure to regain possession.

Attacking Out of Defence

When a team gains possession of the ball deep in defence, a full-court attack swings into action. The defenders and centre must transport the ball quickly and safely out of the danger zone and deliver it to the frontcourt. Court spacing should be in check before or immediately after possession has been won and the principles of attack (as discussed in chapter 5) applied to ensure a smooth transition from defence to attack. Defenders should look for the opportunity to run a fast break if possession was unexpected and opposition players are out of position. The player with possession should immediately scan for a free player in the vicinity to quickly pass to, while team-mates should drive forwards, maintaining their court spacing to power the ball forwards into attack. If possession was predictable and no opposition players were caught out, then the team should proceed with the regular ideals of looking down-court first, providing three options and maintaining mobility.

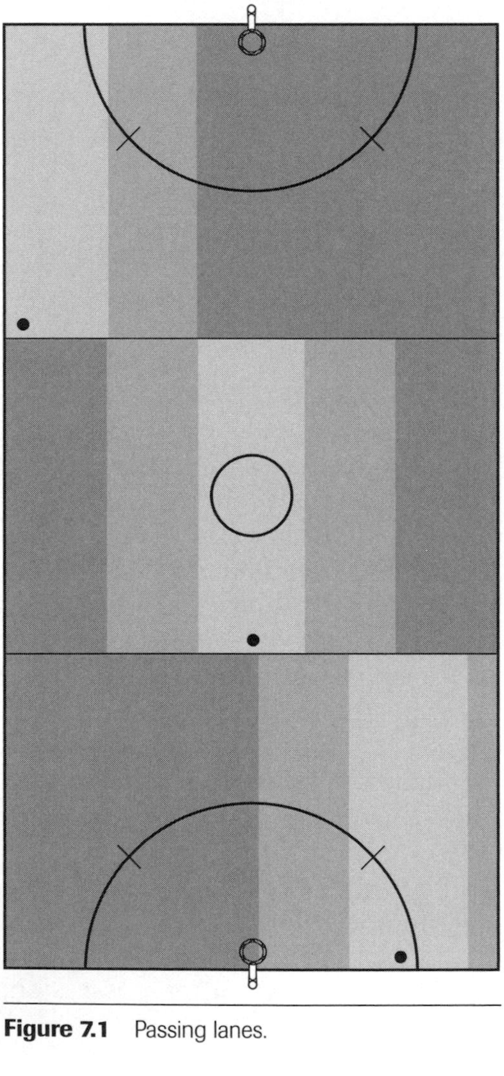

When attacking out of defence, a team should be aware of crossing passing lanes or corridors (see figure 7.1). For example, a goal keeper who intercepts deep in the left corner of the court should scan for a target in the left or middle corridor. A pass that crosses to the far side of the court carries a high risk of attention from the opposition because of the breadth of angle and air time for the ball. Of course, at times the cross-court pass is the best option out of defence, such as when a driving team-mate is completely unattended, with no encroaching opponents in front of her. These situations are rare, and most of the time, the safest and quickest option is the same-side or middle corridor target to get the ball moving.

Figure 7.1   Passing lanes.

Some teams utilise a short–long pattern of play out of defence from a back-line throw-in, where the first pass out is short, and team-mates position for the second pass to go long. This is usually a lob to cover some distance and get the ball clear of the opposition goal area. Teams that adopt this procedure often reverse it as well to complete a balanced initiation of attack. If the first ball out of defence is long, possible receivers for the subsequent pass will cut forwards to the ball to balance the move. Although these plans can work well, close-marking opponents often alter pre-set strategies, and the principle of improvisation overrules. A team must above all keep possession. It is not realistic to plan exactly where a ball is to be caught and by whom in such a fast-moving, high-tempo game. Having a basic plan, however, provides structure and balance.

Attacking through anything other than one-on-one defence can present quite a challenge to a team. In attack, the team may be faced with flooding, offline defence, sagging, defensive-third zones or split-circle zones (see chapter 6 for details). Playing against these defence configurations requires a very different approach to the fast-running attack possible against one on one. In fact, the more dependent a team is on a fast flow-on style of attack, the better a zone or floating defence is likely to work against the team. Playing through defences other than one on one is not difficult if a team is prepared, is flexible and has well-rehearsed strategies.

- **Attacking through flooding.** Attacking through flooding can cause a loss of rhythm if the team is caught unawares. The aim of flooding is to close down space by crowding opposition attack ends. This can help defenders by slowing the pace of the attack, driving opponents to the flanks and making scoring more difficult. Three ways to play effectively through the congestion that opposition flooding creates are to take advantage of unguarded players, move through the flood and match up on a defender to create space individually, and work in pairs to set screens on opponents for team-mates. One of the biggest mistakes an attacking unit can make is to stand in the spaces created by the flooding configuration, effectively rendering themselves unusable because then every space is occupied. Attackers need to move with purpose and authority through the flood and defend a defender to claim and protect space for themselves. They may need additional vocal communication with the passer, as the cues are not as obvious in such a congested area. The passer should try to pick the leads ball-side rather than cross-court to reduce the chance of interception in a flood.

- **Attacking through offline defence.** In offline defence, the defender takes a few steps away from the attacker to give the illusion of space and freedom. If a defensive unit plays this version well, it can upset the timing and judgment of an attacking unit. The defence can guide the opponents in the direction of a team-mate for an interception by purposely creating trap spaces for them to move into, so it is essential that players look around them and use fake passes to attack their way through. An offline defence often contains holes, so attackers should take advantage by drilling any long target that becomes available (the passer should continue to look down-court first). As with any alternative to one-on-one defence, attackers can match up to destroy the defenders' configuration of playing in the spaces. Getting close to a defender to get open as a target takes on heightened importance against offline defence to reinstate the thrower's spatial cues. Fake passes can be potent in throwing through offline; a slight step on the fake by an opponent exposes an attacker as an easy primary target. All players should keep eyes up and maintain mobility.

> *"Transitions are imperative to the success of the team. A smooth transition is delight-ful to witness when it flows down-court and results in a goal."*
>
> ~ Margaret Angove OAM, Greatest Win–Loss Record as a Coach in the
> Australian National Netball League

- **Attacking through sagging defence.** In a sagging defence, the opponent of an attacker forfeits the chance to defend the pass to defend the next lead, taking out the primary target. This creates a sometimes unexpected mobile double defence on the nearest primary target. The defenders behind the sagging defender position themselves such that the next pass has to be made cross-court, enhancing the chances of a deflection because the passing angle is shut down. By thinking proactively, the attacking unit can take advantage, and one advantage is that the passer has an unobstructed view of play. Another is that if an attacker is occupying two defenders, the unguarded passer is a prime candidate for the double play if she passes away from the double defence and opens up space for herself to receive the next ball down-court. The thrower should fake to the double-defended target, then take off for the double play, using a short, ball-side option.

- **Attacking through zones.** If the opposition is playing a zone, the attacking team should be clear of the first plan for playing through it. A team's options for blitzing a zone include matching up on positional opponents and forcing them to revert to one on one; penetrating the front of the area and throwing the ball over it; or attacking the weak spots (the joins, or seams) and playing through the zone. As soon as a zone is identified, the attacking team must communicate with team-mates. Some zones are very unobtrusive and hard to spot. The team with possession should start the attack quickly so the defence has limited time to set the zone properly, and the attackers should be clear on a united strategy (pre-determined before the game).

Attacking through well-executed zones and floating-style defence takes a little planning and practice at training. The notion of taking advantage and being proactive rather than reactive helps in attacking through any alternative defence configuration. A team needs to be patient while configuring the attack and be prepared for a few lateral passes until the whole team is set. Once a primary strategy is chosen, a team can confidently attack through by being patient, keeping possession and moving with purpose.

Defending out of Attack

When the attacking team loses possession deep in attack, the players need a default plan for full-court defence. The easiest plan is to play one-on-one or split-circle defence (see chapter 6 for details) if the opposition intercepts the ball in a live-play situation, and turnaround from attack to defence mode must be instant. If the turnover is in the form of a missed goal or overthrown ball and a back-line throw-in is awarded to the opposition, the team has time to set up any defensive system. Full-court defensive options off a deep defensive-third throw-in include one-on-one, flooding, offline, sagging, centre-court zone or systems defence (see chapter 6). Half-court options can include a combination defence of any of the full-court methods (e.g., one on one to halfway followed by sagging in the back half). The primary team defence should be decided before the game, with the team reverting to alternatives if the opposition starts to get on top.

- **Goalers' role.** The goalers dictate how smoothly the ball is delivered to mid-court. They are the first line of defence, and their role needs to be identified and specified so they can patrol their territory with success. The goalers, wing attack and centre should have a plan for the back-line throw-in and a specific objective, otherwise defending becomes generalised and ineffective. Their objectives are to either win back possession before the ball crosses the transverse line or apply so much pressure to the leads and passes that an error is made in the centre third. The first line of defence has several options. The simplest is one-on-one hands-over defence on every pass. Done properly, this puts every opposition move under pressure. Double defence on the opposition goal defence or wing defence directs play through the single marked defender or centre, and team-mates take advantage of increased pressure on the two possible receivers by directing them to wide angles on the non-ball side. Another option is to allow the first (inbound) pass but attack the second one. The goalers come off the opposition goal defence, let the opposition receive an easy inbound pass, then double defend the throw while their team-mates direct their opponents to the wide angles. A change-up of pace for the back-line throw-in is a centre-court block (zone), where the five players allowed in the centre third retreat to their set-up position (see chapter 6). The goal shooter either heads the teeth of the zone to cover the join between the goal attack's and wing attack's areas or chases down balls in the goal third to apply hands-over pressure on incoming passes to the centre third.

- **Engine-room role.** The engine room, consisting of the wing attack, centre and wing defence, is the second line of defence and must be ready to pounce on inaccurate opposition passes as a result of defensive pressure applied by the first line. These players must work in unison with the goalers and read the play off an opponent's back-line throw-in, positioning themselves to enhance the chances of intercepting or deflecting. Their objectives are to intercept and slow the play with pressure shadowing and hands-over defence so the ball is not delivered smoothly or directly to the goal third. In a zone, the engine-room players must quickly rush back into place to allow maximum set-up time and react to calls from their team-mates behind them.

- **Circle defenders' role.** The goal defence and goal keeper are the last line of defence—the last chance to prevent the opposition from scoring. Their objectives are to read the play up-court, position themselves to benefit from their team-mates' pressure, intercept, pounce on any stray balls, apply maximum body and hands-over pressure, defend shots at goal and rebound. They should also attempt to prey on any perceived opposition weaknesses and take away their opponents' strengths with clever positioning and persistence. An important aspect of their role is supporting each other by calling, backing up and working as a team within the team. The defending pair also carries the load of calling and communicating the systems, switches or methods of defence the team will run throughout the game.

A special assignment a circle defender might have is to tag a player. Usually a tag is applied to a goaler dominating play and scoring the majority of goals, but any player can be tagged. Tagging is a very self-sacrificing and thankless task, as the defender focusses all her energies on her opponent by shadowing the player with a facing or closed stance (see chapter 6, Defensive Stance Positions), giving up her chance to intercept or even sight the ball. This may be effective in shutting down one player, but the rest of the defending unit must be prepared for their opponents and step up their workload accordingly.

Performance Points for Smooth Transitions

- React instantly to take advantage of turnovers in possession.
- When team possession is gained, balance up the court, get the ball moving and use the three-option strategy.
- When team possession is lost, pick up personal opponents quickly and aim to regain possession as soon as possible. Do not waste first-line defensive opportunities by lamenting errors.
- Practise team drills that link all units, and highlight connections between court areas.

Transition Drills

The following drills work the connecting skills needed to smoothly link defence to full-court attack and attack to full-court defence. They also highlight the mini-transitions across goal circles and transverse lines. With the focus on whole-team play, the quality of individual skills executed by each player within the drill must be emphasised, and coaches need to keep reinforcing these skills.

ATTACKING OUT OF DEFENCE

OBJECTIVE

For defenders to replicate driving the ball out of defence past blockers and to hit the correct moving target down-court. The drill develops use of the double play, fluent movement through blocks, quick judgments and maintenance of a direct focus in attack.

REQUIREMENTS

Seven to 12 players, two balls, one set of bibs, full court

METHOD

The workers (A, B and C) form a queue behind the baseline, between the goal arc and sideline. Two blockers (D and E) set up on court in front of the workers' queue, two and five metres back, respectively, behind one another. A feeder (F) positions herself on the first transverse line on the opposite side of the workers and blockers, with one ball in hand and another resting nearby on the ground. Two same-team attackers (G and H) position themselves at the middle of the far transverse line, one behind the other. The shooter (I) starts in the middle of the goal circle (see figure 7.2 for complete layout).

1. On "go" from F, A drives forwards, negotiating D and then E cleanly. D and E apply delaying pressure at half strength initially, increasing the pressure on subsequent turns.

2. As A clears the second block, F releases a lob just forward of the centre circle for A as G completes a preliminary move and breaks clearly to one side.

3. H reads off G and offers a complementary lead to the other side. A chooses one lead, passes and returns to the back of the workers' queue.

4. If H receives, G digs in and drives to the pocket on the ball side to connect with a lob from H. I stays in the

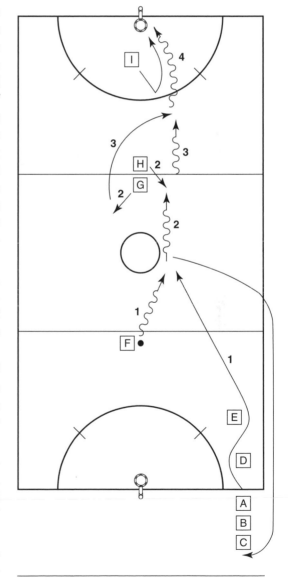

Figure 7.2 Attacking out of defence.

circle, making several preliminary moves and reading off G and H to time a finishing move to collect on the way to the post from G. (If G receives from A, H's and G's roles are reversed.)

5. I completes the drill with a shot for goal.

6. When the ball enters the goal circle, B begins the drill at the other end as F throws in the next ball. I returns the first ball to F after F has released the pass to B.

Players rotate roles regularly.

VARIATION

Add a defender with a bib to cover G's and H's read-off leads to challenge A's and B's decision-making ability. A or B should choose the unopposed option. Add a goal keeper to defend I in the goal circle. Netball footwork and ball-handling rules apply.

TRAFFIC JAM

OBJECTIVE

For each player to improve her ability to execute smooth plays in "heavy traffic", or crowded situations. The drill also hones players' ability to "look over the mess" and scan for a long target.

REQUIREMENTS

Twelve players, one ball, two sets of bibs, full court

METHOD

Seven players set up as a team with bibs, in position for a back-line throw-in taken by GK. Four opposing players set up in the team of seven's defensive third, picking up an opponent or floating, creating heavy traffic.

1. On "go" from GK, GD, WD and C lead to create a target for the goal keeper.

2. GK passes to the best target to open within three seconds.

3. All players break again to provide options for the receiver until a target is chosen. (The team must have two passes in the defensive third.)

4. The ball is then cleared to the centre third, where the team plays out until a goal is scored, obeying all netball rules.

5. Repeat for four more throw-ins, then move the traffic (four defenders) to the centre third. Begin the drill again with GK at the baseline. The team must make two passes in the congested centre third.

6. After five down-court plays, move the traffic to the goal third for the team to get two passes through before the shot.

Rotate the group of four defenders into the team of seven. Increase the traffic to five players to further challenge the attacking team to increase difficulty.

FIVE-PERSON FAST DRIVE

OBJECTIVE

For defenders to improve the movement patterns of contesting, reorientating and using a direct focus when driving the ball out of defence to choose the best option on the run

REQUIREMENTS

Minimum of seven players, two balls (if there are fewer players, the coach can act as a feeder)

METHOD

Two workers (A and B) set up on either side of the goal arc at the defensive baseline. Other workers queue evenly behind A and B. The feeder (C) positions herself at the defensive transverse line near a sideline with the ball; the second ball is nearby on the ground. Two attackers (D and E) set up near the attacking transverse line for the split read-off lead, and a goal shooter (F) and goal keeper (G) set up one on one in the goal circle (see figure 7.3).

1. C releases a loose ball to the top of the circle. A and B compete for the ball. If A gets it, she passes back to C and drives down-court for a double play as B becomes the defender and tries to shadow and pressure A. (If B is the recipient of the first loose ball, A and B swap roles.)

2. As A receives down-court, D and E split for a read-off lead. A passes to either D or E and returns to her original position. (If A chooses E, D digs in and drives to the ball side for a pass to the 45 mark. D balances, turns and delivers to F on a precisely timed hold.)

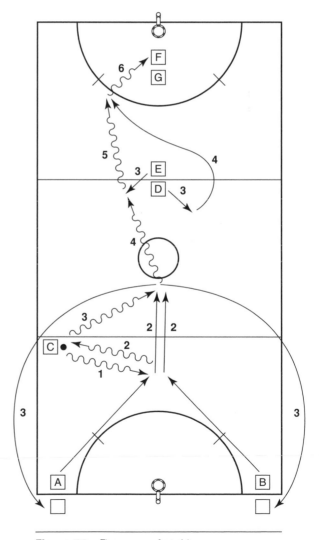

Figure 7.3 Five-person fast drive.

3. F shoots and contests any rebound with G. (G pressures the lead, contests the pass and defends the shot.) C picks up the second ball to restart the drill with the next wave of workers as the shot goes up.

4. F returns the first ball to C after C has passed to the next driver.

Players rotate roles regularly.

THREE-AND-THREE DOWN-COURT

OBJECTIVE

For defenders to sharpen their skills in reaction to a loose ball and work as a unit, using the short–long strategy to deliver the ball to the goal third

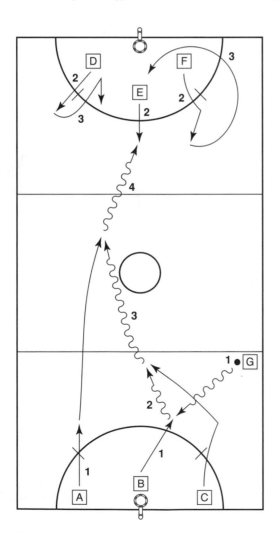

Figure 7.4 Three-and-three down-court.

REQUIREMENTS

Minimum of six players plus a static feeder, one ball, full court

METHOD

The three defenders (A, B and C) position themselves at the baseline, evenly spread across the goal arc origins. The three shooters (D, E and F) start in the goal circle at the other end. A feeder (G) sets up at the nearest transverse line to the defenders, on the sideline with the ball (see figure 7.4).

1. A, B and C begin fast foot taps on the spot until G throws a random ball into the goal third. A, B and C take off and call the nearest player to gather the ball.

2. The nearest player retrieves, and the remaining two provide one short lead and one long lead on opposite sides of the ball.

3. The pass goes quickly to the short option, who then unleashes a long lob to the opposite side as D, E and F begin preliminary moves in the goal circle.

4. As the final catch from the defenders is made, D, E and F break forwards for the ball, maintaining court spacing and staggering.

5. The defender chooses and passes to a target, and the remaining two break in complementary leads to the post. (The first two shooters to enter the circle become GA and GS; the receiver from the defender becomes WA.)

6. Play out until a goal is scored, using at least one catch each. Repeat from the start.

VARIATION

Add one, then two, then three opponents to defend the shooters. Add or swap the opponent defenders to A, B and C to cover the short–long play. Also change the short–long to long–short to test the range and timing.

SECONDARY OPTION

OBJECTIVE

For each player to consider the secondary, or back-up, options if the primary target is unavailable while bringing the ball out of defence. The drill promotes the critical skill of improvisation and ball mobility using variations of pathways.

REQUIREMENTS

Seven players, one ball, one set of bibs, full court

METHOD

The seven players set up as a team positioning for a defensive rebound.

1. One defender throws the ball at the goal ring so that it rebounds back into play to be snapped in by a circle defender.

2. The defensive unit spontaneously sets up a down-court attack, considering court spacing and the three-option strategy, while scanning down-court first for direct options.

3. The coach stands on the sideline and calls, "Second option," at regular intervals so that the player with the ball has to fake to the preferred target and select the best second option, or the back-up lead.

Players must be prepared to reset their timing and to balance up the court to maintain momentum. Play out until a goal is scored.

VARIATIONS

1. Add three opposition defenders to the defensive third to congest the area deep in defence. Add three defenders to the centre third to float and sag to increase perceptual demands in mid-court. Build up to seven on five, six and then seven on seven.

2. Randomise the start by having the coach throw in a loose ball in the defensive third so play transitions spontaneously.

CHAPTER 8

Set Plays and Strategies

In netball, there is rarely time in live-ball situations to create exact attacking conditions that best suit a team. Play happens too fast, and those who hesitate will be lost. Non-live-play situations, or dead-ball time, occur at designated game breaks (quarter, half, three quarter and injury time), after a goal before a centre pass, before a throw-in or when the umpire blows the whistle to award a penalty or free pass. This time presents an excellent opportunity for teams to set the play and place players exactly where they would like, exploiting strengths and rebalancing court space. All teams should have a few basic strategies in place to take advantage of set-up time in a game, setting conditions to maximise success. Set plays replicate familiar movement patterns and minimise the chance of error from misreading a team-mate's move. They can override existing systems (e.g., goalers' leads) or link in with them. Each team needs to consider the individuals in the line-up and tailor a blueprint for success, stamping the team's uniqueness and character on the game. This chapter examines possible strategies and provides many examples of team plays that can be run from dead-ball situations, including centre-pass set-ups; throw-ins; penalties; and free-pass tactical plays in the defensive, centre and goal thirds. The final section discusses defending against set plays.

Centre Passes

Because centre passes are taken alternately throughout the match, both teams are given an equal number of chances to start with possession and launch the ball into attack. A team that can consistently move the ball forwards smoothly at a centre pass gives its goalers the best possible chance to set up to score. The centre pass has four possible recipients who set the play and work as a receiving unit to get the team's attack underway. Many centre passes can be taken through holes in the opposition defence. To rely on this method for every centre pass, however, can lead to critical errors in pressure situations if no immediate gaps are evident. Employing a few proactive strategies adds structure and variety as well as increases the concentration and motivation levels of the team.

Strategies give structure, direction and the satisfaction of working together as a team to create success. Too many strategies in one game, however, can cause confusion and deflect concentration from the core objectives of the game—to obtain possession and score. Some plays need signals from the centre, and others can be set spontaneously between the goal attack and wing attack. It is up to the coach and style of players as to which strategies will be employed and how they will link in with possible goalers' systems. Several basic strategies are available for the centre pass. With all centre-pass strategies, the objective is for the ball to be received in the frontcourt. If the wing defence or goal defence is to receive, the player should time a fast-driving lead to enable her to catch the ball forward of the centre circle, otherwise ground is immediately lost. In subsequent sections of this chapter, the positions are designated by the abbreviations that appear on the bibs.

- **Split read-off strategy.** The primary target is WA, so the entire space at the transverse line is allocated to WA to lead either side. GA positions herself two metres behind WA and times a lead in the opposite direction to WA as the second option (see figure 8.1; note that in figures 8.1 through 8.7 and figure 8.12, the solid arrow line represents the primary lead, and the dashed arrow line represents the secondary, back-up, lead). GD and WD move forwards and hold their leads behind the centre circle until needed for back-up, in which case they accelerate forwards into the frontcourt on their respective sides. If WA and GA are both unavailable, they must clear out to allow room for the back-up options to enter the frontcourt. WA and GA then quickly reposition themselves to offer the next wave of leads according to the team plan.

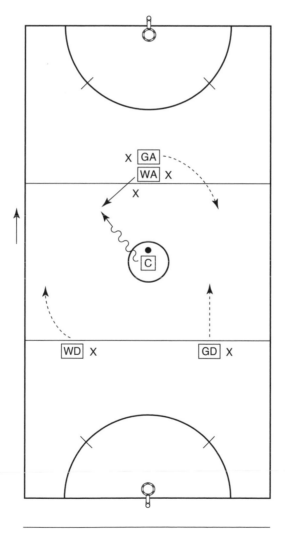

Figure 8.1 Split read-off strategy.

• **GA and WA screen strategy.** WA and GA set up very close to each another, one metre behind the middle of the transverse line. The player in the best position to screen protects the space for the other attacker to drive over the line to receive (see figure 8.2). The screening and driving roles will be determined by the positioning of the opposition defenders. A modification of this manoeuvre is to nominate the player who will screen, and she sets the screen on her attacking partner's opponent. This version gives the move more direction when learning it and assists with timing and spacing. If the screen is not successful and the driving player does not present as a clear target, the second option is the screener, who moves forwards over the line. GD and WD position themselves in the backcourt as third options.

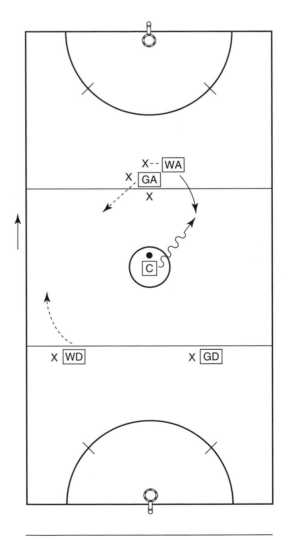

Figure 8.2 GA and WA screen strategy.

• **GA fade strategy.** WA is the primary target and has the complete run of the line as GA retreats four metres back from the line (see figure 8.3). GA is not in the receiving plan for this play but should disguise her role by feigning interest to lead, retaining attention from her positional opponent. If the opposition GD loses interest in GA, WA may become triple defended. The second option is the backcourt player positioned on the opposite side to which WA has led. It will be GD or WD depending on which side WA ends up. This play is a good one to choose when the opposition centre elects to defend the pass of her opponent at the centre pass rather than double defend the lead of the WA. This gives WA the total forward space and only one player to beat.

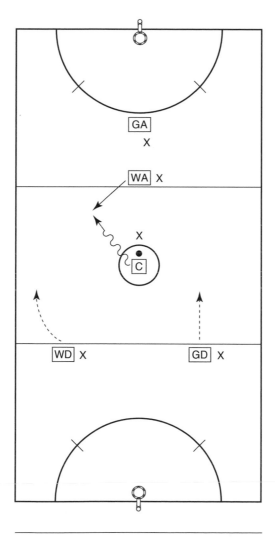

Figure 8.3 GA fade strategy.

• **Double-clear strategy.** WA and GA start up at the transverse line on their respective sides, accelerate forwards, then transform their leads to a clearing move towards their respective sidelines, opening up the centre corridor (see figure 8.4). GD and WD try to position themselves to the inside of their opponents at the defensive line and drive forwards into an open frontcourt created by WA and GA. GD and WD present as dual primary targets for this play. C has two options and chooses the best one. The next pass should connect with GS on a forward drive through the goal arc, as GD and WD are running full pace in the direction of the goal, and WA and GA are on clearing leads at the sides of the court.

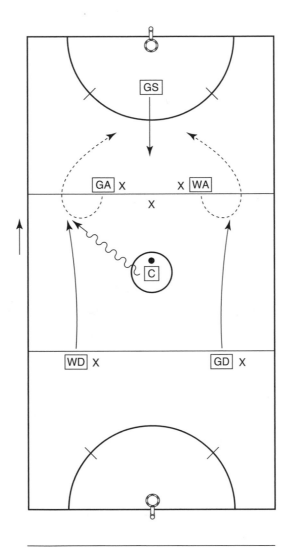

Figure 8.4 Double-clear strategy.

• **Forward-to-forward strategy.** GA is the primary target and is allocated the prime central transverse line space. WA must still feign interest in offering a lead to occupy the opposition WD and ideally the opposition C. WA starts wide to maximise space for GA's primary lead. GA leads forwards over the line for the ball, needing to beat only her direct opponent (see figure 8.5). Upon reception, GA turns rapidly to release a quick ball to WA on the drive to the goal circle. GS should try to position herself against the opposition GK on the side of the drive to protect the space and prevent an interception over the unsighted WA.

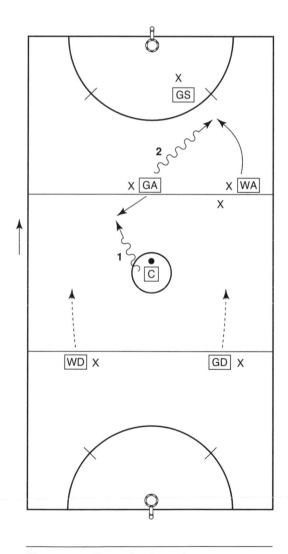

Figure 8.5 Forward-to-forward strategy.

- **Corners strategy.** All four possible recipients set up in the corners of the centre third (see figure 8.6). This formation opens up maximum space for all leads and splits the defence right open to create big gaps. GA and WA drive towards the thrower, and GD and WD head down the sidelines, ready to cut in if needed. C chooses the best of the four options that open up in the frontcourt.

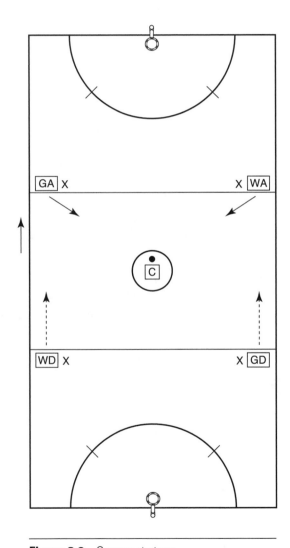

Figure 8.6 Corners strategy.

- **Overload strategy.** Overloading players, or clustering them all on one side, opens up a huge space for a team-mate to lead into. WA and GA overload by positioning themselves in the same corner of the goal third, immediately behind the transverse line (see figure 8.7). They simultaneously break forwards at the umpire's whistle but remain on their side. By overloading one side, the backcourt player on the opposite side has the full vertical split of the centre third to receive the ball and becomes the primary target. If the backcourt driver is unavailable, WA and GA have created a frontcourt space to move into, and one should step up as the second option. GS should be ready for the next pass if the backcourt player receives at full stretch.

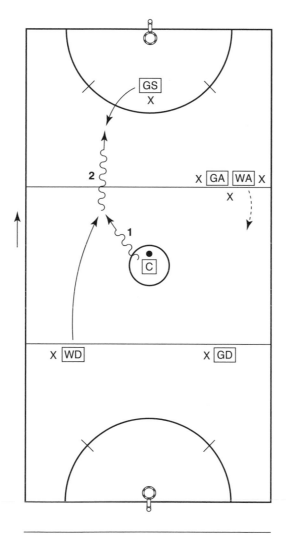

Figure 8.7 Overload strategy.

Defensive-Third Throw-Ins

An opposition turnover in which the ball is judged out of bounds in the goal third results in a defensive-third throw-in for the team. In such a situation, a full-court attack can be run, linking play through all areas of the court. It is essential that the team get the attack off to a good start by clearing the ball swiftly and safely out of deep defence. There is always time to set the play at a defensive-third throw-in, as the goal keeper retrieving the ball can control the speed of the throw-in set-up, providing she is not obviously slow and deemed to be delaying the play. Gaps in the opposition's configuration in a full-court defence set-up will often dictate where the initial pass goes, and a quick start to the play is possible. If the opposition has set a solid defence, the team should set up conditions in a more organised fashion. Teams setting up for a back-third throw-in need to keep in mind court spacing, principles of attack, the three-option strategy and avoiding crossing passing corridors. Following are several strategies for defensive-third throw-ins. Teams should keep them simple at first, then add variations.

Most plays can be adjusted if the throw-in is from the sideline (rather than the baseline) in the defensive third. Strategies operate exactly as for baseline throw-ins, with a slight modification of angles and a shuffling deeper of attacking-unit players. As the throw-in position nears the transverse line, WD or GD can act as the thrower, reducing crowding and reassigning GK to a lateral back-up role.

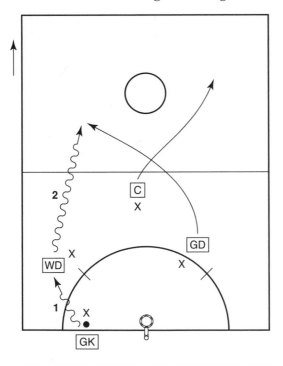

- **Short–long strategy.** When GK throws in from WD's side (right as facing the thrower), a sensible option is to play short–long. WD uses the goal circle to advantage to position herself as the primary target to offer a direct short lead. GK should hit this lead with a crisp shoulder pass as GD breaks long for the connecting clearing pass out of defence (see figure 8.8). C needs to read GD's move and clear to the side GD is vacating to balance up the court and offer the next lead. If WD is double defended well by the opposition for the throw-in, she should attempt to keep both defenders busy and draw them low and wide to clear space for the second and third options.

Figure 8.8 Short–long strategy.

- **Long–short strategy.** Assume GK takes the throw for all baseline throw-ins. For baseline throw-ins on GD's side of the court (left as facing the thrower), GD positions herself as the primary target to set for a drop-back lead to be met with a lob pass (see figure 8.9). GD should be positioned behind the opposition GA, with plenty of room behind in which to lead. WD is the second option and should be positioned well away from GD to maximise leading space and use the goal arc to hold the opposition WA on the side for a safe crossover pass if needed. WD's role is especially important if GD is double defended. C should be high and middle, on the transverse line for the third option. The pattern of play is long–short. As GD drops to receive the lob from GK, WD cuts in towards the thrower while moving down-court to offer a short lead in the centre corridor.

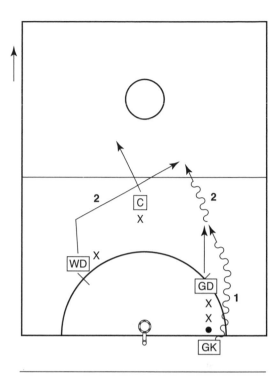

Figure 8.9   Long–short strategy.

- **Centre-drive strategy.** GD and WD position themselves on their respective sides, with C slightly forward of the transverse line in the middle corridor (see figure 8.10). C cuts hard in front of her opponent and connects with a long, straight pass from GK. GD and WD peel off to their respective sides and drive down-court to offer staggered leads in the two adjacent corridors. This play works well for teams with a tall centre who likes to play the middle.

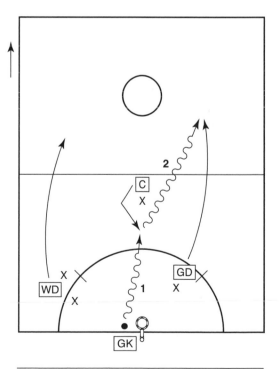

Figure 8.10   Centre-drive strategy.

- **Cut-across strategy.** GK takes the throw-in on GD's side as GD sets up for a short- to mid-range pass from the thrower and masks as the primary target. Ideally GD attracts the opposition GS in a double-defence situation. GD makes a short dummy lead, remaining close to the thrower as WD cuts across high on the same side into the open space behind to receive the pass (see figure 8.11). C starts high and central and offers a second option on the side WD has vacated, cutting back into the action for the next pass. If the throw-in is on WD's side, GD and WD reverse roles. Another version of this play entails GD's setting a screen behind the opposition GA instead of offering a dummy lead to ensure GA does not drop into WD's lead to contest the ball.

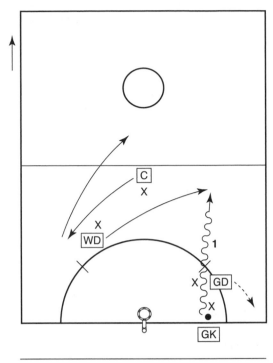

Figure 8.11 Cut-across strategy.

- **Middle-screen strategy.** This play works if the opposition GS is defending GK's throw from a reasonably central position. If the opposition GS is anywhere but over the ball, switch to another play. GD and WD set up very close together in the central corridor for a mid-range pass. One player sets a screen for the other, who drives into the protected space to the side to receive the pass (see figure 8.12). The screener can be pre-determined or called on the spot according to the opposition's defen-

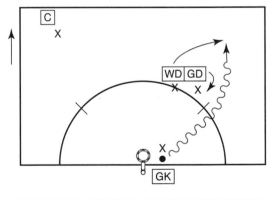

Figure 8.12 Middle-screen strategy.

sive arrangement. After the driver takes off for the ball, the screener drives down in the adjacent corridor to offer the next lead. C must position herself high and to one side of the action to maximise space for the screen. C is the second option should the screen be ineffective.

Centre-Third Throw-Ins

Throwing in from the centre third presents a different set of conditions for the attacking team. Choices regarding who will take the throw are more open than in the defensive third, where apart from very close to the transverse line, GK should take the throw because she has limited space in which to lead. In the centre third, a team can format throw-in set-ups according to four basic factors: (1) who has the best pass or vision, (2) whose side the ball is on, (3) who is closest to the play and (4) whether the team is keeping the frontcourt free for the attacking unit. The coach and team members should experiment with the different methods and decide which priorities suit their style of play and maximise their strengths. Strategies for centre-third throw-ins should be simple and effective. The following strategies detail the short-lob, clear-out and link-in strategies.

- **Short-lob strategy.** For throw-ins awarded in the back half of the centre third, GD or WD takes the throw according to the team's decided format. For throw-ins deep in the back half, GD and WD use a short lob between them. The player not taking the throw sets up behind her opponent in the same passing lane to receive a lob down the line. Other players in the vicinity protect the space for the inbound pass by clearing or holding their players to the non-ball side. C balances up the court on the opposite side, and WA and a goaler position themselves for the next leads down-court according to their systems.

- **Frontcourt clear-out strategy.** If a team's priority is to clear the front half of the court for the attackers, this play ties in nicely with the concept. For throw-ins awarded level with or forward of the centre circle, C takes the throw. WA and the goaler on the lead position themselves to cut hard into the ample free spaces available to them, with GD or WD positioned behind the centre circle for a back-up lead.

- **Frontcourt link-in strategy.** If a team prefers to have more depth in its frontcourt, this play should be favoured over the frontcourt clear-out. As the ball is starting in the frontcourt, players arrange themselves in perfect position for goalers' systems (see chapter 5) to operate and move the ball directly down-court deep into attack. WD or GD takes the throw. The non-thrower of these two retreats to the backcourt to clear space for the attacking unit. C sets up wide in the far lane to read off the goalers' system lead and drives opposite side to WA. WA offers the first lead, to which the goaler on the system lead makes a complementary lead. The thrower chooses the deepest open target, who receives and looks to the post for the goaler in the circle. If she is not open, then the driving feeder should present for a quick release to the goal circle's edge.

Goal-Third Throw-Ins

Goal-third throw-ins from outside the circle need to be carefully designed to ensure that the ball reaches its destination smoothly. The advantage of pre-setting the team in ideal position is offset somewhat by the opposition defenders' starting with full coverage on the attacking unit, aided by restricted space. As the throw-in location moves towards the goal line, angles are narrower and space is more cramped. This section details link-in plays for open areas, as well as restricted-space plays such as the second-pass screen and the baseline squeeze.

- **High-third link-in strategy.** For throw-ins closer to the transverse line than to the baseline, goalers' systems can be run straight off the pass. C or WA takes the throw according to the team's format, and the non-thrower positions herself well off the circle in the adjacent or far corridor, leaving room for the goaler on the lead. The primary target is the goaler on the lead; the secondary target is the on-court feeder. If the opposition defenders are sagging, the primary target should take two defenders wide to open space for the secondary option or a back-up player (WD or GD).

> *"Set plays can be a way of challenging players to think about the team's strengths to create 'power plays'—something quite special that they may only use once every few games, but that really expands or enhances their normal game."*
>
> ~ Ruth Aitken, Silver Ferns' Coach, World Champion, Commonwealth Games Gold Medallist

- **Mid-third link-in strategy.** Mid-third throw-ins as well as any taken closer to the baseline change from a preferred-receiver situation to hitting the first available option because of the lack of space and the increased difficulty of leading. The primary movement patterns should still be strong, but back-up leads will be used more often. When the throw-in is around the middle of the goal third, it is still a wise option to hit the goaler on the lead to create a possible one-on-one situation in the goal circle in close-range play. This situation often results in a scoring opportunity with the next pass, on a goaler-to-goaler connection or feeder-to-goaler connection, with the lead goaler out of the circle. WA or C takes the throw, the non-thrower positions herself off the circle in the middle or far passing corridor, and the goaler on the lead is the primary target driving out of the circle. To take advantage of the tight angle, the opposition will often use a defender to sag back on the goal circle to pick up outgoing leads from the goalers. The lead goaler should still offer her lead and try to beat the sagging opponent or at least drag two opposition defenders out of the action to open up prime space. WD or GD provides back-up.

- **Second-pass screen strategy.** For the tricky sideline throw-ins taken close to the baseline, this play works well. WA or C takes the throw, and the two goalers position themselves mid-circle, a metre apart. The goalers must keep both circle defenders interested and be prepared to call for the direct ball if they become open. The primary target is the on-court feeder, who sets up well off the circle, aiming to cut in front of her opponent and on to the goal arc (see figure 8.13). The thrower must be careful when throwing over circle defenders and try to avoid crossing passing lanes. When the pass goes to the feeder, the goalers position themselves to screen, so one receives the next pass.

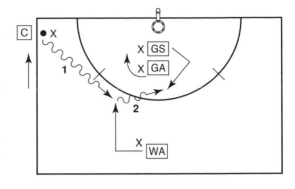

Figure 8.13 Second-pass screen strategy.

The goalers must remember that one of them must offer a lead out of the circle on the throw-in if the on-court feeder is not clear immediately.

- **Baseline squeeze strategy.** Baseline throw-ins outside the goal circle are always a very tight squeeze. It is a challenge to thread the ball through small gaps, so goalers need to come up with configurations that create space. One play that maximises space available in the circle is a squeeze play. WA or C takes the throw, and goalers and the on-court feeder align themselves diagonally with the thrower to form a line, creating deep linear spaces on either side of the formation (see figure 8.14). As the thrower is set to pass, the nearest player to the thrower breaks hard left or right, with the second and third players reading off for a lead in the opposite direction to the team-mate in front. The break must be fast

and sudden to create a gap for the thrower to thread the ball through to the first available target. The best option is a direct pass into the circle; however, the circle will not open up every time. Frequently the ball is swung out to the on-court feeder, who has a huge space available and only one player to beat. This feeder must get into a free passing lane and not end up directly behind the congestion in the goal circle to avoid a contest from a circle defender.

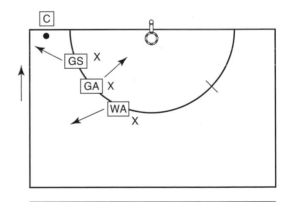

Figure 8.14 Baseline squeeze strategy.

Goal Circle Throw-Ins

Throwing in from the baseline within the goal circle reopens width available in passing angles because of its central location. These throw-ins are much easier than those nearer the sidelines, and if designed and executed well should result in a scoring opportunity within two passes. Goalers throwing in should always seek the other goaler in the circle as the primary target for a one-pass scoring opportunity. As both circle defenders cover this option thoroughly with the aid of restricted space and a goal ring in the way, the pass most often has to go out of the circle before it comes back in again. Two base strategies, the ball-side double play and the triangle play, from which individual variations can be added, are discussed in this section.

• **Ball-side double-play strategy.** This is a great play for throw-ins farther than halfway out from the post to the circle's edge. GA or GS takes the throw according to team format. The non-throwing goaler sets up just on the other side of the post, positioning for a hold and aiming to attract a double defence from the opposition circle defenders. The nearest feeder attempts to hustle for ball-side position on the goal circle so the ball does not have to cross an opponent to get to her. She should aim for a distance short enough for a quick chest or sling pass to be executed. The thrower fakes to the holding goaler and swings a fast sling, chest or bounce pass (bounce passes take longer, so use only if needed to avoid an interception) to the ball-side feeder and enters the court quickly, grounding the feet and turning to protect some space at the baseline for the return pass (see figure 8.15). One foot needs to be grounded on court before the goaler can play the ball in accordance with the laws governing re-entry to the court. The receiving feeder either bats the ball back in a controlled manner or catches and releases rapidly to the goaler to complete the double play. The goaler should strive to receive with a split-foot landing to minimise distance to the post.

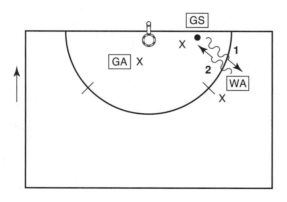

Figure 8.15 Ball-side double-play strategy.

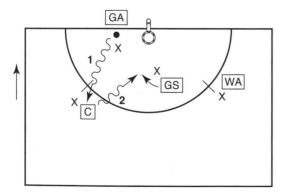

Figure 8.16 Triangle play strategy.

• **Triangle play strategy.** This play works well for throw-ins closer to the post. GA or GS takes the throw as the non-throwing goaler positions herself behind her opponent on the other side of the goalpost. The feeders set up on the goal arc as near as possible to the respective 45 marks (see figure 8.16). As the throw is released, the holding goaler maintains a strong position behind her opponent as the ball swings to the closest feeder. When the holding goaler hears the catch, she rolls out to lunge towards the ball for a quick pass in. The ball travels in a triangle path, with GS, the receiving feeder and GA forming the points.

Penalties and Free Passes: Defensive Half

When a penalty pass is awarded to a team, the offending opposition player must stand out of play for one pass. Wherever possible, teams should exploit this by freeing up their unopposed player to lead down-court and using a player with limited forward space allowable to move in to take the pass. This sets up for a four-on-three attack in the centre third. Any player on the team allowed in the area can take the penalty or free pass, so teams again have the opportunity to set up play exactly as they would like.

- **Defensive-third penalty or free pass.** It is always advantageous to get the ball moving quickly out of defence, so GK should pounce on the ball and set the penalty quickly. With maximum space and possibly a clear view (if an opponent is standing out of play), GK takes the pass and uses the three-option strategy, with the primary target being the unopposed player. The other possible receivers should position themselves to draw their opponents away from the target. For a free pass, the same action is taken, but there will be no unopposed target, so the thrower defaults to the primary lead.

- **Centre-third penalty or free pass.** WD or GD takes the pass; the non-passer of the two sets up in the far corridor behind the thrower. The three-option strategy applies again, with C, WA and GA being the three options. If the infringing opponent's player is free because of a penalty, this player becomes the primary target. C and WA offer primary and complementary leads. The back player must read off the front player (as she has the vision) to ensure the leads are in different spaces. GA plays deep on this play to give the mid-court players room and to keep from advancing too far up-court and out of position. GA is the third option if the first two leads are unusable. An alternative for this play is for the goalers to run a closed-circle lead system in which they both remain in the circle and use the WD or GD, whoever is not taking the throw, as the back-up.

Penalties and Free Passes: Attacking Half

Penalties and free passes in the attacking half can really make use of a team's collective strengths. The best passer can always take the throw, and the best mover can always take the lead. This concept must be weighed against passing to the nearest player to get a quick play underway as well as using an unopposed team-mate whose opponent is out of play because of the penalty. For penalties in the centre third with the opposition GD, WD or C standing out of play, a four-on-three situation should be created in the goal third.

- **Centre-third standard penalty or free-pass strategy.** For a penalty, if the infringing player is GD, WD or C, the team should run a four-on-three play. For a free pass, if the team favours depth in the attacking half, WD or GD takes the pass and the team can run a three-option strategy, with C, WA and the goaler on the lead. The goaler is the primary target, and who is in the next best position to lead for the ball depends on where players are positioned at the whistle.

- **Centre-third free-pass clear-out strategy.** In this free-pass alternative for teams that operate well in open spaces, C takes the pass in the centre third, with GD and WD both behind the centre circle on their respective sides. This arrangement, if the pass is taken quickly before the opposition GA and WA float into the frontcourt, creates huge spaces for the WA, GA and GS in which to lead. The opposition C may float back into the goal third but will likely be ineffective if the pass is taken quickly. The goalers run their system leads off the pass, with WA offering an alternative to the lead goaler using the ample space available. After the pass is released, C drives hard down-court to balance up and offer in the next wave of leads.

- **Goal-third penalty and free-pass strategies: off the goal circle.** Goal-third penalties should be one- or two-pass plays to get to a shooter in good scoring position. When GK or GD is out of play, a two-on-one situation that should be exploited is created in the goal circle. WA or C takes the pass; the non-passer balances up the court, ready for a back-up lead if the play is unsuccessful. The pass may still need to beat the defence over the ball, so it will most likely need to be aerial or wide. GA and GS set up in the goal circle for a ball-side screen (see figure 8.17). One goaler protects the ball side by putting a screen on the circle

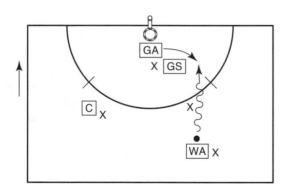

Figure 8.17 Ball-side screen.

defender still in play. The other goaler runs into the protected space to receive the ball uncontested, ideally in the goal circle. The screen must not be set before the thrower is ready, or the opposition defender can move out of the screen. When the pass is released, if not received in a shooting position, goalers should seek a quick pass to each other or give to the nearest feeder for a short double play into scoring range before both opposition defenders are back in position.

When the WD or C is out of play, WA or C takes the throw, checks the goal circle for a possible direct feed and then hits the goaler on the system lead out of the circle if the direct feed is covered. The feeder not taking the pass offers a complementary lead to the goal circle wide of the central passing corridor, and the goaler not on the lead must position herself in the circle for a back-up lead. As it is a penalty set-up, the thrower should have clear vision and be able to give a quick, accurate pass to the best target before accelerating to the goal circle. For a free pass in this region, the same plays apply. The attackers need to make their leads so that they clear opposition hands in passing lanes to ensure that the thrower has adequate vision of them as a target.

- **Goal-third penalty and free-pass strategies: on the goal circle.** Penalties and free passes from the edge of the circle provide great opportunities to get the ball to a goaler in a good scoring position in one pass. When GK or GD is out of play, WA or C takes the pass. There is a two-on-one situation in the goal circle, with the ball in the hands of the feeder poised on the goal circle and no defence over the pass. The goalers need to take maximum advantage by arranging themselves so that one of them receives an uncontested ball in a scoring position. The strategies available for this play include the *sandwich*, *split* or *screen* set-ups. To execute the *sandwich* play, GS and GA align themselves between the thrower and the post and trap the opposition defender between them (see figure 8.18*a*). The front player lunges forwards to the ball, and the back player sets for a hold and drop to the post. The thrower can further assist the play by fake passing to the option she does not choose. Because of the vertical depth of this strategy, one defender cannot cover both options. The *split* is best used when the penalty is awarded in the central corridor. To run the split, GA and GS move quickly to the extremities of the goal circle, one positioned high and one low (see figure 8.18*b*). When the passer is ready, they sprint towards each other, changing direction or passing through when they get near the middle and forcing the defender to decide which one to defend. The ball goes to the first available target in shooting range. Again, a good fake pass helps. This move should be pre-planned and practised so that each goaler has a specific side to pass through so they do not collide. Adopting the *screen* technique in this situation is straightforward as long as the timing is right. As soon as the passer is ready, one goaler defends the opposition defender (as for the ball-side screen technique), creating a space for the other goaler to receive the ball unopposed in scoring range. It is good to practise all three of these strategies and decide on a best option to run in games.

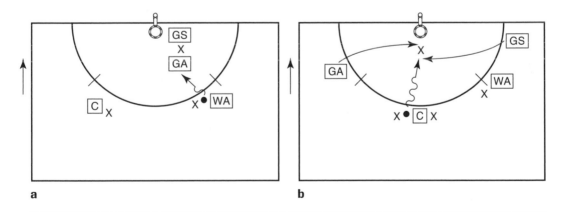

a   b

Figure 8.18   *(a)* Sandwich strategy and *(b)* split strategy.

When WD or C is out of play, WA or C takes the pass. In this case, it should always be the nearest player of the two to the infringement to allow opposition defenders minimal set-up or recovery time. The primary target is the first goaler open, with the back-up being the non-passing feeder holding on the goal circle. There are a few ways to play this out: one is to *split* the defenders and offer two

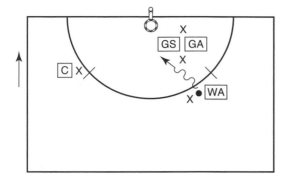

Figure 8.19 Double lateral hold.

options, another is to set up a *double lateral hold*, and the last is to *screen*. To *split* the defenders, GS and GA situate themselves near the circle edge in a staggered position. When the feeder is set to throw, they both offer simultaneous explosive movements, and the feeder hits the first one open. To set a *double lateral hold*, GS and GA position themselves side by side, halfway between the thrower and the post, with very wide stances, their outside feet touching (see figure 8.19). The feeder fakes one way and delivers to the open target on the opposition defenders' reaction to the fake. The goalers should not need to move unless the defenders do not buy the fake. To *screen*, one goaler defends the shooting partner's opponent to protect a space for her to pop in and receive the ball, ideally so the pass does not have to cross an opponent.

Goal Circle Penalties and Free Passes

Goalers should always look to shoot any penalty shot or pass awarded to them rather than pass back out of the goal circle and forfeit their two-on-one advantage. For free passes awarded to the attacking team in the goal circle, goalers may not shoot but must pass the ball only in accordance with the rules. GA or GS takes the pass and checks quickly for the shooting partner near the post. As this area is likely to be heavily guarded, WA and C should position themselves for a pass out and either double play with the player who took the free pass or set a triangle play from goaler to feeder back in to the other goaler on the hold. This section discusses long- and mid- to short-range penalties as well as final-whistle penalty strategies.

- **Long-range penalty strategy.** For penalties set from the perimeter or up to a metre in, GA or GS should take the shot, stepping in on her second grounded foot and taking the shot from mid-range reasonably unopposed. The non-shooter should set up for an off-load pass (a short-distance pass from the other goaler) on the opposite side of the post, forming a triangle with the shooter and the post. When the non-shooter positions herself well for the off-load, the opposition defender needs to guard her, or the shooter will whiz the ball over the defender's head to her partner, who will shoot from under the post. Setting a good triangle option clears the path for the shooter to take the step-in shot towards goal. WA and C need to maintain a receiving position (ball-side if possible) on either side of the shooter on the goal arc. If the defender overcommits to the shooter on the step-in, the shooter off-loads to the non-shooter under the post. Set up properly, it is a win–win situation for the goalers. If neither goaler is proficient at the step-in shot from long range, the secondary option is to flick the ball out to the closest ball-side feeder and lunge towards the post for a double play. The situation will immediately revert to a two on two in the goal circle. If this is more likely to be successful for the team than the step-in shot, it becomes the primary strategy for a long-range penalty.

- **Mid- to short-range penalty strategy.** GA or GS takes the shot, with the non-shooter adopting the ROS approach (see chapter 4) of setting up for rebound or as an off-load target or screening the shot for the shooter. Which role the non-shooter selects depends on the distance of the penalty from the post, the position of the defender in play and personal preferences of the shooting pair. As a rough guide, mid-range penalties (about three metres out from the goal) could use an off-load option (to give the shooter space to step in for an easy shot). A screener is appropriate for short-range (two-metre) shots, and a rebounder is a good choice for shots under the post (to one metre out). WA and C should remain on the arc until the goal is scored to cover any tap-outs or loose balls that come their way from a rebound contest.

- **Final-whistle penalties.** Many a nail-biting match has come down to the last shot of the game. Under all extremes of pressure, the shooters must remain clear-headed and confident, knowing that for every situation, they have a plan that has been discussed and rehearsed, ready to swing into action when it's time to deliver.

The coach and the team's shooters must develop clear plans for penalties awarded on or within 10 seconds of the final whistle and guidelines for playing out the dying seconds when the result is in the balance. After all parties have had input before the game, a decision needs to be made on the course of action in all possible circumstances. For penalties awarded on the bell or taken as the last possible shot of the game, who will take the shot needs to be determined. The considerations could be factors such as the most experienced player, the player awarded the shot, or the player who has shot the most accurately in the game. The role of the non-shooter also needs to be clear. For a short-, mid- or long-distance penalty, what aspect of ROS is most appropriate? These decisions make every team unique because there is no set formula to maximise chances of success that will be the same for every team.

Performance Points for Attacking Set-Play Strategies

- For open spaces, use running leads and dynamic plays.
- For closed or tight spaces, use holds and screens.
- Rehearse plays in gamelike simulations during training. Know the plays and everyone's roles.
- Balance the court with feeders on opposite flanks and one goaler always in the goal circle.
- Use a variety of set plays and strategies, but have a limit. Complicating the game plan causes attackers to lose their instincts.

Defending Set Plays and Penalties

A defensive unit that is well prepared and well drilled can foil many set plays. Set-up familiarisation, logic, teamwork and unit practice can force the opposition to run a second (less potent) option. The defence of set plays needs to be discussed and practised in training. The situations need to be rehearsed at half pace so they become familiar, then at game pace under full pressure in a half-court or practice-match situation to perfect technique, strategy and timing. This section outlines general strategies for successfully defending set plays.

- **Opposition centre passes.** Defending opposition set plays at a centre pass can be an absorbing challenge. As a general rule, players should try to figure out the other team's plan and how to foil it. There are some general guidelines to increase difficulty for the opposition and some specific counterplays that will ruin a good attacking plan. Generally, the defenders should always hustle for the inside position on the opponent at the transverse line to lengthen the pass and force the ball to cross them before it is received by the opponent, giving them a greater chance of deflecting the ball. The defensive team should also scan the set-up to see where the attackers are trying to open up space and shut down that space by playing offline. Any time the attackers attempt to move together, the defensive team should intervene and keep them apart. These general tactics will force the opposition to at least rethink the first options or will make the pass more difficult.

    More specific opposition tactics (e.g., screens) should be noted and counterplayed. To defend screens at a centre pass, defenders should try to prevent the opposition attackers from getting together in the first place. The defence should split the attackers by side, defending and directing them apart to prevent the screen. Another option to foil a screen is for defenders to step away from the set-up as the opposition attacker moves to face them.

    To defend wide starts such as the corners configuration, defenders should play offline in the central space into which the opponent is going to run. If defended tightly, the opponent need only slip past in the first second of the play to run into a wide-open central corridor to receive an easy centre pass. Playing offline will challenge her to pass within the three-second limit.

    To defend a centre-pass set-up where only one attacker is at the line and the other has faded deep for the subsequent lead, the defender of the deep opposition player can support the defence of the centre pass by working a double defence on the attacker at the line, forcing the pass to go backwards if covered well. The defender who moves up for the double defence then has plenty of time to track her opponent, as the pass will not go directly forwards. In an overload situation where the attacking team stacks the receivers on one side of the court to open space for other team-mates, defenders should play offline in the central space, decreasing the size of the space and increasing the time taken for attackers to cut through it.

- **Opposition throw-ins in the defensive and centre thirds.** Although set plays allow the attacking players time to set up conditions that suit them, defending set plays, such as throw-ins, also allows the defensive team time to counter the set-ups. For full-court opposition attacks from a back-line throw-in, defensive teams run their regular options of playing one on one, double defending the thrower, flooding, sagging or using a zone. For sideline throw-ins, defending teams should take advantage of the narrow passing angles and concentrate the defenders one on one, directing opponents to the same sideline as the thrower. This forces passes high and long to a predictable target, and defenders in the far corridors should play offline in the central corridors for reinforcement. Attending to these details in set-up time gives defenders an advantage they are not afforded in live-ball situations.

    Players down-court from throw-ins should always note the position of a team-mate's arms when she is defending the thrower to establish which passing lane she is impeding. Defenders down-court should then adapt their stances in anticipation of a pass in the free lane. For example, a WD who has good defensive position over the ball with her arms in the wide lanes should indicate to the team-mate behind to play in front, as the pass is likely to go high and direct. Teams should familiarise themselves with basic attacking strategies (e.g., the short–long and the three-option strategies) to anticipate likely opposition movements when in defence. If an opponent from the attacking team deliberately clears away from the action to create space for up-court team-mates, the defensive team should flood the spaces.

- **Opposition throw-ins in the goal third.** Sagging by the WD or C on to opposition forward leads concentrates the defence configuration in the goal third and can frustrate the goalers. An extra player to negotiate as well as the positional opponent directing them into the sag often takes away their primary option. If the defensive team does sag on a throw-in, the sagging defender must be quick to pick up her positional opponent once the pass has been released to halt a double play on to the goal circle. Double defending on a shooter when her partner leaves the goal circle forms a constellation of defenders near the goals. The circle defenders resume one on one when both opposition goalers are back in the circle.

    For throw-ins from the baseline, defenders must protect the goals first by guarding the post-option player. At the same time, the thrower should not be given too much latitude or she will run a sizzling double play with the near-side feeder right in front of the circle defenders as soon as they enter the court. Defenders outside the circle arc should hustle for ball-side position so the ball must cross them to get to their opponent, as for defending the centre pass. In a closed-circle situation, with all players in or around the goal circle, circle defenders should be on the lookout for opposition player movement towards them as a cue for setting up a screen or hold and shuffle out of it.

• **Opposition free passes and penalties.** The first thing to do when an attacking team turns the ball over is to recover and move quickly into defence mode. Teams relish the chance to run a quick play with the defensive team out of position for an easy route to the goals. Teams should react quickly to the whistle, anticipate the call and scramble to pick up positional opponents. If a penalty results in a four-on-three situation, the defensive team has two basic options: (1) either forgo defending the first pass and attack the second one or (2) play offline and create indecision for the opposition thrower. Attacking the second pass allows the free opposing player to receive an easy ball but then face full one-on-one coverage with the next pass, when the infringing player re-enters the action. Playing offline can create indecision and mask perceptual cues as well as buy time for the infringing team-mate to re-enter play. Whatever option is taken, the defensive unit must communicate so that all players work together, not against each other. If a circle defender must stand out of play, WD or C should apply extreme pressure on the pass or support as deep as she can on the circle edge. The remaining circle defender should keep moving so the goalers cannot set up an easy two-on-one play and receive the ball unopposed. To combat fake passes coming into the goal, circle defenders need to keep their feet moving all the time and can even fake their own move—so the thrower will be fooled into thinking they have taken off—and pass back the other way just in time for the defenders to dig in and spring back towards the ball.

Performance Points for Defending Against Set Plays

- Players should familiarise themselves with and rehearse possible opposition strategies and set-ups.
- Where the opposition players try to create space, try to invade it.
- Support defensive efforts by team-mates by creating extra defensive presence in the vicinity.
- Be proactive. Take advantage of breaks in play to set counterplays.

CHAPTER 9

Transfer Games

Games in team training sessions are always popular. They are a great way to finish off the session, and if chosen carefully, games not only provide enjoyment for players and coaches but also satisfy a number of fundamental objectives in a court session. The objective of including a game needs to be clear. Is it for a bit of light-hearted fun, or is it an absorbing way to include some pertinent netball skills in the session? If the team needs a lift, a laugh, some lightening up or some team bonding, a short, quirky game or challenge that does not relate to netball at all can achieve the desired effect. Transfer games, however, are different from games played purely for fun; transfer games contain skills that have positive transfer to netball and expand elements of a player's repertoire that can be incorporated into match play.

> *"Playing cross-sport combination games at training provides a medium for working outside the comfort zone and transferring new skills to the netball court."*
>
> ~ Natalie Avellino, Australian Wing Attack and Goal Attack, World Champion

Playing half-court netball or netball against the same players every week to end a training session can get monotonous after a while and cease to be productive. Transfer games keep court sessions fresh and provide an outlet for creative thinkers and competitive souls. Well-designed games promote critical thinking, require decision making, create leadership roles, solidify teamwork links, challenge fitness work, satisfy competitive urges and encourage a positive attitude to training. Transfer games also balance out a session if they include a lot of intense one-dimensional conditioning work. Thoughtful programming of court sessions with a games theme woven through them can be a clever way to keep motivation fresh while satisfying a range of skill objectives. This chapter provides examples of games that can be played on a netball court with little equipment that have similar elements to netball, providing positive transfer to the players' game play. The games are designed for 20-minute periods (two 10-minute halves) but can be lengthened or shortened to suit the training session.

BASKANET

A cross between basketball and netball, the objective of this game is to score more goals than the opposition by dribbling, passing, shooting and using teamwork. The major skills targeted are ball handling, cutting forwards past opponents, spatial awareness, shooting, screening and defence.

REQUIREMENTS

Netball court, 8 to 10 players for two teams, netball, two sets of bibs, whistle, umpire

GAME SET-UP

Game starts with a jump ball between two players at the centre circle; other players may start anywhere.

RULES

Netball rules with the following alterations:

- Players may move in all court areas.
- Players can bounce the ball up to three times before passing or shooting.
- Anyone can shoot; two points are awarded for a shot scored in the goal circle, four points for shots taken from outside the circle.
- After a goal, the opposition throws the ball in from the goal line at the same end.
- No obstruction penalties are called, but players cannot steal the ball from opponents' hands or reach around their bodies to gain possession.

VARIATIONS

The first two attackers in the goal circle are the only two allowed in the circle until a goal is scored or the ball is turned over and moves down-court. Another variation is to allow zone defence only (practise the diamond, box or any goal-third zone).

MODIFIED KORFBALL

This game is a slightly modified version of korfball, the popular European sport similar to netball, with a few interesting twists to the rules. The aim is to score more goals than the opposition by passing, shooting and using teamwork. The major skills targeted are ball handling, spatial awareness, shooting, screening, one-on-one defence and cooperation.

REQUIREMENTS

Netball court, 12 to 16 players for each of two teams, netball, two sets of bibs, 10 markers, whistle, umpire

GAME SET-UP

The court is divided into two halves by markers. Each player is assigned a personal opponent, who wears the same bib letters. Pairs of opponents are divided equally into the two halves, where they must remain. Toss a coin to determine who starts with possession. The game starts with a centre pass taken from the thrower's attacking half, just in front of the centre line. The game restarts after a goal in identical fashion.

RULES

Netball rules with the following alterations:

- No physical contact whatsoever is allowed.
- Shots at goal can be taken anywhere in the attacking half, with three points counting for shots taken outside the goal circle.
- Strictly one-on-one defence is played at all times; a player may not defend any opponent other than her own as indicated by bib lettering. Penalty for this infringement is a free pass to the player who was defended by the "wrong" defender. If the "wrong" opponent defends a shot for goal, a penalty shot is awarded to the player shooting. For a penalty shot, the shooter lines up at the midpoint of the goal arc with the ball, steps in on one foot and shoots underarm style (players can use any shooting technique in live play). All other players must remain outside the goal arc until the shot is released, then they may run in for a rebound.
- After every two goals netted, all players change halves, as indicated by the umpire, staying with their positional opponents so attackers become defenders and vice versa. Teams shoot towards the same end all game.
- The no-shot rule: the umpire must call, "No shot," and award a pass to the opposition if a player takes a shot when her personal opponent is positioned directly between the shooter and the post with her arm raised less than one metre away. These three conditions must be in place to call a no-shot.
- After a goal, play restarts at the centre line; the team that did not score starts with possession.

NETBALL PINBALL

This game is standard netball with the addition of players on the sidelines as rebounders to change angles of play. This speeds up the game, as the ball is rarely out of bounds. The major skills targeted are ball handling, double plays, spatial awareness, shooting and challenging defence.

REQUIREMENTS

Netball court, 12 players for three teams (or 10 plus 2 permanent non-playing rebounders), netball, three sets of bibs, whistle, umpire

GAME SET-UP

Game starts with two teams on court and a toss-up between two players; other players may start anywhere. If playing with three teams, each member of the third team stands at a transverse line intersection along the sidelines, just outside the court, so that there are two members on each side; these players are the 'rebounders'.

RULES

Netball rules with the following alterations:

- Players may move in all court areas.
- Players are allowed to throw to the rebounders, but two passes must separate handling by a rebounder.
- Rebounders must pass back to a player on the team of the person who threw the ball to them.
- Anyone can shoot.
- After a goal, the team that scored stays on, the opposition players become the rebounders, and the rebounders enter the game with possession to restart the play. A team stays on as long as it keeps scoring.

THREE-ON-THREE NETBALL

This game is identical to netball but restricted in space to one-third of the court, with three players on each team. Both score at the same goalpost. The objective is to score more goals than the opposition by passing and shooting using limited space. The major skills targeted are ball handling, decision making, fitness, spatial awareness, shooting and one-on-one defence.

REQUIREMENTS

Netball court third, six players for two teams, netball, two sets of bibs, whistle, umpire

GAME SET-UP

Game starts with a player on the transverse line with the ball; other players may start anywhere.

RULES

Netball rules with the following alterations:

- Players may move in all areas of the third.
- After a goal, the ball is returned to the transverse line by the non-scoring team to restart play.
- Only two players on any team are allowed in the goal circle at one time.
- Place a strict time limit on play to keep the focus sharp (e.g., five-minute bursts).

VARIATION

Add another pair to play four on four, and take the transverse line boundary out three metres.

FOUR-WAY NETBALL

This game is netball with bi-directional scoring zones. Each team plays with two goalposts and tries to score more goals than the opposition by passing, shooting and using teamwork. The major skills targeted are ball handling, spatial awareness, court balance, refocussing, shooting and defence.

REQUIREMENTS

Netball court, 10 to 14 players for two teams, two portable netball posts (safely anchored), two sets of bibs, whistle, umpire

GAME SET-UP

Game starts with a toss-up between two players; other players may start anywhere. Two portable posts are set up behind each sideline, level with the centre circle.

RULES

Netball rules with the following alterations:

- Players may move in all court areas.
- Players may score at either of their two goalposts. One team is assigned the northern and western goals, the other team the southern and eastern goals.
- Anyone can shoot.
- After a goal, the ball is returned to the centre circle for a toss-up to restart play.

VARIATIONS

Assign one goaler to each goalpost; goalers are the only players that can score. Rotate scoring duties frequently. Another variation if portable posts are not accessible is to put a goaler in a hoop two metres back from the sideline; to score, the goaler must make a one-hand catch with both feet in the hoop. No defender can exit the court to defend in the goal zone.

TOUCH NETBALL

This game is an adaptation of touch football (touch rugby). The team advances the ball by running it forwards towards the goal line while using only allowable backwards passing. The aim is to score more tries than the opposition by running, weaving, passing and using teamwork. The major skills targeted are ball handling, court balance, spatial awareness, decision making, fitness and defensive cover. This is an advanced game that may be beyond players with no touch experience.

REQUIREMENTS

Netball court (if width can be increased by using markers, add three metres), eight players for two teams on court (plus substitutes if necessary), netball, two sets of bibs, whistle, umpire. It helps if the umpire has some touch experience to assist players with rule knowledge and flow of the game.

GAME SET-UP

Game starts with both teams in their defensive halves. Toss a coin to determine who starts with possession. The player in possession starts with the ball in the centre circle, and team-mates spread laterally behind, two on one side, one on the other. The opposition players must start in their defensive third until the ball is played. Play begins with the ball carrier tapping her foot up to the ball and running forwards.

RULES

Modified touch rules:

- To start play a player must either tap (raise the ball to her toe and run) or use a roll-back (put the ball on the ground and roll the ball backwards up to one metre with her foot for a team-mate to pick up). Taps are taken to start the game, after a try (score) and at a penalty. Roll-backs are used after a touch by an opponent or from one metre in from the sideline when the ball goes out.

- The team in possession tries to touch the ball down over the goal line to score. Players need to do this before the opposition tags them on the arms or torso on six different occasions. Every time a player is tagged, she must stop on the spot and restart play with a roll-back. The defensive team must retreat 10 steps immediately after a tag and not tag an opponent until she gets her distance. If they do not, they are offside, and the opposition gets six more touches (i.e., the touch count reverts to zero) and a penalty tap.

- Players may move in all court areas and should aim to stay behind the ball in attack.

- If a player passes after she has been tagged, "touch and pass" is called, and the team loses possession.

- Players can pass only backwards or level with a team-mate. Forward passes lose possession.

- To receive a roll-back, a player (known as the dummy half) moves up immediately behind the person who is playing the ball and must pick it up cleanly before it rolls a metre, then take off to gain ground and look for a passing option.

- If the attacking team does not score before six team touches, the opposition gains possession from where the last touch was called.

ZIPBALL

This fast-moving thinking game is a cross between a number of sports including netball, basketball, touch and football. The aim is to score more points than the opposition by accumulating possession points and throwing, hand passing or kicking the ball to the team goaler. The major skills targeted are ball handling, leading, spatial awareness, teamwork, decision making and defence.

REQUIREMENTS

Netball court (best suited to a larger area if one is available, such as two adjacent courts), 8 to 12 players for two teams, netball, two sets of bibs, 12 markers (cones), whistle, umpire

GAME SET-UP

Markers are set in a three-metre-radius semi-circle around the goalposts. The goaler for the attacking team stands in this area, and no other player may enter. The game starts with a jump ball between two players at the centre; other players may start anywhere.

RULES

- Players may move in all court areas.
- No physical contact is allowed.
- Players must cooperate to transport the ball to their goaler to make a catch to score. Players may handle the ball for only three seconds and must throw, hand pass (hold the ball in one hand and tap it out with the other in an underarm action) or kick (from the hands) to a team-mate. Throws are worth 1 point, hand passes worth 2 and kicks, 3. When a team accumulates 10 team points, the players may attempt to score.
- Players are allowed to run two steps, bounce the ball and run two more. This is the maximum handling allowable for one possession.
- If a team drops the ball, possession is lost.
- All lost possessions result in a free possession to the closest opposition player on the spot, who may kick, hand pass or throw the ball to a team-mate.
- Balls that are contested and knocked to the ground by a defender are awarded to the attacking team, but the attacking team's accumulated point tally reverts to zero.
- The scoring system is the same as for accumulating points when delivering to the goaler, who must make the catch cleanly to add one, two or three points to the scorecard.
- Goalers are rotated regularly.

FANTASY GAMES

Fantasy games are situational netball games involving task cards that give a team a fictional game circumstance and a time limit to play out the result. The aim is to measure up the predicament, make some decisions and win the game. The major focus is to execute all netball skills effectively and calmly in a simulated pressure environment.

REQUIREMENTS

Netball court, 14 players for two teams, netball, two sets of bibs, written task cards made up by the coach, whistle, umpire

GAME SET-UP

Set up as for regular netball, with the score, time and possession adjusted to task card requirements.

RULES

Netball rules. Teams must both take a turn as team A. The team that starts with possession for the first task card starts without it for the second one. Some cards can be repeated a few times to encourage improvement in decision making and cementing concepts.

SAMPLE TASK CARDS

1. Team A is three goals up with two minutes remaining. Team B starts with possession at its attacking transverse line. There will be one major incorrect umpiring call that goes team B's way.

2. Team A is one goal down with 90 seconds remaining. Team B has the centre pass.

3. Scores are level and team A has a penalty shot or pass three centimetres in from the goal arc. Forty-five seconds remain in the match.

4. Team A is two goals down with five minutes remaining. Team B has a throw-in in its defensive third. Two major incorrect umpiring calls go against A in the final five minutes.

5. Team A is one goal down with the centre pass. Fifteen seconds remain.

CHAPTER 10

Peak Physical Conditioning

Attaining peak physical fitness for netball is a challenge for every player and a foundation element in the quest to become the best player possible. Physical fitness is a controllable aspect of the complete netballer. High-quality netball-specific physical training has a very direct effort–outcome relationship. When a player commits to a well-designed conditioning program, the training effect on the body's energy systems and fitness components will be measurable. To attain and maintain top physical shape for netball requires effort, dedication, focus, responsibility and the ability to train hard without supervision. These factors, coupled with knowledge and application of a conditioning program tailored specifically for netball, will prepare the player for the season ahead and help maintain high fitness levels once competition begins.

Coaches and players need a basic understanding of the body's energy systems and how to train them. Knowledge of the components of netball-specific fitness is essential to ensure the program addresses the development of all components for a balanced training effect. This chapter discusses how to incorporate netball-specific fitness into a seasonal conditioning program. It also discusses recovery and injury management.

Conditioning Phases and Programs

The major fitness components relevant to netball are speed, agility, endurance, strength, power, flexibility and balance. It is impossible to develop each component every session, so a total fitness program planned for the season is a good way to ensure that players receive a balanced, effective conditioning program. (For tips on planning effective practices and training sessions, refer to Appendix A, Training Guide.) To plan an effective conditioning program, it is necessary to divide the entire year into training blocks called phases. One way of allocating the phases is pre-season, pre-competition, competition, post-season and off-season. Conditioning programs should be designed specifically for these phases. When dates for the match fixtures become available, they can be allocated for the year-long program and planning can begin. All netball-playing nations run their major competitions at different times of the year, and different associations within every nation differ again, so dates will be specific to each team's netball calendar. An example of a training program for a five-month season with competition beginning in the first week of May follows:

- Pre-season from February to the first half of April
- Pre-competition for the second half of April
- Competition from May to September
- Post-season in October
- Off-season from November to January

Different playing levels require modifications in time allocation for some phases, the pre-season in particular.

Fitness work (particularly during the pre-season phase) can make players feel uncomfortable at times. For a player to improve, she must overload the exercise time or intensity. However, a conditioning program should never push players to the point of any kind of muscular pain or medical danger. If a player begins to look or feel sick, dizzy, pale or faint, or begins to compromise technique to protect an injured body part, she should cease the activity immediately. Players 18 years or younger will need concessions if their bodies are not yet fully developed and ready for adult strength work such as weight training. As with any strenuous physical activity, players with pre-existing injuries or health problems should be screened and cleared by a sports medicine professional or physiotherapist before participating in the programs.

The tables in this chapter provide examples of training session plans for the different phase blocks of the season. Content and length should be modified to suit the level of the performer.

Pre-Season

The body is powered by two energy systems, anaerobic and aerobic. Netball, as with most other team sports, calls on a contribution from both systems. To effectively condition players' anaerobic and aerobic systems, coaches must know how each system works. For movements that are explosive and short (e.g., a fast-breaking sprint for the ball or an explosive leap to intercept), the body uses the anaerobic system, meaning without oxygen. For movements longer than 90 seconds (e.g., repeated efforts of leading, passing and defending in the mid-court), the aerobic energy system takes over. As the body is continuously in motion for repeated efforts, it requires a constant supply of energy while exercising. The aerobic system achieves this through the muscles' absorption of sufficient oxygen from the bloodstream to produce energy. As the body becomes fitter, the cardiovascular system becomes more efficient at transporting oxygen in the bloodstream to the muscles. This means the muscles can absorb oxygen at a greater rate, allowing the body to exercise for longer without tiring. It is important to train both systems to work towards peak physical condition.

The first part of pre-season training focusses exclusively on the aerobic system, creating an endurance base from which to maintain total fitness over the season. Three-quarters of the way through the phase, the focus swings to anaerobic work. Pre-season programs can encompass running, swimming, cycling, gym work (conditioning machines) and weight training to build a solid aerobic base. A qualified instructor at the local gym can put a netball-specific pre-season weight-training program together. Developing core stability and flexibility is critical in the initial pre-season stage. A sports physiotherapist or qualified gym instructor can set a core-stability and flexibility program specific to each player's needs after a basic screening procedure. Aerobic, weight-training and core-stability sessions should take the form of extra individual work independent of team sessions.

> *"A player in peak physical condition can concentrate all her energy on the skills required on the court; a player that has cut corners will be exposed at crucial times in a game or may struggle to last the match."*
>
> ~ Karen Atkinson (Aspinall), England Wing Attack, Commonwealth Games and
> World Championship Bronze Medallist

Sprinting and plyometrics-based exercises (e.g., depth jumping and some medicine ball work) are beneficial in the lead-up to the pre-competition phase. Simple sprint programs and jumping work can run independently of team training when the program introduces anaerobic work. After incidental exposure to speed in off-season pursuits, specific speed training presents itself in the latter half of the pre-season, after the acquisition of a solid aerobic base. In this phase, the goal is to improve technical aspects of the sprinting action, and sprint drills should be based on very short distances of 10 to 20 metres, incorporating some changes of direction to make the drills netball specific. With the introduction of anaerobic work, Fartlek training should be considered as a high-transfer training method, integrating the netball-like movement pattern of a sprint within a running effort, changing up the speed requirements. Fartlek running involves interspersing short bursts of high-intensity work with medium-intensity exercise. It is an extremely effective training method for many team sports, particularly netball, because of the stop–start nature of the game. Fartlek training has excellent fitness transfer to game situations for players in all positions and is very important in the overall conditioning program.

Variety is important to keep motivation levels fresh, especially if a coach has the same basic squad of players for a number of years. Sports such as boxing, martial arts, triathlon and surf life-saving can be used as alternative content or as a supplement to the pre-season program. A qualified instructor needs to teach some activities, but it can be well worth the effort and investment. Non-weight-bearing options such as swimming and cycling should be occasional as they do not have the training transfer of running or weight-bearing activities.

Tables 10.1 and 10.2 provide sample sessions detailing possible content of a 90-minute team training workout in both parts of the pre-season phase. Table 10.1 carries an aerobic development objective, and table 10.2 reflects content of sessions introducing anaerobic training, given an established aerobic base.

Pre-Competition

The pre-competition phase is a short segment of the calendar reflecting a tapering of the conditioning program to have the team in peak condition for the first game of the season. The aerobic work ceases temporarily as short-distance speed and agility training takes over in combination with ball handling and court work. The number of weekly training sessions drops off, but the sessions last longer, as they combine mixed skills and conditioning. The conditioning segments in these team training sessions are shorter in time (to fit in court work) and more intense in content. Pre-competition sessions include lots of agility and explosive power work (e.g., jumping or medicine ball work) as well as high-intensity endurance. The final preparation stage of speed training is in the pre-competition phase, when distances shorten to 5 to 15 metres and incorporate agility. Once speed training is underway, it takes the form of various court sprints that can be included in the weekly team session. Weight-training programs continue but shift their focus to power. Table 10.3 details possible content of a pre-competition team training session. Note that court work would be a priority at this time of the season, so a high percentage of the 120-minute session is devoted to court skills, game drills and tactics.

Table 10.1 Sample Pre-Season Team Training Session

Theme: aerobic training
Duration: 90 min
Squad: 16 players aged 18 to 30
Venue: school soccer pitch
Equipment: 1 ball between 2, 8 markers, bench

Activity	Details	Time
Warm-up	Jog 2 easy laps of the pitch, changing direction at every corner.	
	Pass on the move with a partner up, down and across the pitch. Players and balls are in constant motion, maintaining an easy pace.	7 min
	Perform stretching exercises.	10 min
Conditioning	Run at 60% effort around the grounds.	6 min
	Complete 4 stations of an 8-station strength circuit. Place markers at eight circular locations about 10 metres apart. The stations are 1. push-ups, 2. sit-ups, 3. triceps dips, 4. step-ups on the bench, 5. lunges, 6. oblique crunches, 7. broad jumps (5 two-legged continuous jumps forwards, pausing for 5 sec in between efforts), 8. burpees.* Two people work at each station. Work for 1 min at each station.	4 min
	Run at 60% effort around the grounds.	6 min
	Complete remaining 4 stations of the 8-station strength circuit. Work for 1 min at each station.	4 min
	Run at 60% effort around the grounds.	6 min
	Complete each station of the 8-station strength circuit. Work for 30 sec at each station.	4 min
	Rest and recover.	6 min
	Game of touch netball (see chapter 9) on the pitch, 6 on 6. Use a netball and modify the rules if necessary. Every player must be actively involved at all times. The remaining 4 players complete a ball-handling drill for approximately 2 min each and tag with 2 other pairs on the pitch. The drill must keep all players constantly moving at varying paces.	22 min
Cool-down	Walk or slowly jog 2 laps of the pitch.	5 min
	Perform stretching exercises.	10 min

* Coaches should demonstrate all station techniques to ensure athletes understand the correct technique to be used before commencing the circuit.

Table 10.2 Sample Pre-Season Team Training Session

Theme: anaerobic introduction training
Duration: 90 min
Squad: 16 players aged 18 to 30
Venue: park or oval with a long ramp or hill
Equipment: medicine balls

Activity	Details	Time
Warm-up	Jog 4 lengths of the oval at an easy pace, alternating V-cuts, grape-vines, side-stepping, backwards running, diagonal slip-stepping, skipping and shadowing a partner.	
	Pass on the move with a partner (any ball-handling work that keeps both players on the move).	7 min
	Perform stretching exercises.	10 min
Conditioning	Fartlek 3x3s: run at 2 min low intensity, then 1 min high. Repeat 2 more times.	9 min
	Rest and recover.	2 min
	Fartlek 3x3s: run at 2 min low intensity, then 1 min high. Repeat 2 more times.	9 min
	Rest and recover.	2 min
	Fartlek 3x3s: run at 2 min low intensity, then 1 min high. Repeat 2 more times.	9 min
	Medicine ball passes in pairs or threes: chest, shoulder, overhead. Change passes every minute. Emphasise correct passing technique and smoothness.	6 min
	Ramp sprints. Start at the bottom, sprint uphill for 20 sec, walk or slowly jog back down for 25, rest for 20.	15 min
	Medicine ball passes in pairs or threes: chest, shoulder, overhead. Change passes every minute. Emphasise correct passing technique and smoothness.	6 min
Cool-down	Walk or slowly jog 2 laps of the oval.	5 min
	Perform stretching exercises.	10 min

Table 10.3 Sample Pre-Competition Team Training Session

Theme: mixed session (taper conditioning and skills)
Duration: 120 min
Squad: 10 players aged 18 to 30
Venue: netball court
Equipment: netballs, medicine balls, 5 long towels

Activity	Details	Time
Warm-up	Ball handling in pairs, moving up and down the court, using a range of passes and movements: both facing down-court; facing each other; short and medium distances. Use all passing types, maintaining an easy pace.	5 min
	Perform stretching exercises.	10 min
Conditioning	Sprint drills: run-throughs (see chapter 3 drills).	2 min
	High-intensity Fartlek: 1 min blocks. Run at medium intensity for 50 sec, sprint the last 10 sec.	5 min
	Rest and recover.	2 min
	High-intensity Fartlek: 1 min blocks. Run at medium intensity for 50 sec, sprint the last 10 sec.	5 min
	Medicine ball work: depth drops; chest, shoulder and overhead passes. Work in pairs.	7 min
	Agility courses (see chapter 3 drills). 1:1 work:rest ratio. Incorporate passing a ball in for some of the sequences. Work at full intensity: 30 sec bursts.	10 min
	Medicine ball work: depth drops; chest, shoulder and overhead passes. Work in pairs.	7 min
	Resistance running: pairs with towels. Work at full intensity.	10 min
	Rest and recover.	4 min
Court work	Skill work and various drills on current theme. Specialist areas work, tactical concepts, down-court team drills.	40 min
Cool-down	Slowly jog laps of the court.	3 min
	Perform stretching exercises.	10 min

Depth drops and resistance running are very effective components of pre-competition sessions. They are included in table 10.3 and detailed here:

• Depth drops require partners and a medium-size medicine ball. One player (P1) lies on her back, hands in front of her chest. Her partner (P2) stands at P1's feet, holding the ball out over P1's chest. P2 drops the ball, and P1 catches it and propels the ball straight back up with maximum force so her partner can catch it. The person on the ground should have her hands ready at all times to protect her face. Only players who have mastered general medicine ball work and who have adequate strength to handle the ball should do depth drops. These exercises develop power for passing by combining strength with speed, with the added benefit of muscular coordination required to handle the medicine ball.

• For resistance training, players form pairs. The worker loops a long towel around her waist and sprints to a marker 10 to 20 metres away with her partner following, pulling on the ends of the towel to create resistance, staggering with a wide stance to avoid the worker's feet. The worker must maintain correct sprinting technique and run at full pace. The worker completes five repetitions, walking back in between each set. She finishes the set with two non-resistance sprints over the same distance. Players reverse roles. Repeat three times. An alternative is for the partner to stand in front of the worker and apply resistance with her hands to the worker's shoulders while she sprints on the spot for 10 seconds, then move out of the way so the worker can sprint forwards 10 to 20 metres.

Courtesy of The Advertiser.

Being in peak physical condition allows players to focus purely on skill execution in competition.

Competition

The aim of the conditioning program during the competition segment of the netball season is to maintain the body's fitness after building a strong base. Attention must still be on fitness to validate the hard work done in the preseason. Skill-based drills can be designed with conditioning in mind for smart time management and to replicate the execution of game mechanics in a fatigued state. Players who wish to maintain peak fitness need to complete conditioning sessions outside of team training as well.

To get the most out of conditioning during the competition phase, the phase is divided into conditioning training blocks that vary in objective from aerobic to anaerobic. It is like starving one energy system periodically to maximise the other, then reversing the situation to get the full training impact from both systems. This strategy is called periodisation. The basic rationale behind periodisation is that once the body adapts to the training type, performance gets stale after a while and stops improving. Programming aerobic and anaerobic conditioning training in blocks keeps the body adapting, as fresh demands are placed on the body just as "adaptation saturation" is kicking in. This approach works well for netball, with its combination energy system demands, and is much more effective (as well as interesting and easier to plan) than attempting to train both systems all the time. Training blocks are longer at the start of the competition phase and become progressively shorter as the end of the season approaches. Shortening the training blocks ensures that players return more rapidly to speed work and short, sharp agility work. The solid foundations of aerobic work are maintained throughout.

Taper weeks involve lightening the physical training load in terms of sessions per week as well as session length. This ensures that players are fresh and energized for big games. Some teams also taper for particularly significant games during the season, which works well.

Table 10.4 presents a periodisation schedule for the competition phase of netball conditioning. Tables 10.5 and 10.6 contrast aerobic and anaerobic conditioning content of the team training sessions during the competition phase.

Table 10.4   Periodisation in the Competition Phase

Training period	Training block
Pre-season, week 1	Anaerobic
Pre-season, week 2	Anaerobic
Game 1	Taper
Game 2	Aerobic
Game 3	Aerobic
Game 4	Aerobic
Game 5	Anaerobic
Game 6	Anaerobic
Game 7	Anaerobic
Game 8	Aerobic
Game 9	Aerobic
Game 10	Anaerobic
Game 11	Anaerobic
Game 12	Aerobic
Game 13	Anaerobic
Game 14	Taper
Semi-final	Taper
Preliminary final	Taper
Grand final	Taper

Sample is based on an eight-team draw playing each opponent twice, with a top-four, three-week final format.

Table 10.5 Competition Team Training Session (Sample Aerobic Training Block)

Theme: court work and aerobic conditioning
Duration: 120 min
Squad: 10 players aged 18 to 30
Venue: netball court with stairs nearby
Equipment: netballs, 6 skipping ropes, 5 hoops

Activity	Details	Time
Warm-up	Minor game: Island Tag. Five hoops are set out randomly in a goal third. One player stands in each hoop, and 3 players stand in the spaces in between. The remaining 2 players are sharks. On "go", the sharks try to catch players who are not on an island. If the sharks tag a player, the tagged player is the new shark. To claim an island, a player runs to a hoop and forces the occupant to leave. After leaving the island, the runner quickly moves to claim a new hoop.	5 min
	Perform stretching exercises.	10 min
Conditioning	Team ball-drill medley: Precision Passing drill and The Triangle/Square drill (see chapter 2 drills) and Four Corners Rotation drill (see chapter 3 drills). Drills are done at medium intensity with precision ball handling. Each drill lasts approximately 6 min. Players should be in constant motion.	20 min
	Ten, Nine, Eights: Players start at the baseline and do 10 push-ups, 10 sit-ups and 10 shuttle runs (1 court length = 1 shuttle run), then 9 of each, 8 of each and so on until 1 of each.	10 min
	Rest and recover.	5 min
	Aerobic circuit: 2 players at each of 6 stations; leave 1 free on each rotation. Stations 1, 3 and 5 are rope skipping; mix up style for each rotation. Station 2 is mirror work on a line (partner A does series of aerobic movements mirrored by B over the line). Station 4 is partner passes up and down the court, close range, no stepping. Station 6 is stair runs. Rotate after 1 min at each station.	15 min
Court work	Skill work and various drills on current theme. Specialist areas work, tactical concepts, down-court team drills.	40 min
Cool-down	Slowly jog laps of the court.	5 min
	Perform stretching exercises.	10 min

Table 10.6   Competition Team Training Session (Sample Anaerobic Training Block)

Theme: court work and anaerobic conditioning
Duration: 120 min
Squad: 10 players aged 18 to 30
Venue: netball court with stairs
Equipment: netballs, 10 markers

Activity	Details	Time
Warm-up	Minor game: Shrink the Court. Players move about, changing directions and avoiding each other over the full court. Every 30 sec a court area is eliminated (start with a goal circle, then a third and so on) and the area continually restricted. After 2.5 min, expand the area back out.	5 min
	Perform stretching exercises.	10 min
Conditioning	Specialist areas conditioning drills (see Attacking-Unit Split Conditioning drill in chapter 5 and Defenders' Conditioning drill in chapter 6), splitting up into goaler, centre court and defender position groups.	10 min
	Rack sprints: Set cones along a sideline at 5, 10, 15 and 20 m from the baseline. Work in 2 groups of 5, staggered start, sprinting to the 1st marker and running through at 50% intensity to the final marker. Walk back to start. On 2nd time through, sprint to the 2nd marker, 3rd time through to the 3rd and so on. After sprinting to the 4th, work the drill in reverse, starting with a sprint to the end marker, shortening the sprint every repetition. Repeat x 2.	10 min
	Rest and recover.	5 min
	Stair work: Run up a set of stairs quickly and safely. Walk back down till 3 steps from the end; drop down from the 3rd last step to the ground, landing safely, and spring up vertically as soon as feet hit ground. Repeat drop phase 5 times. Repeat whole sequence 8 times, pausing 20 sec in between repetitions.	10 min
	Perform agility courses (see chapter 3 drills).	13 min
	Rest and recover.	2 min
Court work	Skill work and various drills on current theme. Specialist areas work, tactical concepts, down-court team drills.	40 min
Cool-down	Basic 3-person weave drill: 1 ball between 3 standing along baseline. Middle person passes to an outside person and follows the ball, cutting around that player. Repeat to the end of the court. Easy pace. Complete each length with a running shot.	5 min
	Perform stretching exercises.	10 min

Post-Season

The post-season is the period immediately following the last match of competition. It is important for players to use this time to switch off and revitalise themselves physically and mentally after a rigorous commitment for most of the year. Players who have a dual commitment to another team (e.g., a representative team) sometimes need to switch straight back into a pre-competition phase for an upcoming tournament. Coaches need to carefully manage a program for these players to ensure that some time is allocated for recovery to avoid burnout or overuse injuries. As a time for rest and rejuvenation, the post-season period is quiet on the conditioning front. The body needs a break from the high-impact world of netball to give players the best chance of bouncing back at full strength in the next season. Some teams are lucky enough to use the post-season phase purely to celebrate their victory!

Off-Season

For serious competitors, off-season means preparing themselves for pre-season. The off-season presents the opportunity to play another sport or engage in physical activities other than netball. Players should try to stay active by participating in a range of lower impact physical activities such as walking, yoga, cycling and swimming. Special attention should be paid to resting the body (striking a balance between active and passive rest) and re-evaluating sleep patterns and healthy eating habits. The drop in time commitment in the off-season allows players to take care of niggling injuries properly and prioritise their healing with icing, rest and treatment. The goal is to stay in reasonable shape so all the hard work done during the season still counts and the hard work in the upcoming pre-season is not a huge shock to the system.

Recovery

An increasing area of focus for competitive players trying to get an edge over their peers is the field of recovery. Recovery is particularly important for players training intensively or playing more than three times per week, as well as players involved in a tournament situation, with many games in a short space of time. With the onset of muscular fatigue and the production of lactic acid after taxing the anaerobic energy system, 20 minutes to 2 hours is required for a player to recover completely. The aerobic system's recovery can take up to 48 hours to completely replenish glycogen stores after a demanding workout. If no cooling down period takes place, with movement and stretching, the large supply of blood in the muscles after an intense physical workout can pool. If blood does not return to central circulation, a player can faint because of lack of oxygen to the brain. Therefore, it is very important to cool down properly as the first step of recovery. Walking or light jogging for a few minutes directly after a game or intense training, followed by a whole-body stretch, will benefit the body in its quest to bounce back fresh for the next assignment. During cool-down time, players should rehydrate and start replacing some of the fluids that have been lost (water or a sports drink with glucose are recommended). A low-fat, carbohydrate-rich post-match snack such as a sandwich, piece of fruit or cereal bar will begin to replenish energy supplies and should be consumed as soon as a player feels she is able to eat. After the game, any sore spots should be iced (through a wet towel) and elevated. Ice baths to sit in for a few minutes at a time, contrast baths (alternating cold bath and hot shower a few minutes at a time) and light massage promote muscular recovery and reduce swelling. Finally, the best recovery method after a tough match or session is sleep. Regular sleeping patterns are encouraged, and a bit of extra sleep after the match or session is the best way for the body to repair itself.

Injury Management

The downside to every sport including netball is injury. Injuries can be minor, moderate or major for the purposes of injury assessment. Minor injuries include cuts or grazes, muscular strains, sprains and general soreness. Any injury that can be treated by basic first-aid procedures where the player is able to resume playing comfortably classifies as minor. Each team should have a well-equipped first-aid kit and an adult with a first-aid certificate on hand to treat injuries. Some associations have a first-aid officer on the premises at fixtures. It is an advantage, however, to have team resources instantly available to treat minor complaints so the athlete can resume play within the allowable injury stoppage time of two minutes, within which the team's officials must make a decision as to the player's ability to continue. After the match or session, further examination of the injury should be undertaken and fresh dressings or ice, compression and elevation applied as needed. For full current first-aid procedures, officials should contact their local service providers and enrol in a basic or senior first-aid course.

Moderate injuries include such complaints as a severely strained muscle, a twisted ankle or soreness from a heavy body clash. When attended to, if these players cannot walk and hop on the injured limb correctly, or cannot catch and throw with strength in the case of upper-body injury, or cannot see or breathe normally, they should be removed from the game. Moderate injuries are the most difficult to assess, as often a player will insist she is able to play when sometimes she should not. That is another reason why having someone with basic sports injury knowledge on hand is a distinct advantage. The injury should be treated according to official first-aid procedures on the sideline as the player rests, and if rapid improvement does not occur after rest and treatment, the player should be referred to a sports medicine practitioner in the first instance.

Major injuries include mainly concussions and knee and ankle injuries involving stretched or torn ligaments, torn cartilage, soft tissue tears and even fractures. In this case, the player is usually in a great deal of pain and should be reassured and protected from possible elements and not moved until a qualified medical person has the situation under control. Ice can be applied straightaway, but anything that may twist or move the injured part should be avoided (such as taking a shoe off) until a qualified medical person has checked the extent of the injury. Under his or her guidance, the player should be carefully removed from the court and taken to a medical centre for assessment. The player should then follow the sports medicine practitioner's advice and embark on the prescribed rehabilitation program. All players returning from a major injury should have a clearance from a medical professional to return to modified training and to resume matches.

Long-term injured players will feel better about their situation if they set themselves attainable recovery goals and develop a positive attitude towards rehabilitation. Most of the time, the injury will keep them out of the game only temporarily, and they should use their time away from competition to strengthen other game skills. Recuperating players could undertake a short course in mental training, study some tactics or take statistics for the coach and apply the knowledge to their own game. There are usually things injured players can do at team training sessions (e.g., develop passing skills if their lower body is injured or do strength work on their legs if they have an upper-body injury). Much can be gained by positive thoughts and ticking off progress goals during the recovery process. Players who aim to return to the game better than when they left it quite often will be.

Performance Points for Attaining Peak Physical Condition

- Follow a well-balanced, netball-specific conditioning plan with periodised training blocks and season-phased plans.
- Be prepared to do extra training at the gym or on your own outside team sessions to maintain above average fitness.
- Test for fitness at prescribed intervals to monitor progress and adapt programs.
- Develop a working knowledge of fitness principles, and self-monitor intensity with pulse rates.
- Look after your body, and adopt sound recovery and injury management techniques.

CHAPTER 11

Mental Skills

Netball has scaled new heights in the past decade, inviting a new wave of professionalism only previously seen in national representative teams. Once-peripheral aspects of the game such as mental preparation have become mainstream in the sport's escalated expectations. Mental skills form a massive area of largely untapped potential in players. With discipline and regular practice, mental programming can significantly enhance consistency and physical performance by training the body to cope with any competition stresses placed upon it. Match pressure can cause the most physically skilful players to self-destruct into a bundle of nerves and render movement hazy, error-ridden and ineffective. By tapping into their mental skills, players can create unshakable self-belief. This empowers them to perform consistently close to their maximal level, or just as they do in their best training sessions without game pressure. This chapter examines the dominant psychological factors in netball and their relationship to performance. It also outlines practical mental pre-competition techniques including goal setting and visualisation, as well as pro-vides effective mental strategies for use in the heat of performance.

Mental Factors for Netballers

Several external factors prey on the minds of the competitors before and during a match. Internal factors such as self-doubt; perceived pressure about winning; or worry about recent poor form, injury or holding a spot on the team can cripple a player's focus and flow, greatly reducing chances of success. External factors such as weather conditions, umpiring decisions or an intimidating opponent can also transform ideal focus and flow to panic and errors in skill execution. Each athlete is different with respect to how internal and external factors affect her. Some pressure and nervousness is good—it means the player is ready to go, alert and excited about the game. Too much pressure can lead to problems, from missed cues to upset rhythm and unforced errors. A basic understanding of the mind–body relationship and practising a range of stress-management techniques can be the saviour of many highly strung competitors as well as benefit more laid-back players seeking consistency in their performance. This section discusses some chief psychological factors at play in netball: self-image, self-confidence, concentration and attention.

• **Self-image.** How players see themselves and perceive how others see them are two of the most fundamental factors in triggering improved performance. If a player does not have a realistic concept of herself, her place on the team and in the game, it can put a ceiling on her achievements. Many female netballers tend to err on the side of poor self-image rather than inflated self-image. It takes a concentrated effort and a lot of work to change a player's self-image, often requiring returning to what caused the poor image in the first place. Once this can be unlocked, the player, with help from the coach or a sport psychologist, can reform a more realistic self-image and begin to scale new heights, taking away previous limitations that the player put on herself. With a realistic self-image, all mental training techniques are much more effective.

• **Self-confidence.** The confidence factor can be a very circular paradox. If an athlete struggles in a match, she loses confidence. If she plays well, then she is confident. However, it is not much use having confidence after an event when players need it during the match! Players whose confidence varies erratically usually perform erratically. It is important to nurture self-confidence in players so they are less dependent on external factors such as winning and comments of others and more dependent on what they think about themselves. A focus on process is important with self-confidence—how well players match up against their own personal goals for the match or training session. Meeting targets generates positive feelings, and players can remain positive and self-confident about their next performance after losses and below-par performances. If performance targets were not met, written goals give players tangible reasons for a sub-standard performance and avoid the "I'm not good enough" or "I never play well against them" or "It was someone else's fault" excuses and destructive thought patterns. The experience can be turned into a learning opportunity that empowers players with new information and wisdom to put into action, while self-confidence remains intact.

Something that is critical for the development of self-confidence in matches is the regular opportunity to simulate game pressure during training. The feelings of mastery and genuine confidence in their own ability need to come from overcoming difficult and mentally challenging situations in training. Physical conditioning needs to challenge players' resilience and perseverance (this may be different for each player on the team), and drills and practice matches should put players under pressure of decision making and physical intimidation if they are to develop the confidence to flourish under match conditions.

Building self-confidence is a long and gradual process. Players who set themselves apart from their peers will typically have a solid, unwavering confidence in themselves that is relatively unaffected by what others do or say. Self-confident players exhibit a number of common traits, including focussing on performing the fundamentals of their position well and talking positively to team-mates and themselves. They set goals for each match, evaluating and modifying them at the end of each quarter. Self-confident players apply maximum effort at all times with the team or by themselves and accept that some errors are inevitable, ensuring that they learn from them and refocus instantly on the next task. An important skill of self-confident players is the ability to train themselves to remain calm and clear-headed in competition by practising dealing with adversity. These players seek challenges and enjoy overcoming difficult tasks. Self-confident players acknowledge approval and soak up advice from coaches but focus on their own expectations—the small goals they have set for themselves.

- **Concentration and attention.** It is possible for players with acute concentration to be affected by nerves, let a winning position slip and "choke" at the crucial point in the match. Their concentration might have been intense, but they were probably attending to the wrong cues. At pivotal stages in the match, usually when a personal opponent starts to get on top or the result is in the balance, attention to the cues that will see a continued calm execution of skills is challenged. Often, panic and choking follow, resulting in errors that may well cost the result. The good news is that players themselves are in charge of how much they allow pressure to affect them and whether they mentally drift from the task. Athletes need to understand that the focus must remain on the execution of

Courtesy of The Advertiser.

The ability to narrow one's focus and attend to one skill at a time is critical when shooting goals.

physical skills, that attention outside these cues confuses the body and output is adversely affected. Once players realise that their minds can effectively cause pressure errors, they can set about ways to turn attention back to the process and let the outcome take care of itself. It is a waste of physical and emotional energy to calculate chances of winning and losing or worry about what an opponent may do. Narrowing the focus back to attending to one skill at a time gives players the best chance of getting their desired result. Great attention skills allow players to enjoy their performances and play "in the zone" or stress free. Champion players are able to focus on executing their own tasks perfectly whatever the circumstances and use pressure to sharpen their awareness and motivation. They compete against themselves rather than opponents, effectively blocking out distraction and simplifying their focus to task quality.

Pre-Match Mental Techniques

Players can train their mental skills just as they train their physical skills. With belief, a desire to tap into their full potential and consistent high-quality practice, players can use their minds to enhance physical outcomes. When mental-skill practice is a part of the training program over time, players come to trust their mental preparation, knowing that for every perceived problem, there is a solution. This empowers the players to perform uninhibited and worry free, greatly enhancing their enjoyment of the game.

Mental training is easy to fit into the weekly schedule because it can be done anywhere, any time players have a moment to themselves. Team and individual training time presents an excellent opportunity to practise overcoming distraction and rehearse for game situations. Because it is usually quiet and uninterrupted, bedtime can be a very effective time for mental rehearsal, and the mostly calming nature of mental training techniques can be beneficial for insomniacs. This section discusses techniques players can use to build up their mental skills before performance. These techniques include goal setting, visualisation and imagery, positive self-talk and relaxation. They can be done at training sessions and during the week, building up to match day.

- **Goal setting.** Players should be mindful of their long-term or season goals in order to define their purpose for being on the team and the sacrifices they will need to make to be successful. Their chief focus from week to week should be short-term goals. Players can set goals for pre-season sessions, training sessions, matches and finals. Writing the goals down in a goal-setting diary or logbook adds considerable weight to their importance by reinforcing the goals and serves as a visual reminder during the goal period. These diaries are powerful confidence tools for recording success, and players should keep them in their training bags, available for action and evaluation. Ideally, the coach should assist with each player's goal setting to keep every player headed in the right direction for the role she has on the team. Goals should be measurable, with most able to be validated by statistics (e.g., every centre pass moves forwards; get five defensive touches or use at least three different preliminary moves in a quarter). They should be realistic—challenging but achievable. Goals should include physical and mental objectives and be restricted to a maximum of three at a time to avoid overloading the performer. Evaluating goals after each performance adds confidence and direction to performance and provides the opportunity to reset new goals to achieve next session.

- **Visualisation and imagery.** Our bodies act in accordance with what we imagine to be true. In a pressure match, players' bodies often cannot distinguish between what is real and what is imagined when calling on previous experience, so it is important that players imagine the task vividly and positively. This gives the players' minds a clear snapshot or action replay of themselves doing the task perfectly, down to the last detail, including the unhurriedness and the emotions of confidence and accomplishment that go with it. Having a clear picture of themselves performing a skill in their minds' movie library has a high correlation to the quality of physical execution.

Visualisation is the ability to create mental pictures. The better a player is at this skill, the more vivid the image in the mind. Imagery is multi-sensory, affecting more than one sense simultaneously (e.g., visual, aural and tactile). A player mentally rehearsing well can elicit actual physiological responses such as increased heart rate or muscular twitching in the area of the body that is used to perform the actual skill. Visualisation is an extremely powerful medium for improvement in performance and a skill that is well worth the time investment to get right. It has been suggested over the years that high-quality mental imagery practice on given closed skills is at least as powerful as physical rehearsal. Players with advanced mental rehearsal and imagery skills devote time to practise them regularly at training and at home, calling on them effectively in performance.

These athletes can see themselves through an "eye view" perspective vividly performing skills with attention to detail and proficiency in a calm, unhurried manner.

• **Positive self-talk.** The little voice inside a player's head may as well be a deafening stereo announcement to all, with the magnitude of effect it has over physical action. It is imperative that players recognise the messages of their subconscious and train themselves to assimilate only what is positive. Using techniques of positive self-talk will benefit confidence, attention and output. When players can dismiss a negative thought as soon as they catch themselves entertaining it, they are on the way to positive self-talk. When they can transform the negative thought to a positive affirmation on a consistent basis, they have created another powerful mind tool to use whenever negative thinking or self-criticism creeps in. An example of this would be a shooter's thinking, "Balance, eyes, elbows, swish!" instead of "I hope I don't miss this goal." Self-talk has an excellent chance of becoming a self-fulfilling prophecy; it is a big risk for players seeking maximal performances to constantly berate themselves or have doubt in their minds. Athletes who are interested in improving their positive self-talk and consequently self-image can record themselves on tape saying strong, confident affirmations about themselves and their skills. Listening to the tape over and over while using mental imagery will help cement belief in the statements and increase the likelihood of transfer to positive self-talk in a game situation.

• **Relaxation.** Followers of Eastern religions and martial art practices continue to demonstrate the powerful mind–body connections in their faith or craft. The Western world can learn much from these amazingly skilled people whose discipline and ability to concentrate allow them to achieve amazing feats. Their capacity to relax their minds and bodies and channel their focus is something we can aspire to adapt and incorporate in sport. It will not happen overnight, but with commitment and practice, netballers too can benefit from heightened awareness in mind–body connections. Relaxation during the week assists in the overall well-being of players' mental health. Setting aside some time to do what they enjoy each week outside of netball and work or study can balance the mind and benefit performance.

Performance Points for Pre-Match Mental Techniques

• Write two or three process-specific goals for every training session.
• Adopt the mind-set of challenging yourself to get the most out of each training session.
• Apply gamelike concentration, attention and effort to training situations.
• Visualise skills, match situations and opponents during training.
• Use each session to practise stress-management techniques.

Match-Day Mental Techniques

Mental techniques that can be used during a match reflect the techniques used during the week and in pre-match routines. They are just abbreviated instant cueing techniques reflective of the full processes. A player can start the game well, then make a few mistakes, fall in a hole and lose confidence, triggering the onslaught of doubt and panic. A few errors are normal in such a fast-paced game where the ball changes hands at a rapid rate. It is almost impossible for a player to play a perfect game, making every pass, interception or shot. However, when a series of errors occurs, a player needs to take stock of her emotional state and refocus. Symptoms that identify a player who has lost focus can reveal themselves physically, physiologically and emotionally. Physical symptoms include unforced errors, lack of talk, hesitation, increasingly early-timed moves or hazy leads. Physiological symptoms include muscle tension around the neck and shoulders, clenched jaws, furrowed brow, sweaty palms, shortness of breath and fast and panicky talking. Emotional symptoms include an argumentative demeanour, lashing out in contests, lack of discipline and looking as if on the verge of tears.

> *"When an opponent starts to get on top, a smart defender uses her mental talk to resort back to her major game goals. She comes back to her three primary goals against this strong opponent and concentrates on doing them very well."*
>
> ~ Michelle den Dekker OAM, Australian Goal Defence and Captain,
> Two-Time World Champion

An experienced player will recognise symptoms early and begin the thought-stopping process, positive self-talk, breathing techniques and external talk to encourage team-mates. Trouble-shooting techniques and a positive frame of mind will enable the player to overcome adversity and make minor hiccups out of potential disasters. Practical techniques to use on court during a game to refocus include deep breathing, tension–relaxation contrasting, switching to external focus and thought stopping. Each player can develop her own short refocussing technique to calm her down and redirect her energies to the task.

- **Pre-game routine.** Pre-game routines start from the night before the match and finish with the first whistle. Every player is different and will vary in her routine. The main thing is to find and stick to a routine that is sound physically, mentally and nutritionally. Players should experiment with their physical routines to determine what places them in their optimal mental state when they begin the match. A good pre-match routine provides familiarity and helps the body arrive in this state. A familiar pre-match pattern puts players in control of their surroundings, clears the mind and reduces the unpredictable factors that can create stress counterproductive to the controlled, calm state desired.

The team warm-up caters for physical preparation, while the mental preparation will be different for each player. Each player should seek her ideal level of arousal; some players will need firing up when they arrive for the game, while some will need calming down. All team members arrive in a different mental state, and it is quite a task to have all seven on-court players in their peak state at the first whistle. Players can increase their arousal levels by listening to lively music or talking with others. It is more challenging to decrease levels. Relaxation is difficult to accomplish if a player is feeling excessively nervous and edgy before the match, especially if the rest of the team is in firing-up mode. A coach must be sensitive to the needs of all team members and allow the players time to relax, perhaps away from the group if necessary to help them achieve their optimal pre-match state of calm aggressiveness and clear-headedness. Some pre-game relaxation options include sitting in a quiet place listening to peaceful music or affirmation tapes, visualising peaceful scenes, concentrating on deep breathing techniques and relaxing muscle groups that may be tense.

• **Deep breathing.** Deep breathing can be an instant refocussing cure. When the ball is away from a player's section of the court or there is a brief break in play, the chance for refocussing presents itself. The player should stand comfortably balanced, with knees and arms slightly flexed, drop the shoulders and relax the neck to release muscular tension in that region. She should then drop the jaw and smile to release facial tension. Next, she inhales a deep, slow breath into the body's centre as shoulders and face (especially the jaw) remain relaxed. Finally, she exhales slowly, draining the tension from the body. When the wave of calm takes over, the player should say a positive cue word (e.g., "strong"), visualise the cue with a positive image featuring herself and direct attention to the next skill.

• **Tension–relaxation contrasting.** Sometimes players are unaware of their stress on court. A way to check and refocus is to contrast what tension and relaxation feel like. As for deep breathing, athletes select an appropriate moment when the play has moved away. Isolating the face, shoulders and arms (including hands), players inhale while creating maximum tension in the muscles, screwing up the face, clenching the jaw, hunching the shoulders, flexing every arm muscle and making two tight fists. After holding this for three seconds, they let the tension go, exhaling for five slow seconds while dropping the shoulders, jaw and fingers, imagining the tension being drained out of their bodies. If time permits, they can repeat the procedure. Players should not worry about spectators of the ritual; all eyes will most likely be on the play.

• **Switching to external focus.** When a player starts to feel the pressure building, redirecting her focus from internal to external can have similar effects to breathing techniques. This refocussing technique involves getting verbal and bolstering team-mates with loud, clear encouragement. The effect is twofold. First, it gives team-mates a lift and heightens their awareness of the player's plight, and second it breaks the building negative thought patterns, creating a gap to transform thoughts to positives and redirect attention to appropriate process cues.

- **Thought stopping.** When a player can use a deliberate cue such as visualising a stop sign as soon as she catches herself attending to negative thoughts, she is on the way to refocussing. A deliberate action to dismiss the thought before it gains momentum will pay off in performance with practice and regular use. The thought-stopping action must be sudden and forceful to have an effect, and it needs to be something that suits the player involved.

Performance Points for Optimal Mental Match State

- Rest the body and mind adequately before performance.
- Use the same pre-match routine from the night before the game to the first whistle.
- Train several stress-management techniques to deal with any circumstance or pressure that may arise.
- Have a refocussing routine ready for distraction or for when attention slips from process to outcome.
- Employ a post-match evaluation process, and reset goals for the next week.

CHAPTER 12

Teamwork

Netball is one of the ultimate team games. Seven players must combine to deliver the ball to their goal with severe space restrictions and frugal time limits. For this process to happen intrinsically time after time, each player must be in tune with the other six. Teamwork needs to be implicit both on and off the court. Players, coaching staff and other club personnel must make connections that make the team work as a synergistic unit. Teamwork does not just happen. It takes effort from all involved to successfully fuse physical abilities, communication skills and different personalities into a functional, integrated unit. Teams that have successfully fused the factors required to be great seem to have a presence and style that just work. You cannot measure it or put a label on it—it is just there. This chapter discusses elements of successful teams. It challenges all players and team officials to think critically about their own roles and skills as a team member as well as outlines ways of fostering better teamwork.

Elements of Successful Teams

Great teams in sport that have experienced repeated success have common core characteristics. These characteristics resonate from the coach and his or her style, the playing group, and the team processes that govern team operations. This section discusses those characteristics that contribute positively to achieving teamwork.

Coaches

The coach is the major facilitator of overall teamwork. Coaches should be well informed and continual learners. They should seek knowledge by completing accredited coach education programs, updating resources, scouting opposition matches, watching higher-grade matches and reviewing video feedback. Players expect their coaches to know what they are talking about and to be well organised at training and on match day (see appendix A for training-session planning). Good communication skills are essential for team-oriented coaches. Great coaches have the ability to get through to the players and to pull rank and discipline a player if circumstances call for it. They must work hard to foster working relationships with the players, with the priority of helping them be the best that they can be. Coaches must be able to listen and assimilate player input while maintaining their role as the chief idea person in charge of pulling it all together. Great coaches show genuine care, interest and concern for their players and adopt the process of working together with them to achieve individual and team goals.

With good knowledge and communication skills, coaches should carry a demeanour of fairness and professionalism at all times. A professional relationship with players is ideal (it is much more difficult to deal with conflict objectively if the coach is too social with the players). Coaches should keep a little distance from the playing group and allow them to develop as an independent unit for ideal team mechanics. To promote an inclusive atmosphere and the well-being of the entire team, coaches must have clear expectations and be able to delegate responsibility to all team members.

Players

Each player on the team has a responsibility to contribute positively to the team work ethic. In team sports, especially one as interconnected as netball, players should aim to develop their skills on two fronts. What players do off court to enhance the team's unity carries at least as much importance as their efforts on court. These two areas are discussed as personal (off-court) and physical (on-court) factors.

A united approach off-court underpins great teamwork and understanding on-court.

Personal Factors

Great teamwork starts with successfully blending the variety of personalities within the team. Coaches need to pick the right people to be involved with the team, or those who have the potential to be great team players and officials. Players come in all shapes, sizes and personality types. A careful blending and understanding of all types of people are required to successfully assimilate the range of personalities and skills into a positive working force. The chief personal characteristic of a truly successful team player is possibly resilience. Great players show resilience in the face of defeat, criticism, non-selection, poor form and personal difficulty. They have the ability to bounce back under crushing pressure, and they know there is a solution to every problem. Belief in themselves and the goals and processes of the team can facilitate the development of resilience. Great resilience involves accepting blame in proportion and then redirecting energies to a positive resolution and moving on. In team sports, resilience is a wonderful characteristic to train, as it will see players through tough circumstances and make them stronger because of the experience.

Being team oriented and unified in their creed, goals and values is something that players on great teams work at. Acquiring this skill involves communication during training, on match days and particularly at team discussion time. Each individual should understand the goals of the team regarding values such as fair play as well as outcome-related goals such as a win–loss record. A difficult skill for some competitive athletes is developing a global view of their place on the team. Sometimes players think that if they believe they have personally improved or played well, it guarantees them a starting position on the team. However, they need to be pleased with their personal goals but understand that the coach or selection panel makes the calls on team placement and selection for the good of the team, and little is to be achieved by allowing destructive behaviour to interfere with the smooth running of the team and the rest of its players. Athletes must do their best in the role the coach assigns to them on the day. If the team has good communication systems, then dealing with disappointment becomes easier, which can be a major factor come finals time. Players who with maturity have developed a more global view of their roles on the team contribute greatly to positive teamwork.

Great team players take on the role of continuous learners. They develop the ability to listen, process and apply feedback. They welcome the chance to learn or modify their skills to make them better players and add to their repertoire. They use lots of eye contact with coaches and ask questions to clarify understanding. Outstanding team players have made a personal commitment to being their best. Everything they do in training sessions, individual fitness sessions, match play and demeanour oozes quality. Too many players see training as some form of punishment and do not understand that cutting corners comes back to haunt them in the end. Mentally, if players have done their very best, particularly in attending to the little things in their preparation, they can develop an unshakable confidence that serves them well in pressure situations. Win, lose or draw, they will never be left wondering if they could have done more.

> "Quality team players who are successful at the elite level exhibit desire, determination and dedication. They want to be the best they can be. They train hard and never cut corners. They never look for excuses. They **believe** in themselves."
>
> ~ Margaret Caldow, English National Coach, Former Australian Goal Attack and Captain, Triple World Champion

Accepting responsibility is another thing that great team players do well. Blaming others is the easy way to react to hardship, but it will not allow players to grow personally. Accepting responsibility in proportion for mistakes will cement understanding of the correct choices, increasing the likelihood of reacting correctly the next time. It also earns the respect of team-mates and provides a role model for the rest of the team. Players who are able to take responsibility for themselves and their roles on the team—from quality and intensity of activity to off-court matters such as a disciplined lifestyle—are on the way to becoming true team players.

Attitude is a very influential characteristic. It is essentially how players feel and what they show about their involvement in the team. Team players develop positive attitudes towards training, as they understand it is essential to make them better and give them an edge. During a match, even in the heat of competition, these players can be aggressive and tough on their opponents but remain calm, fair and clear-headed. This adds to rather than detracts from their performance. Every player makes a choice when it comes to attitude, and sometimes a player needs to fake it to contribute. It is tough when a player is substituted, beaten or left out of a line-up. Team players with the right attitude will continue to rise above personal disappointment and support the team in every way possible, even if it is by supplying vocal support from the sidelines.

Physical Factors

Great teamwork off the court usually underpins great teamwork on the court. Players who are team oriented work for each other, and team-mates can rely on them to provide physical and vocal support. Three factors indicate how much "team" is in a team player: how much she talks and encourages team-mates during a match, the amount of work she does off the ball, and how she conducts herself after substitution from the game or non-selection.

In attack, great team players use their space wisely (and respect the space of others), back up leads, reoffer to support, talk, understand their team-mates' moves, set screens for a team-mate, use quick passes from shooter to shooter or feeder to shooter, read team-mates' emotions and use confident and direct attacking plays. In defence, great teamwork is reflected by talking and communicating, acting as an extra set of eyes for team-mates, backing up tips and deflections, setting traps for a team-mate to finish off and creating a tough and unified defensive front. Physical teamwork skills can be achieved only through hours and hours of well-structured team drills where players read their team-mates' moves and receive their passes time after time until instinct and anticipation are developed.

Team Processes

Successful teams usually have a set of procedures in place to short-circuit group dynamics problems that inevitably crop up in team sports. Having clearly defined roles for each team member avoids a lot of unnecessary angst and speculation. Individual discussion between coach and players to ascertain where the coach sees athletes at that point of their development and where the players see themselves is a very productive exercise. If a player's and coach's assessments of playing ability are markedly different, there are bound to be problems when team selection and placement arises. Communication beforehand and some guidelines for areas of improvement can detour conflict and accelerate targeted improvement.

Creating opportunities for all players and officials to offer input on team planning for strategy, fitness, training programs, off-court policies, team goals, team values and social events reinforces each team member's value to the team and hints at a democracy rather than a dictatorship. Coaches can learn a lot from players in the heat of the action each match, and the ability to listen and assimilate relevant information into team plans is an asset. Regular team discussions during stretching sessions or more formal meetings help keep communication lines open, as does an open-door policy for players wishing to speak with the coach privately.

Having a clear policy in place for conflict resolution can be a wonderful asset for teams searching for harmony and well-being. It would be remarkable to go through a season without one disagreement or case of tension between members of a competitive team. The problem is not that there is friction—this is normal human group dynamics—but how it is dealt with. If allowed to fester and gain momentum, friction between team members can destroy on-court performances. If a player is continually in dispute with other team-mates and it affects team harmony, focus or performance, then it must be dealt with appropriately. The player and coach might like to meet to discuss that player's options of continuing with the team.

On-court team processes have great bearing on a team's success. Teams that focus on the process of what they are trying to achieve in the game with respect to skills, such as timing, strategy and hitting targets, find that the results take care of themselves. Focussing on non-performance matters such as the score, tiredness, umpires or trying to win adversely affects performance. Great teams have almost pure focus on the immediate task and are process oriented. Teams that stumble or make silly errors at crucial times are often outcome oriented and have lost their focus on the steps needed to achieve the desired result of winning. Great teams work on showcasing their own unique qualities. Each player offers different strengths and characteristics, and a team that uses different strategies and skill variations reinforces that group of players as a team with its own distinct style. Finally, great teams have skilled players with sound physical and mental qualities. Good players on a team with a contemporary, well-designed, motivating skill-development program that addresses the full range of physical and mental skills will be hard to beat. The key that binds the entire process of operating a successful team where members enjoy what they do is teamwork.

Fostering Teamwork

For some people, understanding teamwork and being a team player are instinctive. Others possess a more individual focus, and teamwork needs to be role-modelled and taught. Most players fall somewhere in between understanding teamwork and applying it on and off the court. In addition to providing a great example of team-oriented leadership by their attitude and actions, coaches can structure environments that highlight and teach teamwork. Players can gain personally from such activities and take their newfound sense of cooperation and self-sacrifice into all areas of their lives. Some practical activities to enhance teamwork include camps featuring physical, social and skill-based team-building activities; social events involving different players in organisational roles; and challenges and small-group work during training, such as writing down strengths of a partner's game for her, as well as everyday things such as rotating partners for training exercises. Consistent attention to the little things pays handsome dividends in the ultimate teamwork stakes.

"Teamwork does not just happen, it is the culmination of values and a shared vision that involves the planning and preparation of all aspects of management, coaching and player partnerships, linked with a strong team identity."

~ Kendra Slawinski (Lowe) OBE, Former England Captain,
Most Internationally Capped Player

On-court leadership is a fundamental ingredient in strengthening teamwork. The captain, vice-captain and experienced players must think, act and play by example. Great leaders must radiate a positive attitude, fine sportsmanship, a strong work ethic and an understanding of the strengths and shortcomings of all players. Great on-court leaders have the ability to detect and assist team-mates in trouble, and they sacrifice their own personal glory to support a struggling colleague. These leaders' selflessness allows them to put the needs of the team before their own and think calmly and effectively under pressure. The ideal aim is to create a leader-rich team with shared responsibility and an enthusiasm for belonging to the team that permeates everything that they do. A team of skilled, genuine competitors who operate with the team goals and ideals foremost in their thoughts and actions—in theory and practice—will be hard to beat. The greatest netball teams of all time that have scaled the peaks of success at a high level are often described as playing "as one"; their signature playing style is flawless teamwork.

APPENDIX A TRAINING GUIDE

Team training sessions should provide opportunities for learning, reinforcement, enrichment, support, extension and correction for all players. Training sessions present a forum to take feedback from the last performance and put it into action to modify skills. Coaches owe it to the players to be well organised, with a written plan and theme. They should also arrive at training with the aim of making every minute of the session purposeful. Some of the best-planned sessions sometimes do not unfold as intended, and coaches need to be flexible and modify the plans to best suit the players' needs. It is all part of the grand juggling act that is coaching.

Following are tips for running effective training sessions:

- Set a theme for the training session that is pertinent to the team's current position.

- Prepare a written plan for the session detailing the warm-up, skill practices, drills, conditioning work, tactics, games and cool-down. Keeping a ring-bound notebook is a practical way of referring to previous practices to match details and promote continuity of learning.

- Set the tone for the team by modelling punctuality, organisation, proper dress, sportsmanship, demeanour, enthusiasm and quality in everything you do.

- Always have markers or equipment set up for the first activity by starting time. This motivates players and gets them interested in the action to follow.

- Design activities for maximum individual participation. Avoid activities where players are standing in queues for any length of time. Ensure that drills include enough balls, stations, movement and decision making to actively engage players for the entire drill.

- Have one ball between two players in the kit to maximise individual skill development.

- State the goals and outline the session to the players at the start of training. If they know the purpose of the activities and how they can improve their performance, they can direct their thinking and energy more efficiently.

- When talking to the group, try to eliminate distractions by standing with a wall or something similar behind you. Avoid competing for attention with action that will catch their eyes.

- When teaching a skill, give an overall picture of it and its place in the game, provide an accurate visual model (by demonstration, diagram or video), and supplement by verbalising the key cues. Allow the players to attempt the skill, and then provide specific feedback.

- Build up drills from a basic model. Start with a slow pace until the movement is smooth, then add speed, pressure (defence) and variables (extra balls, stations or decisions in the action).

- Allow time for the athletes to get the drill right on their own before jumping in to redirect. Be prepared to modify the drill if it is not working after a reasonable period of time.

- Always incorporate netball rules into skill practices and drills. Identify the rules and obey them.

- Give a balance of group and individual feedback, general and specific feedback, and make an effort to address everyone in the group each session. Positive feedback needs to balance out constructive criticism.

- Always put safety at the forefront of every activity, regarding the training venue, equipment and nature of the activity (e.g., do not plan running in the direction of brick walls; to avoid collisions, set multi-directional movement drills only for players who can handle them).

- Always practise the fundamentals at each session, no matter what the standard of the playing roster. Ball handling, leading, preliminary moves, timing and defence all need constant development.

- Develop a base set of drills that suits you and your team and go back to them frequently, adding variations so the players get a chance to revisit and cement the skills involved.

- Keep training plans simple. Avoid overcomplicating sessions with too many new drills or ideas. Stick to one or two new concepts per session, and provide chances for reinforcement.

- Finish sessions on a positive note. While stretching to cool down, summarise concepts and skills visited, note improvements, and give the players a chance to comment.

APPENDIX B STATISTICAL GUIDE

In netball, there are seven statistics to be recorded for each player on both teams: turnovers, penalties, rebounds, interceptions, deflections, offsides and pick-ups. Pages 230 and 231 feature a reproducible recording sheet that can be used to record statistics for both offense and defense during a game. Goalers' statistics in the form of goals and misses can be recorded at the end of respective rows. Outlined here is a brief description of each of these elements and when they should and should not be recorded. It is important to have consistency of the statistics across the board.

Turnover (T/O)

- A turnover is a negative statistic.
- If GK passes a ball straight out of court, she would be credited with a turnover.
- If a player passes to another member of her team and the ball is deflected out of court but possession does not change, this should *not* be counted as a turnover. A bad pass is not counted as a turnover if the same team retains possession.
- Turnovers occur for a number of reasons including stepping, replayed ball, offside, poor pass, poor lead and held ball.
- It is not always the player in possession who is at fault when a turnover occurs. Receivers cause turnovers as well.
- Missed goals should not be counted as turnovers.
- The recorder judges which player is credited with the turnover.
- Interpretations should be consistent.

Penalty (P)

- Penalties are either a contact or an obstruction.
- Advantage obstruction or contact calls should *not* be included.

Rebound (Reb)

- A rebound is credited when a defender or goaler rebounds a missed attempt at goal.

- Recorders should be generous with rebounds. For example, if a player deliberately taps a missed goal to a member of her own team without gaining full control herself, the player should be credited with a rebound.

Interception (I)

- An interception is a clear take of the ball (e.g., if GK comes flying out of the goal circle and takes a ball intended for the opposition).
- An interception will almost always result in a turnover by the opposing team.

Deflection (D)

- A deflection is just that—a touch on the ball, whether it results in a turnover or not.
- Deflections should *not* be counted if a player has infringed (e.g., if a player has been called for offside in the attempt to get a deflection). The same rule applies for a player who has been called for a penalty in an attempt to get a deflection.

Offside (O)

- Offside is when a player enters an area other than what the position she is playing allows.
- If WA or C is called offside in her own attack (and her team is in possession), this should be recorded as both an offside and a turnover.
- Advantage offside calls should *not* be included.

Pick-Up (PU)

- A pick-up is counted when a player picks up the ball, whether it is because of a deflection by another player or not. A pick-up may also be the result of a dropped pass or error by a team-mate or opponent. Recorders should be very liberal when allocating this statistic.

Goals Scored (GS)

- The recorder marks a vertical dash for a goal scored, and a dot for a missed attempt.

Note: On the recording sheet, each player's name is recorded in the long box in the Team column, and her position is recorded every quarter in the four boxes immediately following.

Team				Round		Result					
				I		D		PU		Reb & GS	
GS				T/O		P		O			
				I		D		PU		Reb & GS	
GA				T/O		P		O			
				I		D		PU		Reb & GS	
WA				T/O		P		O			
				I		D		PU		Reb & GS	
C				T/O		P		O			
				I		D		PU		Reb & GS	
WD				T/O		P		O			
				I		D		PU		Reb & GS	
GD				T/O		P		O			
				I		D		PU		Reb & GS	
GK				T/O		P		O			
				I		D		PU		Reb & GS	
S				T/O		P		O			
				I		D		PU		Reb & GS	
S				T/O		P		O			

Recording sheet courtesy of Todd Miller. From *The Netball Handbook* by Jane Woodlands, 2006, Champaign, IL: Human Kinetics.

Team				Name & Signature				Umpires		
				I		D		PU		Reb & GS
GS				T/O		P		O		
				I		D		PU		Reb & GS
GA				T/O		P		O		
				I		D		PU		Reb & GS
WA				T/O		P		O		
				I		D		PU		Reb & GS
C				T/O		P		O		
				I		D		PU		Reb & GS
WD				T/O		P		O		
				I		D		PU		Reb & GS
GD				T/O		P		O		
				I		D		PU		Reb & GS
GK				T/O		P		O		
				I		D		PU		Reb & GS
S				T/O		P		O		
				I		D		PU		Reb & GS
S				T/O		P		O		

Recording sheet courtesy of Todd Miller. From *The Netball Handbook* by Jane Woodlands, 2006, Champaign, IL: Human Kinetics.

INDEX

Note: The italicized *f* and *t* following page numbers refer to figures and tables, respectively.

ABOUT THE AUTHOR

Jane Woodlands brings to the book 20 years of netball coaching experience, ranging from the under-eights to the Australian National League. She is a Level 3 nationally accredited coach, the highest awarded by Netball Australia, as well as an advanced coaching workshop coordinator and presenter. Woodlands' coaching credits include a Premiership as head coach with Matrics Netball Club in the South Australian State League and assistant and specialist goaler's coach with the championship-winning Adelaide Thunderbirds in the Commonwealth Bank Trophy, Australia's premier national league competition. A former State League and National Super League Premiership player, she represented Contax Netball Club as a shooter. Woodlands holds a bachelor of education degree in specialist secondary physical education from the University of South Australia. She resides in North Brighton, South Australia.

Photography by Roxy Studios.